MAKING FOREIGN POLICY

Timely Reports to Keep
Journalists, Scholars and the Public
Abreast of Developing Issues, Events and Trends

Editorial Research Reports
Published by Congressional Quarterly Inc.
1414 22nd Street N.W., Washington, D.C. 20037

Library of Congress Cataloging-in-Publication Data

Making foreign policy.

Reports originally appeared in Editorial research reports.
Includes bibliographies and index.
1. United States--Foreign relations--1981-
2. United States--Foreign relations administration.
I. Congressional Quarterly, inc. II. Editorial research reports.
E876.M3   1988   327.73   88-18142
ISBN 0-87187-496-2

CONTENTS

FOREWORD

Few policy areas underwent as much change during the 1980s as the nation's relations with the rest of the world. The decade was marked by a seemingly relentless shift in economic might from the United States to other industrial powers in Western Europe and East Asia. America's widening trade and budget deficits were signs that the overwhelming economic clout the United States had enjoyed since the end of World War II was waning. This volume looks at the ways the Reagan administration and Congress tried to adapt to the country's evolving international role.

As America celebrated the bicentennial of the Constitution in 1987, the unfolding Iran-contra scandal precipitated a new skirmish in the 200-year-old struggle between Congress and the White House over which branch of government should play the greater role in making foreign policy. Our lead report examines the historical background of this debate and its implications for power-sharing between the White House and Congress. The related debate over the proper role of the National Security Council, a key issue in the Iran-contra affair, is examined in our second report.

The signing of the intermediate-range nuclear forces (INF) treaty in December 1987 focused attention on another area where two branches of government share jurisdiction. The Constitution grants the president the power to make treaties "by and with the advice and consent of the Senate." Our report on treaty ratification shows how the vagueness of the Founding Fathers' language has complicated the process of making foreign policy.

In the 1980s, U.S. policymakers faced problems the Founding Fathers never dreamed of, including the growing interdependence of the world economy. As the dollar's value first soared and then plunged after 1985, the Reagan administration took unprecedented steps aimed at stabilizing exchange rates. A report on dollar diplomacy examines how coordination among the industrial world's central bankers and treasury officials has become a key ingredient in the foreign policy repertoire.

The collaboration of five European countries in the American effort to protect oil tankers in the war-torn Persian Gulf was further evidence that the United States and the other industrial nations were on a more equal footing than in the past. A report on the subject shows how the presence of U.S. and European warships in and around the Strait of Hormuz constituted an unprecedented show of Western allied military force outside European territory.

The Reagan negotiating record, examined in another report, has also changed America's relations with her Western European allies. Worried that the United States may be willing to eliminate the nuclear deterrent that has kept peace on the continent since the end of World War II, European members of the North Atlantic Treaty Organization (NATO) spoke of the need to strengthen the "European pillar" of the alliance as the negotiations to remove intermediate-range nuclear missiles from Europe proceeded.

Once signed, the INF treaty prompted calls for a new set of East-West negotiations, aimed this time at conventional, or non-nuclear, forces. The treaty's elimination of nuclear missiles from Europe would leave the West vulnerable to the Warsaw Pact's superior arsenal of tanks and other offensive weapons. Officials on both sides called for new talks to correct the imbalance.

But American lawmakers, eager to find ways to reduce the federal budget deficit, charged that the allies were not carrying their fair share of the cost of defending Europe. They said that increased "burden-sharing" by the European allies should be the condition of their greater say in alliance affairs. At the same time, there was growing awareness that America could no longer sustain the defense buildup Reagan initiated in 1981. But it was clear that neither the White House nor Congress had the political will to make the difficult choices needed to cut defense spending in the 1990s. That task will top the foreign policy agenda of Reagan's successor.

Mary Cooper
Editorial Research Reports

ERR

JUNE 26, 1987

MAKING FOREIGN POLICY

EDITORIAL RESEARCH REPORTS

EDITOR
MARCUS D. ROSENBAUM

MANAGING EDITOR
SANDRA STENCEL

ASSOCIATE EDITOR
RICHARD L. WORSNOP

STAFF WRITERS
MARY H. COOPER
HARRISON DONNELLY
SARAH GLAZER
ROBERT K. LANDERS

PRODUCTION EDITOR
CHARLES J. MOSELEY

EDITORIAL ASSISTANT
DOUGLAS SERY

RICHARD M. BOECKEL (1892-1975)
FOUNDER

PUBLISHED BY
CONGRESSIONAL QUARTERLY INC.

CHAIRMAN
EUGENE PATTERSON

PRESIDENT
ANDREW BARNES

PUBLISHER
WAYNE P. KELLEY

EXECUTIVE EDITOR
NEIL SKENE

The Iran-contra
affair continues
a struggle over

MAKING FOREIGN POLICY.

Is the president
pre-eminent, or
is Congress?

by Sarah Glazer

President Reagan's press spokesman, Marlin Fitzwater, had been assailed by reporters daily with questions about the president's role and culpability in the Iran-contra affair. Repeatedly, he denied any presidential improprieties. Then on May 15, at the White House, Fitzwater took a new tack, asserting for the first time the president's constitutional powers over foreign policy. His target was the series of laws, known as the Boland amendments, aimed at barring U.S. aid to rebel forces in Nicaragua.

None of those laws, declared Fitzwater, "contained any language that limited the constitutional and historical power of the president to set and implement foreign policy."

Fitzwater's assertion didn't go unchallenged. "The president is the president, and the United States is a democracy," declared Sen. George J. Mitchell (D-Maine), a member of the Senate select committee on the Iran-contra affair.[1] "He's not the king, and this is not a monarchy."

It's a debate as old as the country: Who is pre-eminent in the making of U.S. foreign policy — Congress or the president? Though evident throughout most of the country's history, probably never has the debate raged with more intensity than in our own time, as the country struggles with its international identity and its role in a hostile world. In essense, it is a constitutional question, stretching back to such legal matters as the original intent of the Founding Fathers, to decades of practice and precedent in the conduct of foreign policy, and to the smattering of court rulings that have thrust toward the heart of the matter.

But ultimately it's a political question, and it turns on the sum total of popular sentiment in the land at any given moment. Thus, the current struggle between Congress

State's Elliott Abrams testifies (left). Sens. Warren B. Rudman and Daniel K. Inouye listen.

and the president — over U.S. policy in Central America, over "re-flagging" Kuwaiti ships in the Persian Gulf, over arms-control negotiations with the Soviets — is a struggle to marshal political sentiment on behalf of a constitutional interpretation. Politics, not legal niceties, will determine the outcome. As historian Edward S. Corwin, author of the classic work on the subject of the president's control of foreign policy, once wrote, the Constitution set up an "invitation to struggle for the privilege of directing foreign policy."

Added to these ever-present dynamics of struggle are some important institutional changes in government peculiar to our own time. Especially since the Kennedy administration, executive-branch power has increased, with more and more power concentrated in the White House and in ideological political appointees. Responding to this growing power concentration — and to the abuses of Watergate as well — Congress has beefed up its support structure, including its foreign-policy staff. In addition, congressional "reforms" of the 1970s, aimed at reducing the power of senior committee chairmen, have given individual members an independent spirit and freed them from party leaders in casting votes and seeking to influence foreign policy.

Contra aid — whose call?

What's more, the foreign-policy consensus of the 1950s, which guided policy making and diminished political tension over such matters, is gone, obliterated by Vietnam and subsequent revelations of abuse by the Central Intelligence Agency (CIA) and other governmental agencies. One result is that secret operations, such as those carried out by the Reagan administration in Nicaragua, have ceased to be the exclusive preserve of the executive branch. Reporting requirements bring Congress into such matters early and provide lawmakers with leverage they didn't have in the days when the country and Congress felt much more comfortable delegating such matters to the president.

The sour memory of Vietnam also has an effect on the way lawmakers look at violent conflicts today, whether in Nicaragua or the Persian Gulf. Members of Congress remember that U.S. involvement in Vietnam, like the Nicaraguan experience, began with a trickle of American aid and advisers. And they have inherited laws, such as the War Powers Resolution of 1973, passed by a previous Congress bent on reasserting its powers in the face of an "undeclared" war.

It is against this background that the current struggle rages. As Fitzwater puts it, "What we really have is a classic confrontation between the Congress and the president. Congress wants to tell us what to do, and the president wants to do what he thinks is right."

Of course, other elements besides the constitutional power struggle are involved in the Iran-contra controversy. Revelations of deceit by public officials, apparent violations of the law, and the creation of a private war-making machine have stirred outrage among segments of the public, as well as some lawmakers. The White House's secret sale of arms to Iran in an unsuccessful effort to free American hostages resulted, it now appears, in the diversion of weapons payments to the Nicaraguan "contra" rebels, who are seeking to overthrow the communist Sandinista government there.

The congressional committees investigating the affair will try to determine, among other things, whether the president or his staff violated either the spirit or the letter of the Boland amendments' prohibition against the use of federal funds to support the contras. The White House, meanwhile, presses the view that these amendments constitutionally could not proscribe the president's prerogatives in the foreign-policy realm.

So far, the White House has not come up with much in the way of a legal substantiation for its constitutional position. The only White House legal study uncovered by congressional committees has been ridiculed because of its cursory preparation by a novice White House lawyer, Bretton G. Sciaroni. But history tells us that the White House's broad assertion of constitutional power without substantiation continues a long tradition. Presidents frequently have claimed foreign-policy powers far beyond those envisioned by the framers of the Constitution and have exercised those powers even when they recognized the constitutional basis was shaky. (See p. 6.)

Indeed, presidential claims and actions, more than

legal opinions, have established precedents that have shaped the power of the office over time. Abraham Lincoln and Franklin D. Roosevelt have received historical acclaim for successfully attaining new powers in times of crisis. Their famous stands have influenced Americans' expectations for their presidents. On the other hand, an overreaching president, such as Richard M. Nixon, can spark rebellion on the part of Congress and the populace and stir efforts to strengthen the legislative role in foreign policy. The difference is in the nature of the crisis and the political acumen of the president seeking to aggrandize the office.

After the congressional committees dig their way through mountains of paper and witnesses to uncover the entire story of the Iran-contra affair, they plan to address the broad question of the executive and legislative branches' responsibility for foreign policy in the final phase of the hearings in late July. No doubt this review will reflect Congress' own parochial views and interests in this constitutional debate, just as the president's position reflects the institutional outlook of the presidency.

Balancing democracy and global strength

At the root of the debate is a 200-year-old tension between the democratic goal of avoiding a monarchical president and the historical necessity of presenting a strong national position in the international arena. The Founding Fathers resolved the issue by separating the foreign-policy powers, like the domestic powers, among the branches of government. To this day, such foreign-policy veterans as former Sen. J. William Fulbright question whether that is a workable approach in foreign relations, where a nation must present a united front to other nations. And Alexis de Tocqueville, the 19th-century French observer of America, expressed the view in 1835 that "it is most especially in the conduct of foreign relations that democratic governments appear to me to be decidedly inferior to governments carried on upon different principles." Among the indispensable qualities to foreign relations that democracies lack, de Tocqueville said, are steadfastness in a course, efficiency and secrecy — all qualities more easily found in an aristocracy.[2]

The early writers and explicators of the Constitution made a self-conscious decision — in laying out control over foreign affairs — to distinguish the president from the British king against whom they had rebelled. In the power to declare war, particularly, they saw the danger that a despotic leader could plunge the nation unwillingly into a bloody conflict. The result would be the very antithesis of democracy.

The scholarly Virginian James Madison had listed such vices of ancient and contemporary governments in a notebook that he carried to the constitutional convention in Philadephia. ". . . [I]t has grown into an axiom that the executive is the department of power most distinguished

Foreign-Policy Powers of the President and Congress

PRESIDENTIAL POWERS

Article II, Section 1

"The executive power shall be vested in a president of the United States of America...."

"[The president] shall take the following oath or affirmation: "I do solemnly swear ... that I will faithfully execute the office of the president of the United States, and will to the best of my ability, preserve, protect and defend the Constitution of the United States.""

Article II, Section 2

"The president shall be commander in chief of the Army and Navy of the United States...."

"He shall have power, by and with the advice and consent of the Senate, to make treaties, provided two-thirds of the Senators present concur; and he shall nominate, and by and with the advice and consent of the Senate, shall appoint ambassadors...."

Article II, Section 3

"... he shall receive ambassadors and other public ministers; he shall take care that the laws be faithfully executed...."

"The general doctrine of our Constitution then is, that the *executive power* of the nation is vested in the president; subject only to the *exceptions* and *qualifications*, which are expressed in the Constitution."

—Alexander Hamilton

"I cannot accept the view that this clause is a grant in bulk of all conceivable executive power, but regard it as an allocation to the presidential office of the generic powers thereafter stated."

—Supreme Court Justice Robert H. Jackson in the 1952 *Steel Seizure Case*

CONGRESSIONAL POWERS

Article I, Section 1

"All legislative powers herein granted shall be vested in a Congress of the United States...."

Article I, Section 2

"The House of Representatives ... shall have the sole power of impeachment."

Article I, Section 8

"The Congress shall have power to lay and collect taxes ... to pay the debts and provide for the common defense and general welfare of the United States....
To regulate commerce with foreign nations....
To declare war, grant letters of marque and reprisal, and make rules concerning captures on land and water;
To raise and support armies....
To provide and maintain a navy...."

Article I, Section 9

"... No money shall be drawn from the Treasury but in consequence of appropriations made by law; and a regular statement and account of the receipts and expenditures of all public money shall be published from time to time."

"In Article I, what are the legislative powers 'herein granted' to Congress? The answer is you will not find anything in the specific grant of powers [giving foreign-policy power to the Congress]."

—John Norton Moore, professor of law at the University of Virginia

"The power of Congress to declare war doesn't give it power to declare every use of force."

—Eugene V. Rostow, professor of law emeritus at Yale University and visiting professor at the National Defense University

"But Congress does not control the private purse — except through the taxing power."

—Michael M. Uhlmann, former counsel for domestic policy to President Reagan

"The ultimate power is in Congress: they can remove [the president]. He can't remove them."

—former Sen. J. William Fulbright

"The power [of Congress] to control war includes the power to control things closely connected to war."

—Louis Henkin, professor of law at Columbia University

"Congress' control over the purse would be rendered a nullity if the president's pocket could conceal a slush fund dedicated to purposes and projects prohibited by United States law."

—Laurence H. Tribe, professor of constitutional law at Harvard University

Presidents on War Powers and the Constitution

"I think the Constitution invests its commander in chief with laws of war in times of war. . . . I may in emergency do things on military grounds which cannot constitutionally be done by Congress."

Abraham Lincoln discussing the Civil War, quoted in former Sen. Jacob K. Javits' *Who Makes War?*, pp. 130, 131.

"In the event that Congress should fail to act, and act adequately, I shall accept the responsibility and I will act. . . . The President has the powers, under the Constitution and under congressional acts, to take measures necessary to avert a disaster which would interfere with the winning of the war. . . . I will use my powers with a full sense of my responsibility to the Constitution and to my country. . . . When the war is won, the powers under which I act automatically revert to the people — to whom they belong."

Franklin D. Roosevelt in a Sept. 7, 1942, address to Congress. The speech referred to Congress' inaction on the president's proposal to repeal a farm subsidy, which threatened to produce serious wartime inflation. Roosevelt's threat of unilateral action was never put to the test, because Congress later approved the proposal.

"I said early in my presidency that if I wanted Congress with me on the landing of Vietnam, I'd have to have them with me on the takeoff. And I did just that. But I failed to reckon with one thing: the parachute. I got them on the takeoff, but a lot of them bailed out before the end of the flight."

Lyndon B. Johnson in a letter to Eugene V. Rostow, March 25, 1972, quoted in Rostow's "Once More unto the Breach: The War Powers Resolution Revisited," *Valparaiso University Law Review*, fall 1986, p. 15.

"The legal justification [for the 1970 invasion of Cambodia] . . . is the right of the president of the United States under the Constitution to protect the lives of American men. . . . As commander in chief, I had no choice but to act to defend those men. And as commander in chief, if I am faced with that decision again I will exercise that power to defend those men."

Richard M. Nixon in *A New Road for America: Major Policy Statements, March 1970 to October 1971*, pp. 675, 683.

". . . I do not and cannot cede any of the authority vested in me under the Constitution as president and as commander in chief of the United States Armed Forces. Nor should my signing [of the War Powers Resolution] be viewed as any acknowledgment that the president's constitutional authority can be impermissibly infringed by statute, that the congressional authorization would be required if and when the period specified in . . . the War Powers Resolution might be deemed to have been triggered . . . or that the [congressional resolution to retain Marines in Lebanon] may be interpreted to revise the president's constitutional authority to deploy United States Armed Forces."

Ronald Reagan upon signing the April 12, 1985, resolution authorizing U.S. Marines to remain in Lebanon for 18 months.

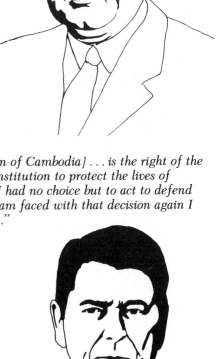

by its propensity to war," Madison later wrote, "hence it is the practice of all states, in proportion as they are free, to disarm this propensity of its influence."

Almost two centuries later, historian Arthur M. Schlesinger Jr. attacked Nixon's conduct of the Vietnam War with the same argument. "Indeed, if decisions of war and peace were not subject to popular control, how much scope and substance did democracy really have? . . . [I]n the nuclear age the power to go to war could mean the power to blow up the planet. Was this dread power, this ultimate power, to be bestowed upon a single fallible man — above all a man systematically withdrawn from reality by the bewitchments of the imperial presidency?" [3]

The unresolved arguments over the vices and virtues of centralized power are seen throughout the history of American foreign affairs. The tension springs directly from the Constitution.

In *Foreign Affairs and the Constitution*, constitutional scholar Louis Henkin points out that the Constitution gives a longer list of explicit foreign-policy powers to Congress than it does to the president. *(See p. 5.)* The Constitution empowers Congress to declare war, raise and support armies, regulate commerce with foreign nations and appropriate money from the Treasury. By contrast, the president's only explicit foreign-policy powers are his role as commander in chief of the Army and Navy, his duty to receive foreign ambassadors and his power to nominate ambassadors, with the advice and consent of the Senate. These concise lists of foreign-policy powers leave many functions in an undefined territory of overlapping powers between the branches. What Corwin called "the invitation to struggle" between the branches was clearly intended by the Constitution's writers to ensure that a potential monarchy would be checked by the separation of powers.

Even Alexander Hamilton, the nation's leading exponent of centralized government at the time the Constitution was drafted, sought to reassure Americans that the "commander-in-chief" power would not create another English king.

In the *Federalist Papers*, a document aimed at winning support for the new Constitution, Hamilton said of the president's "commander-in-chief" role: "In this respect his authority would be nominally the same with that of the king of Great Britain, but in substance much inferior to it. It would amount to nothing more than the supreme command and direction of the military and naval forces . . . while that of the British king extends to the *declaring* of war and to the *raising* and *regulating* of fleets and armies — all which, by the Constitution under consideration, would appertain to the legislature."

Yet ratification of the Constitution, rather than settling the matter of foreign-policy powers, merely set the stage for the ongoing debate.

George Washington, the American Revolution's military leader, was to face this dilemma in his presidential term. He was the first president to take independent action in the realm of foreign policy without congressional blessing. Being keenly conscious of the new Constitution,

he was aware of congressional restrictions and proceeded cautiously. Yet he declared in 1793, during a congressional recess, that the United States would remain neutral in the war between England and France. His proclamation provoked outrage on the part of French sympathizers who marshaled constitutional arguments to buttress their case. They said a declaration of neutrality was too similar to a declaration of war — a congressional prerogative — to be made unilaterally by a president. Washington, in a conciliatory gesture, soon requested approval of Congress for his proclamation. As it turned out, the neutrality stance was popular, and Congress ratified it without much fuss. Thus, politics prevailed.

Hamilton, the most "royalist" of the Founding Fathers, took pen in hand to defend Washington's action in the newspaper under the pseudonym "Pacificus." Hamilton argued that broad foreign-policy powers were intended for the president under the constitutional phrase, "the executive power shall be vested in a president of the United States of America." "Executive power," as defined by Hamilton, contained all foreign-policy powers not explicitly handed to Congress in the Constitution.

Thomas Jefferson disagreed. A French sympathizer and a populist who, unlike Hamilton, tended to see the legislature as the ultimate repository of democracy, Jefferson begged Madison, the constitutional authority, to counter the "heresies" of Hamilton. Madison sallied forth with his own pseudonym, "Helvidius," to counter Hamilton's argument in the same newspaper.

Madison accused Hamilton of equating the constitutional "executive power" with the power of a monarch — counter to the framers' intention. Rather, Madison contended, foreign-policy powers could be said to be "legislative" in nature, because the most important international powers — declaration of war and approval of treaties — had been granted to Congress.

In the end, Washington's decision to seek a congressional vote on the issue rendered neutrality proclamations the prerogative of Congress. But the arguments made by Hamilton established the philosophical basis for the view that the president has broad foreign-policy powers not enumerated in the Constitution. To this day, defenders of presidents quote Hamilton. Defenders of Congress quote Madison.

But institutional factors always come into play, and even Jefferson experienced the lure of military initiative when he himself became chief executive. Becoming the first American president to send a naval force abroad without congressional consent, Jefferson in 1801 initiated an operation to quell the Barbary pirates and the associated government of Tripoli. The aim was to stop the harassment of American merchant ships in the Mediterranean. Conceding Congress' power to declare war, Jefferson requested authorization nine months after he had started the military confrontation. He justified his initial action as defensive, part of the president's unilateral right to repel military attacks, which had been universally accepted at the time of the Constitution's ratification. Though members of Congress expressed skepticism that Jefferson's action was truly defensive, the successful strike against the pirates proved popular, and Congress approved it by resolution. Again, politics prevailed.

Lincoln was the first chief executive to appropriate radically new military powers for his office. "The sudden emergence of the 'commander-in-chief' clause as one of the most highly charged provisions of the Constitution," recounts historian Corwin, occurred almost overnight as Lincoln sought to justify his entry into a civil war without congressional approval. Responding to the Confederates' attack on Fort Sumter in 1861, Lincoln added thousands of men to the Army, Navy and militia and used billions of dollars in unappropriated funds from the Treasury to pay for military equipment. He took these steps while Congress was in recess.

Lincoln's actions clearly fell under the congressional right to "raise armies." However, he justified his actions to Congress under the "commander-in-chief" clause and his duty "to take care that the laws be faithfully executed." Thus, Lincoln derived what he termed the necessary "war power."

Faced with a secessionist crisis, the lawyer in Lincoln struggled to find a rationale for his new reading of the Constitution. An emergency, he believed, validated new powers. "Measures otherwise unconstitutional might become lawful by becoming indispensable to the preservation of the Constitution through the preservation of the nation," he suggested three years into the Civil War.

Franklin D. Roosevelt also cited an emergency threat to the nation as the basis for expanding the president's foreign-policy powers. It has often been noted that he took numerous steps to aid Western Europe against the Nazis before asking Congress for an official declaration of war. His position was bolstered by a major Supreme Court decision in 1936, *U.S. vs. Curtiss-Wright Export Co.*, which conferred far-reaching foreign-policy powers upon the president. The tone of this decision was notably different from the court's stern condemnations of Roosevelt's New Deal programs, seen as federal expropriation of power from the states.

The case stemmed from a joint resolution of Congress that authorized the president to embargo the sale of arms to Bolivia and Paraguay, then involved in a bloody war over a piece of South American territory known as the Chaco. Roosevelt followed the congressional resolution with an executive proclamation of an embargo. The Curtiss-Wright Export Co. was indicted for violating the embargo. In its defense, the company challenged the embargo as a usurpation of congressional power. The Supreme Court, with only one dissenting vote, ruled against the export company, stating that the principles that limit delegation to the president in domestic affairs do not hold equally in foreign affairs.

The decision was based on what historian Schlesinger has called "a highly dubious historical argument." The court stated that the president's foreign-policy powers were not to be found in the Constitution, but that they predated the Constitution, having passed automatically to the nation's leader from the British king at the time of the nation's founding. The court held that the "powers of external sovereignty passed from the Crown not to the colonies severally," but to the nation as a whole and thus to its president.

One could easily imagine Jefferson turning over in his grave upon the application of the monarchical concept of "sovereignty" to the president of a democracy. The decision would have been more likely to meet Hamilton's approval.

Widely quoted still is the court's sweeping reference to "the very delicate, plenary and exclusive power of the president as the sole organ of the federal government in the field of foreign relations."

Though the *Curtiss-Wright* case involved a relatively narrow circumstance of international commerce and the president's power to act under congressional authorization, the sweeping language of the decision fated it to be applied by presidents to much broader circumstances. Congress and the public apparently paid little attention to the decision at the time. Lawyers, including those for President Roosevelt, were well aware of the implications.

Roosevelt cites Supreme Court decision

In 1940, for example, Roosevelt's attorney general cited the case in justifying the famous "destroyers-for-bases" deal that the president undertook without congressional consent. Roosevelt was faced with a desperate plea from British Prime Minister Winston Churchill for naval assistance to hold off the Germans. The president, anxious to help Britain, knew he did not have the votes in the isolationist-dominated Congress to sanction such a move. He did not put the issue to a vote. Instead, he arranged to "lend" 50 aging destroyers to Britain in exchange for the "lease" of naval bases on British islands in the Atlantic. Isolationist critics attacked Roosevelt for overriding Congress' powers to declare war and to approve a *de facto* treaty with Britain. In announcing the trade, Roosevelt echoed *Curtiss-Wright*, saying, "Preparation for defense is an inalienable prerogative of a sovereign state." Roosevelt consulted with congressional leaders and publicly announced the deal, but he did not put the issue to a vote until a year later.

Presidential power to make war was enlarged further when President Harry S Truman intervened in Korea without seeking congressional approval. He did not even meet with congressional leaders until two days after he committed troops to repel a North Korean army that had invaded South Korea. In taking this action, Truman cited a United Nations resolution denouncing North Korea's aggression, but that resolution had not authorized a military response. Within days of the invasion, members of Congress told Truman he should seek a congressional resolution of approval, but he ignored that advice. Instead, he

Milestones in the War-Powers Debate

1793	**Washington's Neutrality Proclamation**	*During a congressional recess, President George Washington proclaimed that the United States would remain neutral in the war between France and England. Because of the neutrality proclamation's similarity to a declaration of war — a power reserved constitutionally for Congress — Washington's action ignited a national debate over the extent of the president's foreign-policy powers.*
1801	**Jefferson and the Barbary Pirates**	*President Thomas Jefferson was the first chief executive to send a naval force abroad without congressional consent. An American naval schooner, sent to the Mediterranean shores off Tripoli to suppress the Barbary pirates, repulsed an attack by a Tripolitanian ship. Jefferson justified his action as purely defensive. Members of Congress, though skeptical, voted in favor of the measure upon his request nine months after he had started the Barbary War.*
1861	**Lincoln and the Civil War**	*In response to the Confederate assault on Fort Sumter in 1861, President Abraham Lincoln called thousands of men to military service and used billions of dollars from the Treasury to finance the Union cause in the Civil War. Lincoln, who took these actions without consulting Congress, was the first president to justify such sweeping measures under the "commander-in-chief" clause of the Constitution.*
1940	**Roosevelt's Destroyer-for-Bases Deal**	*President Franklin D. Roosevelt responded to Britain's request for American naval vessels to help Britain resist the Germans a full year before Congress declared war. Aware that a Congress dominated by isolationists would not approve such involvement in World War II, Roosevelt did not take the issue to Congress. Instead he loaned Britain 50 aging U.S. destroyers in exchange for the lease of some British naval bases.*
1964	**Johnson's Gulf of Tonkin Resolution**	*In 1964, Congress approved the Gulf of Tonkin Resolution, authorizing military action against North Vietnam at the request of President Lyndon B. Johnson. Many members of Congress later claimed that they had understood the resolution as authorizing a limited act of defense against a specific North Vietnamese attack on an American destroyer. Johnson viewed the resolution as the equivalent of a war declaration.*
1970	**Nixon's Invasion of Cambodia**	*President Richard M. Nixon ordered an American invasion of Cambodia in 1970 without asking congressional authorization. He justified the action later on the basis of his "commander-in-chief" power. This was the first time the clause had been cited as giving the president routine powers to initiate war, rather than citing an emergency situation such as that claimed by Lincoln in the Civil War or Roosevelt during World War II.*
1973	**War Powers Resolution**	*Congress passed the War Powers Resolution, an effort to reassert its constitutional power to declare war, in 1973 over President Nixon's veto. The immediate inspiration for the early drafts of the resolution was Nixon's 1970 incursion into Cambodia. Under the resolution, the president must withdraw any armed forces that have been deployed within a specified time period unless Congress legislatively approves or extends the action.*

Yes, said **ALEXANDER HAMILTON**. "The inquiry then is, what department of our government is the proper one to make a declaration of neutrality, when the engagements of the nation permit, and its interests require that it should be done?

A correct mind will discern at once, that it can belong neither to the legislative nor judicial department, of course [it] must belong to the executive.

The legislative department is not the *organ* of intercourse between the United States and foreign nations. . . .

The second article of the Constitution of the United States, section first, establishes this general proposition, that 'the executive power shall be vested in a president of the United States of America.'. . .

The general doctrine of our Constitution then is, that the *executive power* of the nation is vested in the president; subject only to the *exceptions* and *qualifications* which are expressed in the [Constitution]. . . .

The right of the executive to receive ambassadors . . . includes that of judging, in the case of a revolution of government in a foreign country, whether the new rulers are competent organs of the national will, and ought to be recognized, or not. . . .

This serves as an example of the right of the executive, in certain cases, to determine the condition of the nation, though it may, in its consequences, affect the exercise of the power of the legislature to declare war. . . . The legislature is still free to perform its duties, according to its own sense of them; though the executive in the exercise of its constitutional powers may establish an antecedent state of things, which ought to weigh in the legislative decisions. . . .

While, therefore, the legislature can alone declare war, can alone actually transfer the nation from a state of peace to a state of hostility, it belongs to the 'executive power' to do whatever else the law of nations, cooperating with the treaties of the country, enjoin in the intercourse of the United States with foreign powers. . . .

But though it has been thought advisable to vindicate the authority of the executive on this broad and comprehensive ground, it was not absolutely necessary to do so. That clause of the Constitution which makes it his duty to 'take care that the laws be faithfully executed,' might alone have been relied upon, and this simple process of argument pursued."

In 1793, with Congress out of session, President George Washington declared the United States neutral in the war between France and England. In a series of articles in

---

At Issue

In foreign policy, does the president have any authority to declare war or peace?

No, said **JAMES MADISON**. "[U]nder color of vindicating an important public act of a chief magistrate who enjoys the confidence and love of his country, principles are advanced which strike at the vitals of its Constitution. . . .

Those who are to *conduct a war* [the executive as the commander in chief] cannot in the nature of things, be proper or safe judges, whether *a war ought* to be *commenced, continued,* or *concluded*. They are barred from the latter functions by a great principle in free government, analogous to that which separates the sword from the purse, or the power of executing from the power of enacting laws. . . .

A concurrent authority in two independent departments, to perform the same function with respect to the same thing, would be as awkward in practice, as it is unnatural in theory.

If the legislature and executive have both a right to judge of the obligations to make war or not, it must sometimes happen . . . that they will judge differently. . . .

The power of the legislature to declare war, and judge of the causes for declaring it, is one of the most express and explicit parts of the Constitution. To endeavor to abridge or affect it by strained inferences, and by hypothetical or singular occurrences, naturally warns the reader of some lurking fallacy. . . .

In no part of the Constitution is more wisdom to be found than in the clause which confides the question of war or peace to the legislature, and not to the executive department. . . . War is in fact the true nurse of executive aggrandizement. In war, a physical force is to be created; and it is the executive will, which is to direct it. In war, the public treasures are to be unlocked; and it is the executive hand which is to dispense them. In war, the honors and emoluments of office are to be multiplied; and it is the executive patronage under which they are to be enjoyed. It is in war, finally, that laurels are to be gathered; and it is the executive brow they are to encircle. The strongest passions and most dangerous weaknesses of the human breast; ambition, avarice, vanity, the honorable or venial love of fame, are all in conspiracy against the desire and duty of peace.

Hence it has grown into an axiom that the executive is the department of power most distinguished by its propensity to war: hence it is the practice of all states, in proportion as they are free, to disarm this propensity. . . ."

The Gazette of the United States, Alexander Hamilton, writing as "Pacificus," defended the president's action. James Madison, writing as "Helvidius," responded.

accepted his secretary of state's interpretation that the "commander-in-chief" power permitted the president to act alone.

"By insisting that the presidential prerogative alone sufficed to meet the requirements of the Constitution," writes historian Schlesinger in *The Imperial Presidency*, "Truman did a good deal more than pass on his sacred trust unimpaired. He dramatically and dangerously enlarged the power of future presidents to take the nation into major war."

Schlesinger is equally gloomy — for a different reason — about the implications of President John F. Kennedy's bold stance during the Cuban missile crisis. Kennedy did not consult with Congress before making his decision to respond with a naval blockade to the Soviet placement of missiles in Cuba. Schlesinger justifies this lack of consultation as the exception to the rule: a case that combined all the pressures of threat, secrecy and time that are unique to the nuclear age. "Alas, Kennedy's action, which should have been celebrated as an exception, was instead enshrined as a rule," laments Schlesinger.

President Lyndon B. Johnson relied on a congressional resolution as his basis for prosecuting the Vietnam War, but many have argued that he misled Congress.

Johnson asked Congress to pass the Gulf of Tonkin Resolution in a crisis atmosphere, immediately after he reported that the American destroyer *Maddox* had been attacked twice by North Vietnamese torpedo boats. To this day, it is unclear as to whether there were two attacks, or even one, on the ship. The resolution empowered Johnson to "take all necessary measures to repel any armed attack against the forces of the United States and to prevent further aggression." The late Sen. Jacob K. Javits said that "the language of the Gulf of Tonkin Resolution was far more sweeping than congressional intent." "Congress was stunned," Javits said, when the resolution was later used by Johnson to justify a widening war in Vietnam. Most senators, Javits contended, thought they were authorizing a narrow act of retaliation to a specific attack.[4]

Yet at the time of the Senate floor vote, when Foreign Relations Committee Chairman Fulbright was asked if the resolution would give the president authority to "use such force as could lead into war," he replied, apparently with no misgivings about the future, "That is the way I would interpret it."[5] The resolution passed the House unanimously and the Senate with only two dissenting votes.

But the subsequent Vietnam War, which ended in defeat for the United States, spawned some profound changes in American politics. Congress resolved to reassert itself in the realm of foreign policy. A new kind of isolationism emerged among American liberals. And presidents increasingly found themselves on the defensive politically as they sought to press America's geopolitical role in the world.

Indeed, in the past 15 years, Congress has reclaimed a large measure of prerogative in the arena of foreign affairs. Through a series of legislative actions, Congress has curtailed U.S. support for anti-communist insurgencies — in Angola and Nicaragua, for example — that would have

received almost automatic support during the consensus years of the 1950s. And it passed a series of laws that had the effect of clipping the wings of the executive eagle by diminishing executive-branch secrecy in foreign policy and curbing presidential flexibility to deploy troops and mount intelligence operations. This legislative phase began with the tragedy of Vietnam.

As Congress found itself increasingly at odds with President Johnson and later with President Nixon over that bitter war, it sought to reassert its constitutional prerogatives in war-making. Nixon's decision to invade Cambodia in 1970 without congressional authorization inspired the first steps in this direction: the early drafts of the War Powers Resolution. Sen. Javits, the resolution's author, saw it as a way to insert Congress into the initiation of war. Nixon charged that the resolution was an unconstitutional incursion on his power as commander in chief. But by 1973, Nixon's stature had declined precipitously because of Watergate, and Congress overrode his veto of the resolution.

It specified that the president's powers to introduce troops into hostile situations could be exercised only following a declaration of war, specific statutory authorization or a national emergency. Under the resolution, the president must report to Congress within 48 hours after he deploys troops and must withdraw them within 60 days — or 90 days in special cases — unless he receives authorization from Congress. At the time of the resolution's passage, Members of Congress disagreed over whether the language merely restated Congress' war powers, abridged or expanded them.

Since the passage of the resolution, presidents of both parties have complied with its provisions but have refused to concede its constitutionality. For example, Congress issued authorization under the War Powers Resolution for President Reagan to retain Marines in Lebanon for 18 months in October 1982. But, upon signing the Lebanon resolution, Reagan insisted that the document could not "revise the president's constitutional authority to deploy the United States Armed Forces."

U.S. role in Nicaraguan rebellion

In the Iran-contra affair, the president's attempts to support a foreign war fall in the constitutionally disputed territory between a state of war and a state of peace. The Nicaraguan rebellion is not considered a full-scale American war, but it could lead to one.

"Moving the country from a state of peace to a state of war can only be done by Congress," notes constitutional lawyer Eugene V. Rostow, who usually sides with the executive in such debates. "But a show of force in peacetime is under presidential authority," asserts Rostow, referring to Reagan's role in Nicaragua. Rostow is currently visiting professor of law at the National Defense University in Washington, D.C.

Henkin, professor of law at Columbia University, sees Congress as having broader powers in peacetime than Rostow. "The power to control war includes the power to control things closely connected to war," Henkin said in discussing the congressional ban on contra aid.

Because most wars start gradually with incremental shows of force on each side, it has never been clear whether such steps fall under Congress' power to declare war or the president's "executive" power to conduct foreign policy. Of the more than 125 violent conflicts and wars in which the United States has been involved, only five have been "declared" by Congress. Most of those "undeclared" conflicts, however, have been attacks on such non-governmental entities as pirates. Often they have been initiated not by the president, but by lieutenants at sea.

Since the days of the Founding Fathers, presidents have been given the unilateral right to repel invasion. But other kinds of hostile acts remain an area of vigorous dispute. Rostow and other experts who side with presidents argue that the framers viewed the power to "declare war" as a formality under international law. Under this interpretation, Congress' official declaration of war would act merely as the seal of approval on a president's movements toward war. Any step short of a war declaration would be within the president's sovereignty. On the other side of the debate are historians of the Constitution such as Charles A. Lofgren of Claremont College in California. They argue that the framers did not intend to make a technical distinction between "declaring" war and "making" war.[6]

Through history, many presidents have taken action without congressional involvement that could technically be considered in violation of the Constitution. Lincoln and Roosevelt are famous examples. But if the action has proved politically popular, or Congress has been consulted — even after the fact — Congress has usually accepted the president's initiative.

In his book, *The President's Control of Foreign Relations*, Corwin wrote that "the difficulty arising from overlapping powers . . . has been converted from a legal one to a political one, with the result that the real solution has to be sought as each case arises by the methods of compromise and statesmanship."[7]

That picture of comity drawn by Corwin, "can go on without any conflict for generations, where there is mutual cooperation," concurs Rep. George E. Brown Jr. (D-Calif.), who serves on the House Intelligence Committee. By contrast, Brown says, "the present situation represents the most extreme conflict likely to occur. We have a president with the most extreme ideology within my memory and a Congress with the most divergent views of any Congress in my memory."

Reagan's attorneys respond that he is a president whose popular base is independent of Congress. Reagan has a clearly stated policy of fighting communist regimes in Latin America. How are his actions, aimed at circumventing a hostile Congress, any different from Roosevelt's prior to World War II? they ask.

Historian Robert Dallek, author of *Franklin Roosevelt*

and American Foreign Policy, calls the parallel with Reagan "stuff and nonsense."

"Roosevelt understood something that these [Reagan] people have missed: If you're going to have a stable policy abroad, you must have a consensus at home. . . . What's striking is not how secret or overbearing Roosevelt was, but how cautious he was," says Dallek, who teaches history at the University of California at Los Angeles.

While Dallek describes Roosevelt as a "great manipulator" of the political process, he argues that Roosevelt was motivated, not by a conspiratorial plan, but by respect for the democratic process when taking partial steps toward U.S. involvement in World War II.

The current constitutional conflict has focused on the five versions of the Boland amendment, named for its author, Rep. Edward P. Boland (D-Mass.). The spirit in which the Boland amendments are read by opposing sides inevitably evokes the historical and legal debates over who controls foreign policy. The Boland amendments, reflective of the congressional reassertion of recent years, were aimed at limiting U.S. aid to the contra rebels. In the form of riders containing differently worded restrictions, they were attached to one-year appropriations bills covering fiscal 1983-85. Congress later eased and then reversed its position against funding for the contras.

The toughest version of the Boland amendment, enacted in 1984, stipulated that "during fiscal year 1985, no funds available to the Central Intelligence Agency, the Department of Defense, *or any other agency or entity of the United States involved in intelligence activities* may be obligated or expended for the purpose or which would have the effect of supporting, directly or indirectly, military or paramilitary operations in Nicaragua by any nation, group, organization, movement, or individual." (Italics added.)

In response to congressional charges that the Reagan administration violated the Boland amendments, White House lawyers are making a narrow argument about the legal wording as their first line of defense. They contend that the amendments did not apply to the people most directly implicated in raising funds for the contras: the National Security Council (NSC) staff. The NSC, Reagan's lawyers note, is not defined by law as an "agency or entity of the United States involved in intelligence activities." Nor, they argue, can the president be considered such an "entity." Democratic members of Congress retort that since the NSC staff was involved in intelligence activities in practice, the NSC — and possibly the president — would be subject to the amendment's prohibitions.

Although White House lawyers are concentrating their first line of argument on the amendment's specific language, their ultimate defense of the president's role, they say, would be his constitutional pre-eminence in the field of foreign policy.

For example, the president's lawyers argue, under the Constitution even a law that specifically mentioned the president could not prevent him from exercising his diplomatic prerogative of meeting privately with foreign officials to request funding for a foreign war. This example has been the subject of legal interest ever since Reagan acknowledged that he met with King Fahd of Saudi Arabia to discuss Saudi financial assistance for the Nicaraguan contras.

Constitutional lawyer Henkin disagrees that congressional power over the president's foreign-policy activities is so limited. He argues that if the purpose of a meeting was to circumvent the Boland amendments' ban on contra aid, the meeting would be illegal.

"The Congress could regulate pretty much anything he [the president] does," Henkin says, but the interpretation of the Boland amendments depends on how broad Congress intended them to be. "If the Boland amendment meant it's against the policy of the government to help the contras," he says, then it would prohibit actions of the president aimed at overturning that policy. While conceding that Congress could not outlaw meetings, Henkin argues: "If Congress said no assistance to the contras is allowed, then your conversation with Fahd would be a violation."

Those who advocate a strong role for the president argue that the nation's leader should not permit an indecisive Congress to dictate foreign policy, particularly when it diverges from his own policy. The result, they suggest, is a foreign-policy vacuum.

Dean Rusk, who served as secretary of state under Presidents Kennedy and Johnson, believes Congress could not prevent the president from soliciting private funds for the Nicaraguan rebellion. Considering Congress' vacillation over supporting the contras, Rusk says, the president would be justified in construing the Boland amendments as narrowly as possible in order to pursue his own foreign policy. "This is not a matter of broad bipartisan legislation on which the two sides can agree," Rusk notes.

Institutional changes
and covert activities

Perennial conflicts between the president and Congress over the crafting of foreign policy have been exacerbated by recent changes in the nation's political structure. Nelson W. Polsby, a political scientist at the University of California at Berkeley, sees as the root cause of the current conflict a belief on the part of the president that Congress cannot be trusted with foreign-policy secrets. The executive branch points to instances in which members of Congress have leaked classified information about national security to the press. Thus, the executive branch concludes it is necessary to "circumvent congressional will," in Polsby's words. This distrust is heightened by the fact that Congress is in Democratic hands while Republicans control the presidency. At the same time, the number of political appointees who oversee the foreign-policy bureaucracy has grown along with the expansion of such agencies as the State Department over the past 30-40 years. This cadre of appointees has become "a political branch with its own

agenda" and little accountability to Congress, in Polsby's view.

Most experts note that there is distinctly less cooperation between Reagan and Congress on foreign-policy matters than in previous administrations, even when presidents had to deal with Congresses dominated by the other party. Rusk, who suggests that Reagan should have consulted with Congress earlier, recalled that it was easier to have bipartisan consensus when Congress was controlled by a few strong party leaders. "Back in the early 1960s we would go to the Senate and talk to four people" — Senate Democratic leaders Hubert H. Humphrey, Richard B. Russell and Robert S. Kerr and Republican leader Everett McKinley Dirksen — "and then go to the House and speak to old Sam Rayburn," the Speaker. "They could tell us what the Congress would do, because they could tell Congress what to do." With the decline of powerful party leaders, Rusk notes, "You don't have any whales anymore; you have a bunch of minnows swimming around in a bucket."

Covert military operations are a relatively recent phenomenon in the history of the United States, dating from World War II, and so is congressional interest in them. For more than 25 years following the passage of the National Security Act, which created the CIA in 1947, Congress largely ignored the intelligence community. It voted billions of dollars in hidden appropriations for intelligence activities with very few of its members knowing the amounts or the purposes of the funds. Not until the mid-1970s, with the revelations of CIA activities in Chile and abuses of constitutional rights of American citizens by the CIA and the Federal Bureau of Investigation, did Congress enter into a broad-scale scrutiny of the nation's intelligence operations. Investigations by the late Sen. Frank Church (D-Idaho) and by the House gave rise to the creation of permanent intelligence committees — in 1976 in the Senate and in 1977 in the House.

Congress passed a series of laws in the mid-1970s to ensure that the executive branch would report covert actions to Congress. Responding in part to the CIA's role in Chile, Congress passed the Hughes-Ryan amendment to the 1974 foreign aid bill requiring that covert actions conducted "by or on behalf of" the CIA be reported to the appropriate committees of Congress.

The CIA's program to train and support anti-Sandinista Nicaraguans based in Honduras was leaked to the press beginning in early 1982. In response, Congress passed a ban on such aid, first in the secret 1983 intelligence authorization bill and later as a public amendment to the Defense Department appropriation bill.

The current dispute over Nicaraguan aid raises the basic question of whether covert wars are appropriate in a democratic society and whether it is possible to keep them secret. Supporters of covert wars, such as constitutional lawyer John Norton Moore of the University of Virginia, urge that the intelligence committees of Congress keep a tighter lid on secret information. A superior approach, Moore says, is illustrated by the Israeli investigation of the Iran-contra affair. Israel's investigation was conducted by

Past Coverage

■ **National Security Council (NSC)** traces the increasing power of the NSC since its creation in 1947 and presents the debate over its proper role. "Before the Iran-contra affair," writes Harrison Donnelly, "there were no known cases of NSC operatives doing the kind of cloak-and-dagger work normally reserved for the Central Intelligence Agency. . . ." However, notes Donnelly, national security advisers under Nixon and Carter have been entrusted with important foreign-policy missions, often to the extent of elbowing out the secretary of state. "Like his predecessors, Reagan often resorted to the NSC because it was free from congressional and other outside controls," writes Donnelly. The result has sometimes been a crisis resulting from an aggressive NSC, the report concludes. E.R.R., 1987 Vol. I, pp. 18-27.

■ **Foreign Policy Making** reappraises American foreign policy in light of President Richard M. Nixon's policy of détente and the Vietnam War. The report records some famous attempts by presidents to circumvent Congress and takes a look at old and new forms of isolationism. By Mary Costello, E.R.R., 1975 Vol. I, pp. 41-60.

■ **War Powers of the President**, written during the Vietnam War, discussses the conflicts then taking place between Congress and President Lyndon B. Johnson. "The Vietnamese conflict has reminded Congress that its constitutional power to declare war counts for little in today's world," writes Richard L. Worsnop. "Congress virtually abdicated the power to declare war in Vietnam" with its adoption of the 1964 Gulf of Tonkin Resolution, he concludes. Members of Congress "contended that the 1964 resolution was never intended as a blank check to wage unlimited war in Southeast Asia," the report notes. It contains a good, concise history of presidential war powers. E.R.R., 1966 Vol. I, pp. 181-200.

the close of the first phase of committee hearings on June 10, "Privatization of foreign policy is a prescription for confusion and failure. . . . The use of private parties to carry out high purposes of government makes us the subject of puzzlement and ridicule."

Sen. John Kerry, D-Mass., echoed this view when he called the affair an example of recurrent conflict in U.S. history: "On the one side is our deep-rooted commitment to constitutionalism, the understanding that any U.S. military actions must have not merely popular support but the actual public sanction of Congress through a declaration of war and congressional approval as set forth in the Constitution or appropriate statutory authority such as the War Powers act." The other side, Kerry said, views legal restrictions "as irritating limits on a great power's need to exercise power in a dangerous world."

Despite the constitutional currents running through the Iran-contra investigation, the resolution of the struggle will be a political one, depending in large part on how dangerous a picture the American people have of the communist threat that the Nicaraguan contras are fighting.

"Today we don't perceive communism as being the same centrally controlled military force" that the country perceived before Vietnam, says Rep. Brown, who expects Reagan to lose congressional support for contra aid when it next comes up for a vote. "We see an aging, fractionated communism that isn't being bought by very many people."

Dick Cheney, R-Wyo., the ranking Republican member of the House select committee on Iran, agrees that Reagan failed to sell his philosophy to the American people, although — unlike Brown — Cheney shares Reagan's philosophy.

"The most difficult portion [of presidential foreign policy] is building domestic political support. [Reagan] didn't. If there is a failing at this point, instead of going out and doing a massive selling job . . . [the administration] opted for the private covert option."

NOTES

[1] The Senate panel investigating the Iran-contra affair is the Senate Select Committee on Secret Military Assistance to Iran and the Nicaraguan Opposition; the House panel is the House Select Committee to Investigate Covert Arms Transactions with Iran.

[2] See Arthur M. Schlesinger Jr., *The Imperial Presidency*, Houghton Mifflin, 1973, p. 126.

[3] *Ibid.*, p. 284.

[4] See Jacob K. Javits, *Who Makes War?* p. 259.

[5] *Congressional Record*, Aug. 6, 1964, p. 18409.

[6] See Eugene V. Rostow, "Once More Unto the Breach," and Charles A. Lofgren, "On War-Making," *Valparaiso University Law Review*, Fall 1986.

[7] See Edward S. Corwin, *The President's Control of Foreign Relations*, 1917, p. 5.

private committees in secret before a public report was issued. Moore also believes that covert activities provide "an option between peace and war" that can forestall the potential for outright war.

Historian Dallek disagrees. "These secret operations undermine democratic institutions and create terrible cynicism among the public. . . . There's no place for them in a democracy."

For Democratic members of Congress, the perception that secret operations circumvent democracy has been particularly bitter in the case of the Nicaraguan program's apparent reliance on a few, wealthy private citizens.

Rep. Lee H. Hamilton, D-Ind., chairman of the House committee investigating the Iran-contra affair, concluded at

Graphics: cover, p. 6, S. Dmitri Lipczenko; p. 3, James K. W. Atherton/The Washington Post, Murry H. Sill (contras)

BOOKS

Corwin, Edward S., *The President: Office and Powers, 1787-1957*, New York University Press, 1957.

Corwin, considered the authoritative historian on the president's powers in foreign relations, addresses the executive branch's role in foreign policy and in war in Chapters 5 and 6. Corwin explores the intent of the Constitution's framers and traces presidents' uses and abuses of their constitutional powers through history. "The verdict of history," he concludes, "is that the power to determine the substantive content of American foreign policy is a *divided* power, with the lion's share share falling, usually, though by no means always, to the president."

Crabb, Cecil V. Jr., and Pat M. Holt, *Invitation to Struggle: Congress, the President, and Foreign Policy*, 3d ed., Congressional Quarterly, 1988.

A useful reference summarizing recent legislative struggles between Congress and the president over foreign policy. The authors take a sympathetic look at the efforts of Congress to play an increasingly influential role in such areas as intelligence and military conflict up through the Reagan administration. ". . . [B]y the early 1980s many informed students of the American foreign-policy process believed that the era of the imperial presidency had been superseded by almost uncontrolled congressional activism and dynamism in the foreign-policy field," the authors note.

Henkin, Louis, *Foreign Affairs and the Constitution*, Norton, 1972.

A leading constitutional authority in the field of foreign affairs describes the theory and practice of foreign policy from a legal point of view. The clarity of the writing, intended for the layman as well as the lawyer, makes this book a pleasure to read. "The foreign relations of the United States cannot be understood in the light of the Constitution alone, but they cannot be understood without it, for it continues to shape the institutions and the actions that determine them," Henkin writes.

Jacob K. Javits, *Who Makes War: The President Versus the Congress*, Morrow, 1973.

The late Sen. Javits, author of the War Powers Resolution, makes the case that Congress has abdicated its constitutional powers over war and that the president has conquered more

than his fair share. Javits presents his argument through a lively history of presidential power grabs from Washington to Nixon. In recalling the Gulf of Tonkin Resolution, for which he voted, Javits writes, "I am convinced that congressional embarrassment at the failure to weigh all the factors involved in the Tonkin resolution has been responsible for the burgeoning assertiveness of the movement in the Senate at long last to curb the war-making power of the President."

Arthur M. Schlesinger Jr., *The Imperial Presidency*, Houghton Mifflin, 1973.

Tracing the rise and fall of presidential power starting with George Washington, historian Schlesinger argues that the usurpation of power reached its peak with "the imperial presidency" of Richard M. Nixon. This book is a well-written, opinionated history by a former assistant to President John F. Kennedy. "The postwar Presidents . . . almost came to see the sharing of power with Congress in foreign policy as a derogation of the presidency. Congress, in increasing self-abasement, almost came to love its impotence," Schlesinger writes. Of secret operations, he says: "The secrecy system instilled in the executive branch the idea that foreign policy was no one's business save its own, and uncontrolled secrecy made it easy for lying to become routine."

ARTICLES

"Controversy over the War Powers Act," *Congressional Digest*, November 1983.

This issue consists of excerpts from the congressional debate over the 1983 resolution authorizing President Reagan to send Marines to Lebanon. As the editors note, the debate centered more on the War Powers Resolution and the constitutional powers of the president than on the Lebanese situation. Sen. Barry Goldwater, R-Ariz., argued: "History proves we can have no assurance Congress will act when a firm response is needed. Congress would have created an even greater world crisis if the War Powers Resolution had been in effect to tie the hands of Presidents Roosevelt and Truman."

Rostow, Eugene V., "Once More Unto the Breach: the War Powers Resolution Revisited," *Valparaiso University Law Review*, fall 1986.

Legal scholar Rostow argues that the War Powers Resolution violates the spirit of the Constitution by weakening the broad role it envisioned for the president. "Actually enforcing the War Powers Resolution would convert the strong, autonomous president, which is one of the great achievements of the Constitution, into a mere lackey of an omnipotent Congress," Rostow writes.

Lofgren, Charles A. "On War-Making, Original Intent, and Ultra Whiggery," *Valparaiso University Law Review*, fall 1986.

Historian Lofgren disputes Rostow's view, contending that the Constitution's framers intended to give the primary power over war to Congress.

NATIONAL SECURITY COUNCIL

Revelations about secret U.S. arms sales to Iran and the funneling of some of the proceeds to the Nicaraguan contras have raised questions about the NSC's role. *18*

Secret missions of the NSC began with Henry Kissinger's 1971 trip to China, which paved the way for a reopening of U.S.-Chinese relations. *20*

The struggle between the NSC and the secretary of state to be the chief influence on the president's foreign policy is an old conflict. *20*

The NSC's almost complete freedom from outside review and its staffing policies contributed to the Iran-contra affair. *23*

Some analysts argue that the rising power of the NSC in recent years is linked to the shift to the "operational presidency." *23*

Ideas being floated for reforming the NSC include banning covert activities and making security advisers subject to Senate confirmation. *26*

Reagan's Iran-contra crisis
raises questions about the

NATIONAL SECURITY COUNCIL

and its role in
foreign policy-making.

by Harrison Donnelly

When he set up the complex deal that funneled money to Nicaraguan guerrillas (contras) from secret arms sales to Iran, Lt. Col. Oliver L. North did more than touch off a political crisis in Ronald Reagan's presidency. North also set in motion a chain of events that could lead to fundamental changes in the National Security Council (NSC), the embattled agency for which he worked, and thus reshape the decision-making process in foreign affairs.

As a formal decision-making body — composed of the president, the vice president and the secretaries of state and defense — the NSC has played a dominant role in determining U.S. diplomatic and military strategy only occasionally during its 40-year history. Instead, its staff, headed by the national security adviser, has evolved into an apparatus with which the president seeks to carry out his own vision of how the United States should relate to the rest of the world. The chief goals of the NSC have been to advise the president and coordinate the policies of the State and Defense departments and other agencies involved in foreign relations.

The extent to which the staff strayed from that mission will be examined by a three-member Special Review Board appointed by Reagan Nov. 26 and headed by former Texas Republican Sen. John G. Tower. In addition, two special congressional committees and an independent counsel, Lawrence E. Walsh, have been appointed to investigate the Iran-contra affair. The investigations are looking at possible violations of a variety of laws, including those that barred aid to the contras and the sale of arms to nations that support terrorism, and required disclosure to Congress of arms sales and covert actions.[1]

The board, scheduled to issue its report Jan. 29, also will look at the incident in the context of the NSC's structure and role, as they have evolved during four decades. An internal review of the agency's functions has meanwhile been undertaken by Frank C. Carlucci, who became national security adviser Jan. 2, filling the vacancy created by the departure of Vice Adm. John M. Poindexter. He resigned the post Nov. 25 after it was revealed that he had known about the apparently illegal transfer of funds to the contras.

The NSC's plunge into covert operations is one of the many roles it has played since it was created by Congress in 1947. *(See p. 21.)* At times, the agency has been the dominant institutional force in setting U.S. foreign policy — as it was under President Nixon's national security adviser, Henry A. Kissinger. At other times, it has been just a bureaucratic shell, relegated to shuffling papers and little else. But certain trends have been evident throughout the agency's existence. In some ways, the NSC's involvement in the Iran-contra affair represents a continuation of past trends; in other ways, it is a sharp break with the past.

Before the Iran-contra affair, there were no known cases of NSC operatives doing the kind of cloak-and-dagger work normally reserved for the Central Intelligence Agency (CIA). In terms of secret missions abroad, however, a line can be traced at least to Kissinger's trip to China in 1971 to arrange a U.S. reconciliation with that country. Similarly, an NSC dispute with the State Department over the current matter echoes past conflicts, such as those between national security adviser Zbigniew Brzezinski and Secretary of State Cyrus R. Vance in the Carter administration. Tension between the two offices may have reached a new level, however, when NSC staffers bypassed Secretary of State George P. Shultz and enlisted John H. Kelly, the U.S. ambassador to Lebanon, in efforts to free American hostages in Lebanon — the apparent reason, though sometimes officially denied, for the arms sales to Iran.

Like his predecessors, Reagan often resorted to the NSC because it was free from congressional and other outside controls. What remains to be determined about the current affair, though, was whether the council's staff had gone beyond the limits set in the White House, and was acting without control by Reagan or his chief of staff, Donald T. Regan.

Some former staff members of the NSC argue that its plunge into questionable activities has been fostered by flaws in this administration's system for making foreign policy. They say that Reagan had downgraded the agency from the start of his presidency, and consequently contributed to policy disarray within the administration — over the presence of U.S. troops in Lebanon, for example.[2] According to this line of thought, the disarray encouraged disgruntled NSC staffers to assert themselves through covert actions. On past occasions, the worry has been voiced that the NSC was too strong — that the modern presidency inevitably gave it too much power at the expense of other agencies. But Brzezinski insists that "the problem

At Issue

COVERT OPERATIONS

Covert National Security Council operations in the Iran-contra affair, in which NSC operatives carried out activities usually reserved for the CIA, may be unprecedented. But secret missions are not. They can be traced back to the 1971 Kissinger trip to China that paved the way for reopening U.S.-Chinese relations. See page 20.

TURF WARS

Struggles between national security advisers and secretaries of state—recently McFarlane and Poindexter versus Shultz on selling arms to Iran—are longstanding. Part of the reason may lie in the contrasting nature of the two jobs. As the president's personal aide, a security adviser is wedded to the president's goals. A secretary of state is likely to take a longer-range view of foreign policy. See page 20-23.

PRESIDENTIAL AGENTS

Some analysts argue that the rising power of NSC advisers in recent presidencies is related to the "operational" modern presidency. In this view, electronic technology has for the first time given presidents the power actually to implement foreign policy. National security advisers are the logical choice to be foreign policy agents because they aren't accountable to Congress. See page 23-26.

CONTOURS OF REFORM

Examinations into the NSC role in the Iran-contra affair could prompt Congress to consider structural changes in the agency. Among the proposals that are being floated: banning covert NSC activities, making security advisers subject to Senate confirmation, and abolishing or restructuring the job. See page 26.

over the last several years has been not that the National Security Council has been too strong but that it has been too weak." [3]

Carrying the 'black bag' in diplomats' guise

From an institutional point of view, the most significant aspect of the NSC's involvement in the Iran-contra affair was that it was operational, not just advisory. Instead of advising others on what policies to pursue, staff members actually carried them out. Moreover, they did so using the tools not of diplomats but of undercover intelligence agents. In arranging for the delivery of arms to Iran and the secret transfer of funds to the contras, North, Poindexter and others crossed a thin line that past NSC staffers had never quite stepped over. "The potential for this kind of thing has always been there," observed I. M. Destler, a foreign-policy analyst with the Institute for International Economics in Washington, D.C. "The tendency of the staff to implement policy is not new. The element that seems to be new, in terms of what is known about prior action, is the direct management of covert action," Destler said. [4]

Still, there are clear antecedents for the NSC's forays into the international underground. The pioneer in this area was Kissinger, whose 1971 mission to China revealed his taste both for stealth and for dramatic public-relations gestures. After decades of hostility, the United States and China were ready to re-establish relations, but were wary of revealing their intentions to the world. Sent by Nixon to negotiate with Chinese leaders, Kissinger constructed an elaborate ruse to conceal his whereabouts. On a diplomatic stopover in Pakistan, he told news reporters that a stomach virus would force him to rest there for a couple of days. Instead, he flew to China and back before any outsiders realized he had left Pakistan. Soon he and Nixon were ready with an announcement that would shake world power diplomacy — the potential alliance of the United States and China in opposition to the Soviet Union.

Kissinger also engaged in secret diplomacy over the Vietnam War. Even while formal peace negotiations with North Vietnam were going on in one part of Paris, Kissinger went to another section of the city for carefully concealed talks with North Vietnamese leaders. The State Department was not informed about the behind-the-scenes negotiations for months.

Brzezinski displayed a similar penchant for getting directly involved in diplomacy, although he was not given as free a rein by Carter as Kissinger was by Nixon. Brzezinksi's most significant negotiations were also with China, with which he worked out the delicate arrangements to establish formal diplomatic ties in 1978. Another instance came in 1979, when he negotiated with Anatoly Dobrynin, the Soviet ambassador to the United States, for the release of five Russian dissidents in exchange for two Soviet spies held by the United States. Finally, Brzezinski says without elaboration in his memoirs, "I negotiated

some sensitive relationships." [5] Had he been allowed, Brzezinski would have carried out even more personal diplomacy; Carter vetoed trips he proposed to make to Moscow and Tehran.

The antecedents to the NSC staff's role in the Iran-contra affair can be traced even more clearly to the first years of the Reagan administration. Long before arms sales to Iran were approved, North and his colleagues were involved in arranging a variety of secret activities. Those initial forays, however, did not have the Iran-contra's imprint of illegality, nor were they politically explosive. In some cases, they were were quite popular. The NSC served as a nerve center for the October 1983 invasion of Grenada, for example. And North has been credited with the idea for the U.S. seizure of an Egyptian aircraft carrying four Palestinians who had hijacked the Italian cruise ship *Achille Lauro* in October 1985 and killed an American passenger. [6]

North's activities in arranging for private funding for the contras had a more dubious legal and political status. After Congress voted in 1984 to stop government funding for these guerrillas who seek to overthrow Nicaragua's Sandinista government, North helped establish a network of support groups that eventually raised several million dollars for the contras. Reports of North's activities, which appeared to violate the spirit if not the letter of the law, drew strong criticism from congressional Democrats in 1985. But the White House denied the allegations, and congressional investigations made little headway at the time. Another NSC-directed project was aimed at overthrowing Libyan leader Col. Muammar el-Qaddafi. That plan came under sharp criticism in October 1986 after it was revealed that it included efforts to deceive the press. [7]

Fighting with State for influence

The debates within the Reagan administration over the sale of arms to Iran have provided a particularly clear example of an old conflict: the struggle between the national security adviser and the secretary of state to be the chief influence on the president's foreign policy. Along with many other top officials, Shultz strongly opposed the arms sales, which were advocated by Poindexter and by his predecessor, Robert C. McFarlane. Shultz lost that struggle when Reagan decided to approve the deliveries to Iran. The secretary later related to a congressional committee that he was told little about the Iran deal, and nothing at all about the transfer of funds to the contras. [8]

Beyond the specifics, the incident apparently reflects an antagonism inherent in the two positions. Sometimes the clashes that have occurred over the years between the secretary of state and the national security adviser arise from the competing personal ambitions of two powerful individuals. But they also seem to stem from fundamental differences in the two jobs.

The national security adviser is the president's personal aide — his formal title is assistant to the president for

How Powerful Depends on Who's President

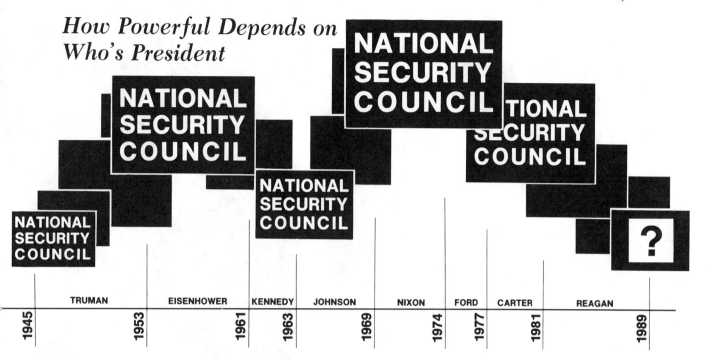

TRUMAN   EISENHOWER   KENNEDY   JOHNSON   NIXON   FORD   CARTER   REAGAN

1945   1953   1961   1963   1969   1974   1977   1981   1989

1947 The National Security Council (NSC) is established by the National Security Act, which also creates the Defense Department, the Joint Chiefs of Staff and the CIA. The council replaces a variety of committees that sought to advise the president and coordinate military policy during World War II. Advocates of the council, led by Navy Secretary James Forrestal, stress the need for a permanent institution to oversee all branches of the government involved in national security.

1950 Preparation of NSC-68, the landmark classified strategic analysis that was to guide postwar U.S. security policy.

1953 President Eisenhower appoints Robert Cutler as the first national security adviser. During his two terms in office, Eisenhower relied heavily on the NSC, both as a forum for consultation with top administration officials and as a system for developing foreign policy studies and positions.

1961 Criticizing the bureaucratic rigidity of the system under Eisenhower, President Kennedy eliminates much of the NSC structure. Instead, he prefers to make decisions after consulting with small, informal groups of advisers. However, Kennedy also appoints McGeorge Bundy, who becomes the first national security adviser with significant personal power in foreign policy decisions.

1966 President Johnson selects as his national security adviser W.W. Rostow, who becomes a leading advocate of greater U.S. involvement in the Vietnam War. But the role of the NSC system continues to diminish, as does the size of its staff.

1969 President Nixon comes into office determined to restore the NSC to the importance it had had under Eisenhower. Nixon appoints as national security adviser Henry A. Kissinger, who quickly overshadows Secretary of State William P. Rogers to become the dominant administration voice on foreign policy. The NSC structure and staff expands rapidly.

1971 Kissinger makes a secret trip to China, during which he arranges for the opening of relations with the United States and Nixon's 1972 visit.

1973 Kissinger replaces Rogers as Secretary of State, while continuing to hold the position of national security adviser.

1975 President Ford appoints Lt. Gen. Brent Scowcroft as national security adviser. Scowcroft avoids the prominent public role played by Kissinger, focusing instead on coordinating policies of State and other departments.

1977 President Carter vows that the NSC will not have as much power, at the expense of the State Department, as it did under Kissinger. But Carter's national security adviser, Zbigniew Brzezinski, soon comes into sharp conflict with Secretary of State Cyrus R. Vance. The disputes continue throughout Carter's term, fostering a public image of foreign policy disarray.

1981 In line with his preference for "Cabinet government," President Reagan de-emphasizes the role of the NSC. He appoints as his national security adviser Richard V. Allen, who is forced to resign in January 1982 because of alleged conflict of interest violations. Allen is followed in quick succession by William P. Clark Jr. (1982-83), Robert C. McFarlane (1983-85) and Vice Adm. John M. Poindexter (1985-86).

1985-86 McFarlane, Lt. Col. Oliver L. North and other NSC staff members implement policy of delivering arms to Iran, in an effort to improve relations with that country and secure the release of U.S. hostages held in Lebanon. On Nov. 25, 1986, Poindexter resigns, and North is fired, following revelations that some of the proceeds from the arms sales to Iran were diverted to contra forces fighting the leftist government of Nicaragua. Poindexter is replaced Jan. 2, 1987, as national security adviser by Frank C. Carlucci.

HOW MUCH POWER ?

Henry A. Kissinger

Robert C. McFarlane

Zbigniew Brzezinski

according to five former NSC chiefs

"[The national security adviser] must separate clearly his own view from his exposition of a problem and of alternative possible actions in response to it," wrote **W. W. ROSTOW,** who was President Johnson's national security adviser from 1966-69. "He must be able to present another man's case as well as the man himself could. A special assistant for NSC affairs who could not do this comfortably — who used his post for explicit or implicit lobbying — would not last in his post for more than a few weeks, at least under Kennedy or Johnson." From Rostow's book *The Diffusion of Power* (Macmillan Co., 1972).

"Though I did not think so at the time, I have become convinced that a President should make the secretary of state his principal adviser and use the national security adviser primarily as a senior administrator and coordinator to make certain that each significant point of view is heard," said **HENRY A. KISSINGER,** who was national security adviser to Presidents Nixon and Ford from 1969-75. "If the security adviser becomes active in the development and articulation of policy he must inevitably diminish the Secretary of State and reduce his effectivenes." From Kissinger's book *White House Years* (Little, Brown & Co., 1979).

"The national security adviser should oversee informally the implementation of presidential decisions to ensure that they are implemented in the manner the president wished them to be," said **BRENT SCOWCROFT,** who was President Ford's national security adviser from 1975-77. "However, I do not believe that the national security adviser should substitute for the secretary of state or the secretary of defense, either as a major public policy explicator or as a negotiator, nor should he head . . . a mini-State Department." From April 17, 1980, testimony before the Senate Foreign Relations Comittee.

"I think that the system would work best if . . . the practical coordination and the definition of the strategic direction would originate from [the president's] assistant for national security affairs, who would then tightly coordinate and control the secretary of state, the secretary of defense, the chairman of the joint chiefs, and the director of central intelligence as a team, with them knowing that he was doing so on the president's behalf," said President Carter's national security adviser, **ZBIGNIEW BRZEZINSKI,** who served from 1977-81. From an interview published in the winter 1982 issue of *The Washington Quarterly*.

"The [national security adviser] must play two distinct roles . . . . He must be an honest broker of advice coming to the president from outside the White House, and he must be an independent adviser and policy manager for the president on national security matters," wrote national security adviser **ROBERT C. MCFARLANE,** who served under President Reagan from 1983-85. "The NSC system must possess a certain amount of centralized strength and authority if it is to have the capacity to coordinate effectively the efforts of the many powerful and contentious components of the policy making community." From McFarlane's essay, "The National Security Council: Organization for Policy Making," in *The Presidency and National Security Policy*, edited by R. Gordon Hoxie (Center for the Study of the Presidency, 1984).

national security affairs — and has no power other than what the chief executive gives him. The position, which was created by President Eisenhower, was not even mentioned in the 1947 law that created the NSC. The secretary of state also is expected to be a loyal supporter of the president. But his office — the oldest and most prestigious in the Cabinet — gives him both power over and a responsibility to a worldwide institution. Inevitably, analysts say, the secretary takes on some of the outlook of the permanent foreign-policy establishment, which was there before the president came into office and will be there after he leaves. As a result, differences with White House aides are almost unavoidable.

During the early years of the NSC, the conflict was subdued. The national security adviser was seen as a coordinator rather than policy maker, and the authority of the secretary was unquestioned. Under Presidents Kennedy and Johnson, the national security advisers became more significant, but still posed little challenge to the department. It was not until Nixon became president that the struggle became a major factor in the internal politics of foreign policy.

The battle between Kissinger and Secretary of State William P. Rogers quickly became a rout, with the national security adviser emerging as the dominant force in foreign policy. Early on, Nixon decided that he wanted to run foreign policy personally, working through Kissinger and a few other aides. Both he and Kissinger mistrusted the State Department bureaucracy and were almost openly contemptuous of Rogers' command of his job. They heaped indignities on Rogers, regularly excluding him from meetings with key foreign leaders and failing to inform him of decisions until just before they were publicly announced. In response, Rogers was limited to bureaucratic guerrilla warfare, sending out cables to embassies that reflected his opposition to Nixon-Kissinger policies and refusing to promote former NSC staff members.

"Rogers must have considered me an egotistical nitpicker who ruined his relations with the president," Kissinger said in his memoirs. "I tended to view him as an insensitive neophyte who threatened the careful design of our foreign policy." [9] Eventually, Nixon ended the battle by appointing Kissinger to Rogers' position. For the next two years, Kissinger avoided NSC-State antagonism by heading both agencies at the same time.

The struggle between Brzezinski and Vance had even more serious consequences. The Carter administration's foreign policy was torn apart by differences between two men with deeply divergent views. Brzezinski favored hardline confrontation with the Soviet Union, while Vance stressed mutual cooperation and nuclear arms control. Carter did not make clear which man reflected his own views, and as a result the American public and other governments were left in confusion about the real direction of U.S. foreign policy.

Brzezinski and Vance worked together on some issues, such as the Panama Canal treaties,[10] and seem to have avoided intense personal antipathy. But their disagreements, reported extensively in the press, contributed to an image of disarray in the Carter administration. The two were drawn into a heated dispute over control of negotiations with China, with Vance arguing that Brzezinski was usurping State Department prerogatives. Finally, after a year of debate over how to respond to the Iranian revolution and the seizure of U.S. hostages, Carter approved Brzezinski's plan for an armed rescue. Vance resigned in protest after the mission, which ended in failure.

The Reagan administration endured arguments between the White House and the secretary of state even before the Iran-contra affair. Alexander M. Haig Jr. ran into overwhelming opposition from Reagan advisers in his attempt to become, in his words, a foreign-policy "vicar" — one who acted in place of the president. But the national security adviser generally was not a major factor in those fights. The first four Reagan national security advisers — Richard V. Allen, William P. Clark Jr., McFarlane and Poindexter — were not viewed as dominant figures, and their differences with the secretary of state were not prominent. McFarlane was the only one who seemed to be establishing himself as an independent power. But he reportedly was felled by battles with Chief of Staff Donald T. Regan, not Shultz.

NSC's freedom from outside review

The NSC's almost complete freedom from outside review was a central element in its participation in the Iran-contra affair. Its actions are not subject to congressional oversight, in contrast to the CIA, whose officials would have been under pressure to inform House and Senate leaders of the covert action — with the danger that it would be publicly disclosed. Like other parts of the Executive Office of the President, the NSC is institutionally responsible only to the chief executive. Over the years, presidents have put increasing emphasis on the council's staff because of their confidence that it could be held accountable only to them.

Presidents also have acted to strengthen the loyalty of NSC staffers to themselves alone. Originally, the staff was thought of as a non-political group of experts, who, like many of the fiscal experts at the Office of Management and Budget, might hold their positions over the course of several administrations. Beginning with John F. Kennedy, new presidents regularly have purged NSC ranks upon taking office, substituting their own allies for those of the outgoing incumbent.

The president chooses whomever he wants for national security adviser without fear of congressional questioning and, possibly, rejection. The position is not subject to Senate confirmation, and by a longstanding Washington tradition that also means the officeholder cannot be compelled to testify before Congress. It was not until 1980 that a national security adviser made his first formal appearance before a congressional committee. On that occasion Brzezinski agreed to answer Senate Judiciary Committee questions

1984

March 16: William Buckley, CIA chief in Beirut, is kidnapped by Moslem militants. In the next two-and-a-half years, nine other Americans will be kidnapped in Lebanon.

1985

August 6: President Reagan approves Israel's sale of U.S. weapons to Iran, as part of an effort to improve U.S.-Iranian relations and secure release of the hostages, according to later testimony by national security adviser Robert C. McFarlane. The White House has denied that Reagan approved the transfer, saying that he was not informed of the action until after the first delivery of arms had occurred. The transfer violated a U.S. embargo on arms sales to Iran that has been in force since 1979. Later this month, Israel begins sending anti-tank missiles to Iran, and shipments continue during following months.

September 14: American clergyman Benjamin F. Weir is freed, but the hoped-for release of other hostages does not occur.

November 22-23: A CIA-supplied transport plane carries an Israeli shipment of U.S. weapons to Iran with CIA logistical help arranged by Lt. Col. Oliver L. North of the National Security Council staff.

December 4: McFarlane resigns as national security adviser, to be replaced by Adm. John M. Poindexter.

December 6: Reagan halts the arms shipments to Iran.

1986

January 17: Reagan signs a secret intelligence "finding" authorizing resumption of U.S. arms sales to Iran. Arms shipments occur periodically during 1986.

May 28: McFarlane, accompanied by North, travels to Tehran with spare parts for Iran's military. The delegation leaves Iran after it becomes clear no hostages will be released.

July 26: Lawrence M. Jenco, another clergyman-hostage, is released.

November 2: Hostage David P. Jacobsen is released.

November 3: *Al Shiraa*, a Lebanese magazine, reveals that the United States has been sending arms to Iran.

November 13: In a televised speech, Reagan says he approved shipment of small quantities of arms to Iran in order to improve relations with that country.

HOW THE STORY UNFOLDED

November 25: Attorney General Edwin Meese III reveals that North had arranged to transfer some of the funds from the sale of arms to Iran to contra rebels in Nicaragua, which was in violation of the 1984 Boland Amendment barring military aid to the contras. North is fired and Poindexter resigns.

November 26: Reagan appoints a three-member Special Review Board, chaired by former Sen. John G. Tower, to study the role of the National Security Council in the arms sales and transfer of money to the contras.

December 9: North and Poindexter decline to answer questions before the House Foreign Affairs Committee, citing the Fifth Amendment's protections against self-incrimination.

December 16-17: Senate leaders appoint an 11-member select committee to investigate the affair. House leaders pick a 15-member investigating committee.

December 19: A panel of judges names former federal district judge Lawrence E. Walsh independent counsel to investigate the Iran-contra affair.

December 26: Reagan names David M. Abshire, the U.S. delegate to NATO, to head a special White House team coordinating the administration's response to the Iran-contra investigations.

about the relationship between Billy Carter, the president's brother, and the government of Libya. Except for Pointdexter, national security advisers have avoided formal testimony since then, although they have given informal briefings to members of Congress. Poindexter appeared before the Senate Intelligence Committee in a closed session Nov. 21, four days before he resigned. In subsequent appearances before that and other committees, he refused to testify, citing the Fifth Amendment's protection against self-incrimination.

Congress has authority over the NSC's budget, setting the current fiscal year's at $4.6 million. But that control over spending is diluted by a White House practice of borrowing staff members from other agencies but leaving them on their former payrolls. Of the 180 current NSC staff members, about half are detailed from other agencies, according to an administration official.

Fault-finding with the system

The use of "detailed" staff members raises questions about staff size and the growing presence of uniformed members of the armed forces on the NSC staff. Both Poindexter and North were military officers officers assigned to the NSC — Poindexter a vice admiral in the Navy and North a lieutenant colonel in the Marine Corps — as were several of their colleagues. The Defense Department reported recently that 17 uniformed officers were serving with the NSC; they constitute about one-third of its professional staff. The number has nearly doubled since 1980, when nine uniformed officers served on the staff. Some critics of the NSC say they detect a military mind-set among the staff members and point to North as someone eager to substitute direct force for careful development of policy.

Although the staff is only about half the size it was under Kissinger, at its peak, it nonetheless has almost doubled since Brzezinski's time. Brzezinski suggested in a recent radio interview that the size of the staff may have enabled North and his colleagues to carry out their schemes without much control even from within the White House. "When the NSC staff becomes that large," he said recently, "the NSC director cannot supervise the staff, in which case some members of the staff can begin to act on their own." [11]

Indeed, a staff that seemingly lacked adequate supervision may be an element in the crucial question still confronting investigators. It is whether Reagan and Regan were aware of North's efforts to divert funds to the contras. The president and his chief of staff have insisted strenuously that they were unaware of the plan until late in 1986. According to press reports, an unreleased study by the Senate Intelligence Committee found no evidence to contradict their claims. But many members of Congress are skeptical that North would have carried out the operation without orders from above. "No one in the country," said Sen. Ernest F. Hollings (D-S.C.) early in December, "believes that either

Col. North or Adm. Poindexter acted without authority."

The organizational structure of the NSC gives some credence to Regan's denial of any knowledge of the contra connection. As did all but one of the other national security advisers, Poindexter reported directly to the president, bypassing senior presidential aides. The exception was Allen, a relatively weak national security adviser who was responsible to Edwin Meese III when Meese served as presidential counselor before becoming attorney general in 1985. On the other hand, formal lines of authority do not necessarily show how the White House system really worked. White House sources say that Regan insisted on being present whenever Poindexter briefed the president.

The fact that within 10 years two presidencies have been weakened by controversy centering on the NSC underscores its importance. Under Carter, sniping between the NSC and the State Department fostered an image of foreign-policy weakness and indecision that, public-opinion polls indicated, contributed to his 1980 electoral defeat. Reagan's popularity has plummeted since the Iran-contra matter has become public. [12]

While opinion is not unanimous (see p. 22), most former national security advisers and foreign-policy scholars agree that the NSC staff should not be a strong, independent force in decision making. According to this view, the national security adviser and his staff should be facilitators rather than policy makers, "honest brokers" who present the views of different departments to the president without prejudice, and monitor the departments' actions to make sure presidential policies are being followed. In this vision, the national security adviser would be a behind-the-scenes figure who would not contest the secretary of state's role as chief foreign-policy spokesman for the administration. The adviser should avoid a direct role in international negotiations and the management of covert operations. [13]

Robert H. Johnson, a former NSC staffer now with the Carnegie Endowment for International Peace, observed: "There's been a persistent tendency for presidents to come into office saying they will give power to the secretary of state and downgrade the NSC. But it never works that way." [14] The early days of the Carter administration, for example, were filled with assurances about how Brzezinski would not become another Kissinger. Carter vowed on the day he took office "to place more responsibility in the departments and agencies," reducing the policy-making role of the NSC. [15] He ordered a cut in the size of the staff, and rejected an initial proposal for a complex system of NSC committees. It was too similar to Kissinger's system, he indicated. Yet, within a little more than three years, Vance was gone and Brzezinski was the dominant foreign-policy voice in the administration. A well-known photograph of the national security adviser brandishing an AK-47 rifle in the Khyber Pass, on the border of Soviet-occupied Afghanistan, symbolized both his emergence as a public figure and the triumph of his anti-Soviet beliefs.

Similarly, Reagan came into office affirming "Cabinet government" as his model. Although he was somewhat more willing than his immediate predecessors to hold formal NSC meetings with the vice president and secretaries of state and defense, he moved to de-emphasize the role of the staff and dismantle much of the existing NSC committee system. Preoccupied with economic affairs during his first year in office, he did not set up a new NSC structure until 1982. He designated the secretary of state as "my principal foreign-policy adviser." [16] Four years later, McFarlane and Poindexter were to persuade Reagan to sell arms to Iran over Shultz' opposition.

For one group of foreign-policy analysts, the reason for the rise of the NSC lies in the nature of the modern presidency. With the aid of sophisticated electronic technology, presidents have gained the ability to monitor and control diplomatic and military communications. That new power has encouraged chief executives to shift to the "operational" presidency — not just to set foreign policy, but to carry it out on their own, through trusted White House aides instead of through bureaucratic professionals in the departments.[17]

Paradoxically, the NSC's ability to interject itself into sensitive issues, such as relations with Iran and support for the contras, occurred even though it had suffered a considerable loss of influence under the current administration. Reagan's preference for Cabinet government — and much-noted lack of interest in policy details — meant that the NSC staff seldom had the authority to impose a single presidential policy on the often widely divergent views of the State and Defense departments. As an institution, the council was relegated to the sidelines, while semiautonomous departments clashed. In that situation, the staff often could do little more than develop ambiguous compromises that merely papered over unresolved differences.

One result of the NSC's demotion was a sense of frustration among its staff members, according to press accounts from the early 1980s. Staffers frequently expressed their feelings of impotence and loss of prestige; low morale made recruitment of talented personnel difficult. Deprived of their power over policy, staff members searched for new ways to develop influence. McFarlane, for example, established the Crisis Management Center, a high-technology monitoring and communications facility that appeared to duplicate the functions of the longstanding White House Situation Room — the facility used since the Kennedy administration to coordinate policy during crises. For ideologically committed staffers, covert action may have seemed like the way out. The loss of clout, Kissinger wrote recently, "tempted the NSC staff into conducting special presidential missions no one else was eager to undertake." [18]

Robert E. Hunter, a Carter NSC staff member now with the Center for Strategic and International Studies in Washington, D.C., argues that the current system did not provide for rigorous internal oversight of the staff. The lack of clear lines of authority over foreign policy encouraged the NSC and other agencies to free-lance their own projects, he said. "Every administration comes up with bad ideas. But if you have things structured properly, they get stopped before they happen," Hunter said. "The president failed to provide himself with a process to help on the 'foul weather' days. He didn't give himself insurance against bad decisions." [19]

Shultz observed recently, "Nothing ever gets settled in this town. . . . It's a seething debating society in which the debate never stops, in which people never give up, including me." [20] In his book *Deadly Gambits*, *Time* correspondent Strobe Talbott provides a vivid account of the bitter internal struggle for dominance over the administration's arms-control policy. His observation might serve as a summary of the NSC's difficulties under Reagan: "The State Department, particularly Richard Burt, fought for compromise against the Pentagon, particularly Richard Perle, while the National Security Council staff, particularly Robert McFarlane, tried to arbitrate, reconcile, synthesize. Now, as before, the result was not so much synthesis as further paralysis." [21]

Abundant ideas for reforms

As it studies proposals for restructuring the NSC, the Tower commission will have no shortage of ideas from which to choose. Some of them will come from the council staff itself, which is already in the midst of significant changes under Carlucci. The new national security adviser has made clear that he sees his role as a coordinator and facilitator of policy who does not seek to be a public spokesman or independent power within the administration. To comply with that model, Carlucci moved soon after his appointment to reduce the size of the staff and abolish some offices, including that of politico-military affairs, where North worked, and possibly the Crisis Management Center.

Other changes in the council might be made through legislation. Although Reagan had already ordered the NSC to halt covert activities, Congress could add insurance against future abuses by making the ban permanent. Congress could also make the national security adviser subject to Senate confirmation. That idea has drawn presidential opposition in the past, and probably will again. Moreover, future presidents could easily evade the intent of the legislation by appointing a nonentity to the national security post and seeking foreign-policy advice elsewhere.

More drastic remedies also are available, and being discussed. The job of national security adviser might be abolished or split into two positions. Some other aide could advise the president on foreign policy, while a management-oriented executive secretary oversaw the operations of the NSC. The NSC staff would be restored to its former status as a relatively non-political group of experts. Another approach suggested in the past by Brzezinksi but unlikely to be considered in the current situation, is to raise the national security adviser to a level above that of the secretaries of state and defense, where he would serve as the undisputed chief, next to the president, of diplomatic and military affairs.

Ultimately, the organization of the NSC will be less important than the way presidents decide to use it. They have always tailored the national security system to meet their own needs, and no structure can force them to employ it wisely. "The burden for management rests in the same place as the burden for policy — with the president of the United States," Hunter has written. "As always, he will be responsible for effective management — or mishap." [22]

NOTES

[1] The other members of Tower's panel are Edmund S. Muskie, former Democratic senator from Maine and secretary of state (1980-81), and Brent Scowcroft, who was national security adviser to President Ford (1975-77). Walsh, 74, a federal district judge, diplomat and deputy attorney general, was appointed Dec. 19 by a special panel of federal judges under terms of the 1978 Ethics in Government Act. The congressional leadership on Dec. 16-17 set up the Senate Select Committee on Secret Military Assistance to Iran and the Nicaraguan Opposition, headed by Sen. Daniel K. Inouye (D-Hawaii), and the House Select Committee to Investigate Covert Arms Transactions with Iran, headed by Rep. Lee H. Hamilton (D-Ind.). Additionally, the House and Senate Intelligence committees, the House Foreign Affairs and Senate Foreign Relations Committee have held hearings on the controversy.

[2] Reagan sent U.S. Marines to Beirut in 1982 as part of an international force to keep peace among Lebanon's warring factions as Israel withdrew its invasion force from that country. Following heated debates within his administration, Reagan withdrew the troops in February 1984, four months after a terrorist bomb killed 241 Marines. See "American Involvement in Lebanon," *E.R.R.*, 1984 Vol. I, pp. 169-88.

[3] Writing in *The New York Times*, Dec. 16, 1986.

[4] Interview with author, Dec. 16, 1986.

[5] Zbigniew Brzezinski, *Power and Principle*, Farrar, Straus, Giroux, 1983, p. 536.

[6] Demanding release of 50 prisoners in Israel, the four Palestinians seized the *Achille Lauro* Oct. 7 and killed Leon Klinghoffer, a vacationing New Yorker, before freeing other passengers and the crew members. Upon surrendering to Egyptian authorities in exchange for free passage out of the country and apparent freedom, they were put aboard an Egyptian plane bound for Tunisia. While en route, on Oct. 10, U.S. jet fighters intercepted the plane and forced it down in Sicily, delivering the four to Italian authorities.

[7] U.S. warplanes from aircraft carriers and Britain bombed "terrorist-related targets" in the Libyan cities of Tripoli and Benghazi, April 14, 1986. For background on U.S. involvement in Libya and Nicaragua, see "Decision on Nicaragua," *E.R.R.*, 1986 Vol. I, pp. 145-64, and "Dealing With Libya," *E.R.R.*, 1986 Vol. I, pp. 185-204.

[8] In testimony before the House Foreign Affairs Committee, Dec. 8, 1986.

[9] Henry A. Kissinger, *White House Years*, Little, Brown & Co., 1979, p. 31.

[10] The treaties, ratified by the Senate after intense debate in 1978, provided for Panamanian control of the canal by the year 2000.

[11] Remark on National Public Radio, Dec. 15, 1986.

[12] According to the Gallup Poll, public approval of Reagan's performance in office fell from 63 percent in late October to 47 percent in early December.

[13] For a description of the "conventional wisdom" on the NSC, see "National Security Management: What Presidents Have Wrought," I. M. Destler, *Political Science Quarterly*, winter 1980-81.

[14] Interview with author, Dec. 15, 1986.

[15] "Presidential Directive/NSC-2," Jan. 20, 1977.

[16] "National Security Council Structure," presidential statement issued by the White House Jan. 12, 1982.

[17] I.M. Destler, et al., *Our Own Worst Enemy*, Simon & Schuster, 1984, pp. 241-58. Leslie H. Gelb, deputy editorial page editor of *The New York Times*, and Anthony Lake, an Amherst College professor, co-authored the book with Destler. Both are former State Department officials.

[18] Writing in *The Washington Post*, Dec. 21, 1986.

[19] Interview with author, Dec. 19, 1986.

[20] House Foreign Affairs Committee testimony, Dec. 8, 1986.

[21] Talbott, *Deadly Gambits*, Alfred A. Knopf, 1984, p. 345. Burt served as assistant secretary of state for politico-military affairs, and for European affairs, before becoming ambassador to West Germany. Perle is assistant secretary of defense for international security policy.

[22] From a revised edition of Robert E. Hunter's *Presidential Control of Foreign Policy: Management or Mishap?*, Center for Strategic and International Studies, due for publication in January 1987.

Graphics: McFarlane and Brzezinski photos p. 22, Wide World.

RECOMMENDED READING

BOOKS

Brzezinski, Zbigniew, *Power and Principle: Memoirs of the National Security Adviser, 1977-1981*, Farrar, Straus, Giroux, 1983. An insightful, if somewhat self-serving, account of the making of President Carter's foreign policy.

Destler, I. M., Leslie H. Gelb and Anthony Lake, *Our Own Worst Enemy: The Unmaking of American Foreign Policy*, Simon & Schuster, 1984. Biting analysis of what they regard as a long-term degeneration of the U.S. foreign-policy establishment. In particular, see chapters "Courtiers and Barons" and "The Operational Presidency."

Kissinger, Henry A., *White House Years*, Little, Brown & Co., 1979. An encyclopedic memoir by the most powerful national security adviser.

Talbott, Strobe, *Deadly Gambits: The Reagan Administration and the Stalemate in Nuclear Arms Control*, Alfred A. Knopf, 1984. How bitter infighting produced chaos in the administration's arms-control policies.

ARTICLES

Destler, I. M., "National Security Management: What Presidents Have Wrought," *Political Science Quarterly*, winter 1980-81. How foreign-policy experts view the job of national security adviser.

Kondracke, Morton, "Out of the Basement," *The New Republic*, Jan. 5 and 12, 1987.

Mulcahy, Kevin V., "The Secretary of State and The National Security Adviser: Foreign Policymaking in the Carter and Reagan Administrations," *Presidential Studies Quarterly*, spring 1986.

REPORTS/STUDIES

Hunter, Robert E., "Presidential Control of Foreign Policy," Center for Strategic and International Studies/Praeger, 1982. Well-written analysis by a veteran of the Carter National Security Council. Reissued in January 1987 with a new introduction commenting on the Iran-contra affair.

Lowenthal, Mark M., "The National Security Council: Organizational History," Congressional Research Service, Library of Congress, June 27, 1978.

Senate Foreign Relations Committee, "The National Security Adviser: Role and Accountability," U.S. Government Printing Office, 1980. Contains reprints of much of the prior literature on the National Security Council.

ERR

JANUARY 29, 1988

TREATY RATIFICATION

TREATY RATIFICATION

Before the INF Treaty can take effect, it must receive the Senate's blessing. The procedure by which the Senate confers or withholds its "advice and consent" is a product of 200 years of controversy, precedent and Supreme Court rulings.

by Mary H. Cooper

"Now that the treaty has been signed, it will be submitted to the Senate for the next step, the ratification process. . . . I am confident that the Senate will now act in an expeditious way to fulfill its duty under our Constitution."[1]

On this hopeful note, President Reagan relinquished the long-awaited intermediate-range nuclear-forces (INF) treaty to the U.S. Senate for its "advice and consent." The agreement, signed Dec. 8 by Reagan and Soviet leader Mikhail S. Gorbachev during their Washington summit, had been six years in the making. If it is ratified, the INF treaty — the first arms control agreement between the United States and the Soviet Union in 15 years — will eliminate an entire class of nuclear weapons.

The agreement has now entered another, perhaps equally precarious, phase in the treaty-making process. The Senate Foreign Relations Committee, which has the authority to recommend approval or rejection of treaties to the full Senate, has called some 40 experts to testify on various aspects of the agreement at hearings that began Jan. 25. The Senate Armed Services and Select Intelligence committees also are scheduled to scrutinize the document before it is submitted to the full Senate for final consideration, probably by the end of February.[2] There, the INF treaty will undergo further discussion as well as likely changes in its terms before coming to a vote, now expected to take place by mid-April. Before the president can ratify the treaty, two-thirds of the lawmakers present and voting must voice their approval. Only then can Reagan and Gorbachev sign the instruments of ratification and the INF agreement enter into force.

As it moved from the White House to Capitol Hill, the

INF treaty entered what Justice Robert H. Jackson once called "a zone of twilight" between the executive and legislative branches of government that repeatedly has been a testing ground for control over the nation's relations with the rest of the world.[3] Indeed, what Reagan referred to as "the ratification process" is anything but an orderly procedure, but rather the continually evolving product of a 200-year-old struggle for authority over the conduct of foreign affairs.

Ambiguity in U.S. Constitution; early disputes over treaty-making

Article II of the Constitution states simply that the president ". . . shall have power, by and with the advice and consent of the Senate, to make treaties, provided two-thirds of the Senators present concur. . . ." Contemporary debates shed some light on what the Founding Fathers meant by their ambiguous language. There is no evidence that Senate involvement in treaty-making was intended to challenge the president's dominant role in the conduct of foreign affairs. Even Thomas Jefferson, the most outspoken critic of Alexander Hamilton and other supporters of a strong executive branch, stated unequivocally that "the

transaction of the business with foreign nations is executive altogether." Rather, the Senate's role as treaty-maker seems to have been aimed at tempering the president's authority, in accordance with the doctrine of the separation of powers evident throughout the Constitution.

At the same time, the Founding Fathers were careful not to extend the treaty-making power to the House of Representatives. In defense of this action, John Jay argued in *The Federalist Papers* that important matters such as treaties should not be placed in the hands of representatives elected directly by the people but rather confined to the judgment of senators, who at the time were elected by the state legislatures. Also, because it was smaller, the Senate was judged to be better suited to consider such sensitive documents with "speed and dispatch."

But the Founding Fathers were ambivalent toward the congressional role in treaty-making. On one hand, they preserved the president's dominant role in foreign affairs by limiting the legislature's power to the Senate alone. But in requiring that two-thirds of the Senate approve treaties, they also made it harder for the president to ratify treaties than would have been possible with a simple majority vote. As it happened, the provision was dictated more by political considerations than by concerns over the separation of powers: Virginia and North Carolina insisted on the two-thirds requirement out of fear that a

The INF Treaty

The intermediate-range nuclear forces (INF) treaty signed by President Reagan and Soviet leader Gorbachev Dec. 8 in Washington calls for the elimination of all U.S. and Soviet land-based nuclear missiles with ranges of between 300 and 3,400 miles.

Under the terms of the treaty, the Soviet Union would have to eliminate four missile categories — the SS-20, SS-23, SS-4 and SS-12/22 Scaleboard — for a total of 1,752 missiles. The United States would be required to destroy its 867 Pershing II and ground-launched cruise missiles.

The INF treaty calls for the most invasive on-site inspection of missile production sites ever anticipated under an arms control agreement. Beginning 60 days after the treaty enters into force, Soviet and U.S. technicians would be allowed to make short-notice inspections to ensure that the designated missiles are destroyed. In addition, teams of inspectors would be based for 13 years on the other side's territory, the Soviets at a U.S. military factory in Magna, Utah, the Americans at a Soviet military factory in Votkinsk, just west of the Ural Mountains.

The Senate debate on ratification will center on critics' claims that the treaty would leave America's NATO allies dangerously exposed to Warsaw Pact superiority in conventional forces, including tanks and other non-nuclear weapons. Critics also say the kinds of weapons covered by the treaty are relatively small, mobile and easily hidden, thus making even the most stringent verification measures inadequate to prevent Soviet cheating.

Only the President Can Ratify Treaties

To ratify, according to *Webster's New Collegiate Dictionary*, is simply "to approve and sanction formally." In this general sense, both the Senate and the president might be said to "ratify" treaties. But in diplomatic parlance, the term is applied strictly to one phase of the executive's treaty-making power, the president's signing of the instrument of ratification. Technically speaking, then, the Senate gives its consent to ratification, but it is the president who ratifies treaties.

simple majority vote would enable the more numerous states of the North to approve a treaty that would deny them the right of navigation on the Mississippi River.

Aside from the "advice and consent" clause, the only other references to treaties in the Constitution are provisions forbidding the states from making treaties (Article I, section 10) and defining treaties as supreme law of the land and therefore binding on the states (Article VI, section 2). No mention is made of what constitutes a treaty or how it should be negotiated, enforced or terminated. More importantly, in light of later debate, the Constitution was silent on the way the Senate was to exercise its treaty-making power.

Reagan's description of the Senate's consideration of the INF treaty as the "next step in the ratification process" did not always apply. George Washington initially interpreted the Senate's role of "advice and consent" to mean its direct involvement in treaty-making from the start of negotiations. On Aug. 22, 1789, he appeared at the Senate and enlisted the lawmakers' advice on a treaty to be negotiated with southern Indian tribes. The legislators, however, viewed his appearance as an attempt to "tread on the necks of the Senate," in the words of Sen. William Maclay of Pennsylvania, and proceeded to exclude Washington from their deliberations. As Maclay recalled, Washington "started up in a violent fret" and withdrew from the Senate chamber "with sullen dignity." [4]

The lawmakers were to regret their behavior. Five years later, Washington excluded the Senate from any role in negotiations leading to the Jay Treaty of 1794, resolving questions with Great Britain that were then threatening to renew the War of Independence. The Senate was asked only to confirm the president's appointed chief negotiator and approve or reject the finished product, setting the precedent that has been followed for treaties ever since. Later administrations even abandoned the practice of seeking confirmation of treaty negotiators.

To be sure, the Senate has not completely relinquished its say in the drafting of treaties. The Foreign Relations Committee, created in 1816, has jurisdiction over all treaties and is often consulted by the executive during the negotiating process. Particularly in the context of recent arms control negotiations, such as those leading up to the INF treaty, the executive often confers with individual senators for advice on complex technical questions. But whether it is solicited by the executive branch or offered spontaneously, the Senate's advice in the treaty-negotiating process is not binding. The Supreme Court gave further weight to precedent in this area in its 1936 ruling in the Curtiss-Wright case: "The President . . . alone negotiates. Into the field of negotiation the Senate cannot intrude; and Congress is powerless to invade it." [5]

Although he may be unable to win Senate approval of the INF treaty without some modification of the text he and Gorbachev signed last December, Reagan is unlikely to fare as badly in his face-off with Senate critics as some of his predecessors. The general euphoria over the future of U.S.-Soviet relations that followed the Washington summit may have worn off somewhat, but the INF agreement appears to enjoy the support of most senators.

Not all presidents have enjoyed the broad bipartisan support for treaties that is essential to win the approval of two-thirds of the Senate. Chief executives ignore at their peril the lesson provided by Woodrow Wilson's refusal to keep senators informed during the negotiating process. He paid for his oversight by losing the opposition Republican Party's support of the Treaty of Versailles, which spelled out the terms of peace with Germany following World War I and established the League of Nations. Republicans led by Sen. Henry Cabot Lodge, chairman of the Foreign Relations Committee, claimed that membership in the League would jeopardize U.S. autonomy in foreign affairs, perhaps drawing the country into foreign conflicts and undermining Congress' constitutional authority to declare war.

Wilson's Democratic supporters refused to compromise, and debate over the treaty dragged on for nearly two years before the Senate in 1920 narrowly rejected a heavily amended version of the treaty. By rejecting the treaty, the Senate also rejected U.S. membership in the League of Nations, a step to which many historians have attributed the erosion of peace in Europe and the subsequent outbreak of World War II.

Executive agreements frequently used as alternatives to treaties

Even before the Senate's rejection of the Versailles Treaty won it a reputation as the "graveyard of treaties," the executive branch had sought ways to sidestep the treaty-making process to conclude agreements with other nations. One such vehicle is the joint congressional resolution. The equivalent of an act of Congress, a joint resolution requires a simple majority of both houses and thus may be easier to obtain than the two-thirds vote of the Senate required for treaties. After the Senate defeated a treaty calling for the annexation of Texas, for example, the transaction was completed by joint resolution in 1845. Likewise, when it appeared unlikely that the Senate would approve a treaty calling for the acquisition of Hawaii in 1898, the islands were bought under the terms of a joint resolution. After the Senate defeated the Treaty of Versailles, the same tactic was used to make peace with Germany.

Another way presidents have avoided sharing the treaty-making power is by entering into executive agreements with other nations without the consent, and sometimes the knowledge, of the Senate. Executive agreements, which include all international pacts the president does not submit to the Senate for approval, have long been used as handy alternatives to treaties, especially for relatively minor matters such as commercial agreements. But because they do not reflect the broad political support that must

be gained for ratified treaties and may easily be repudiated by successive administrations, executive agreements are ill-suited for such weighty political commitments as arms control accords. On occasion, the executive agreement has been used as a temporary solution to an urgent problem and referred later to the more cumbersome treaty-making process. An early example is a U.S.-British agreement to limit naval forces on the Great Lakes, which was implemented in 1817, a full year before President Monroe submitted the pact to the Senate for approval.

Nearly a century later, Theodore Roosevelt abandoned a treaty he had signed with Santo Domingo when the Senate failed to act quickly to approve its ratification. In 1905, the president simply implemented the pact as an executive agreement, thus placing the bankrupt country's customs houses under U.S. control to prevent its European creditors

Alternatives to Treaties

Since 1945 U.S. presidents have increasingly used executive agreements, which don't require Senate approval, as substitutes for traditional treaties. Although most executive agreements concern routine matters, such as the regulation of fishing rights, some have been used to settle significant foreign policy questions.

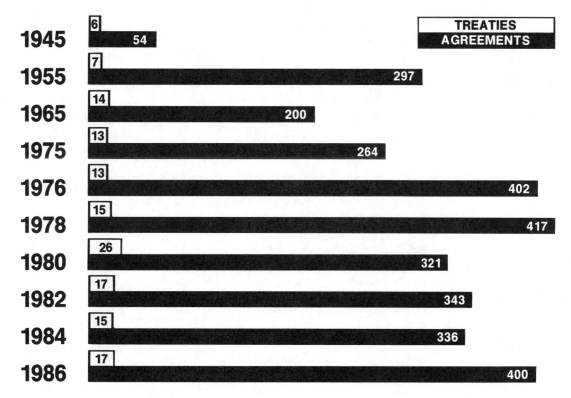

Source: State Department, Office of Treaty Affairs

from seizing their assets. Frustrated by the Senate's delay in approving the treaty, Roosevelt wrote, "I went ahead and administered the proposed treaty anyhow, considering it as a simple agreement on the part of the Executive which would be converted into a treaty whenever the Senate acted. After a couple of years the Senate did act, having previously made some utterly unimportant changes which I ratified and persuaded Santo Domingo to ratify." [6]

Acting under the constraints of secrecy and urgency imposed by World War II, Franklin D. Roosevelt frequently used executive agreements for important international pacts. Some of these — such as the agreements made during the 1945 Yalta conference that determined the postwar boundaries of Europe — had important long-term implica-tions. Presidential recourse to executive agreements be-came more frequent as the United States extended its international reach after the war (see box, p. 33).[7]

More disturbing than the sheer number of interna-tional accords not subject to congressional approval, critics say, is the use of executive agreements for significant foreign policy matters. In the 1960s and early 1970s, the Senate was called on to consent to ratification of treaties covering such relatively minor issues as the preservation of archaeological artifacts in Mexico, international radio regulations and the classification of industrial designs. But President Eisenhower excluded the Senate when he drew up agreements for the postwar construction of U.S. military bases in Europe and East Asia.

Treaties Rejected by the Senate

The Senate's reputation as the "graveyard of treaties" is not altogether deserved. The congressional treaty-makers have approved more than 1,500 treaties in the nation's history, about 90 percent of all they have been asked to consider. Of the 177 treaties that failed to be implemented after being signed by the president and sent to the Senate for its advice and consent, most never came to the vote: They were either withdrawn from consideration by the president or never brought to the vote by the Senate leadership because they appeared unlikely to win approval. About a fourth of the unimplemented treaties were approved by the Senate but left unratified by the president because of amendments or other modifications included in the Senate's resolution of ratification. Only 17 treaties were actually rejected by the Senate, according to the Congressional Research Service:

Date of vote	Country	Votes Nay Yea	Subject
March 9, 1825	Colombia	28-12°	Suppression of slave trade
June 11, 1836	Switzerland	23-14	Property rights
June 8, 1844	Texas	35-16	Annexation
June 27, 1860	Spain	17-25	Claims convention
July 28, 1868	Hawaii	19-20	Commercial reciprocity
Feb. 18, 1869	Britain	54-1	Claims convention
June 30, 1870	Dominican Republic	28-28	Annexation
April 20, 1886	Mexico	32-26	Claims convention
April 5, 1888	Britain	38-15	Extradition
Aug. 21, 1889	Britain	30-27	Fisheries
Jan. 11, 1897	Britain	26-43	Arbitration
March 19, 1920	Multilateral	35-49	Treaty of Versailles
Jan. 18, 1927	Turkey	34-50	General relations
March 14, 1934	Canada	42-46	St. Lawrence Waterway
Jan. 29, 1935	Multilateral	36-52	Permanent Court of International Justice
May 26, 1960	Multilateral	49-30	Law of the Sea Conventions, optional protocol
March 8, 1983	Multilateral	50-42	International Air Carriage convention, Montreal protocols

° The treaty was submitted in two parts. The second part was defeated by a vote of 40-0.

Senate discontent grew during the presidency of Richard M. Nixon, who between January 1969 and May 1972 concluded 71 treaties and 608 executive agreements. Some of these agreements were used to deepen American involvement in the Vietnam conflict, including a secret pledge of U.S. assistance Nixon apparently concluded with South Vietnamese President Nguyen Van Thieu in 1973.[8] In his history of the executive office, *The Imperial Presidency* (1973), Arthur M. Schlesinger Jr. recalls how Sen. Frank F. Church, D-Idaho, "showed understandable irritation when in 1972 the Senate, having been studiously ignored on momentous questions of foreign policy, was asked to ratify a treaty with Brazil concerning shrimp."[9]

Proposals to involve Congress more directly in the treaty-making process appeared after World War II. The first efforts, launched from 1952-57 by Sen. John W. Bricker, R-Ohio, were aimed at granting Congress greater control over both treaties and executive agreements. Concerned about the "pactomania" of the early postwar period, when the United States became party to such agreements as the United Nations Charter of 1945 and the North Atlantic Treaty Organization (NATO) Charter of 1949, Bricker and his supporters proposed several amendments to the Constitution that would have required House and Senate approval of all international agreements.

Although the Bricker amendments were defeated, Congress in 1972 finally acted to curtail the use of secret executive agreements with the Case Act. Named for its chief sponsor, Sen. Clifford P. Case, R-N.J., this measure requires the secretary of state to notify Congress of any international agreement other than treaties no more than 60 days after it enters into force. While the law grants Congress no power to thwart the president's right to conclude executive agreements, it at least assures that the legislative branch will be informed of their existence and content.

Recent moves to involve Senate in treaty negotiations pay off

The most effective brake on presidents' use of executive agreements is the credibility the normal treaty-ratification process lends to international accords. In submitting an agreement to lengthy public debate, a president can more forcefully assure the other party or parties to the agreement that its terms will be honored after he leaves office. Such assurances are vital to the effectiveness of such long-term agreements as the INF treaty and other postwar arms control accords between the nuclear superpowers.

Early in the nation's history, senators were frequently appointed to conduct treaty negotiations. In 1814, for example, President Madison called on Sen. James A. Bayard of Delaware to help negotiate a peace treaty with Britain. Although such direct involvement was less common by the early 20th century, President Wilson's failure to include any senators in the 1919 peace talks aroused

resentment and set the stage for the Versailles Treaty's ultimate defeat. The lesson was not lost on Franklin D. Roosevelt, who began to enlist Senate support for the United Nations long before the organization's draft charter was drawn up at Dumbarton Oaks in 1944. Harry S Truman, his successor, continued to solicit Senate support for the U.N., and included four members of Congress in the eight-member delegation he sent to the 1945 San Francisco conference that founded the United Nations.

The tactic worked. In marked contrast to its dismissal of the Treaty of Versailles just 25 years earlier, the Senate embraced the U.N. charter. "Let us rise to our lofty destiny," intoned Sen. Tom T. Connally, D-Texas, chairman of the Foreign Relations Committee, in one of the more eloquent tributes to the new organization. "The world charter for peace is knocking at the doors of the Senate. We shall not turn it away." Connally's prediction, made June 28, 1945, was accurate; on July 28, the Senate voted overwhelmingly, 89-2, in favor of the U.N. charter.

More recent presidents also have enlisted the Senate's "advice" on controversial treaties. President Carter succeeded in overcoming opposition to the Panama Canal treaties he signed with Panama Sept. 7, 1977, only after he involved senators with exhaustive briefings, meetings with Panamanian officials and "fact-finding" trips to the canal itself, a U.S.-built and -owned facility that the treaties were to relinquish to the Panamanian government by the year 2000. The treaties, which also included a neutrality pact that would permit the United States to defend the 51-mile waterway after it was handed over to Panama, were narrowly approved March 16, 1978, after a heated 38-day floor discussion, the longest ratification debate since the Treaty of Versailles was rejected.

Senate involvement in the negotiating phase of treaty-making has proved especially crucial to the ratification of military and arms control agreements. The pattern was set by Secretary of State Dean Acheson, who involved Sen. Connally and other key lawmakers in drafting the NATO charter. Beginning with the first strategic arms limitation (SALT) talks in the late 1960s and early 1970s,[10] presidents have regularly kept lawmakers informed of treaty negotiations by briefing Senate "observer groups." Carter involved the lawmakers even more directly in arms control negotiations by naming 26 senators as advisers to the U.S. delegation that negotiated the SALT II treaty.

The Senate observer group is an increasingly important agent in the process of ratifying arms control pacts, for its members are called on to explain the technical details of agreements to their Senate colleagues. The role of the observer group has expanded with the growing technical complexity of arms control agreements, and it has been closely involved in the INF negotiating process since it began in November 1981. "One of the major differences from the SALT I days is that the public generally, including the Congress, was not as well versed on all these nuclear questions as they are today," recalls John B. Rhinelander, a Washington, D.C., lawyer who served as legal adviser to the SALT I delegation. In the early 1970s, he says, "there were only a handful who were well informed, whereas today you've got 100 experts in the Senate as well as all their staffers. It's a very different ball game than what we had in those days."

Prospects for INF ratification; memories of 1979 SALT II treaty

The Reagan administration launched its lobbying campaign for Senate approval of the INF treaty as soon as the agreement was signed. Reagan met in mid-December with an 11-member task force of Senate Republicans to enlist their support for the treaty, while he and other members of the administration used the popular support the treaty enjoyed following Gorbachev's visit to Washington to allay critics' misgivings over the treaty's verification measures. "I believe that the Senate will recognize a good deal when it sees one," wrote Secretary of State George P. Shultz. "The administration is eager to work with the Senate to scrutinize this treaty from every angle." [11]

Several potential obstacles could frustrate the administration's hopes for obtaining a vote in favor of ratification by mid-April. One is the emerging struggle between the Arms Control and Disarmament Agency and the Pentagon over control of the new government agency that must be created to carry out on-site inspections of Soviet missile-production facilities. Another is the controversy surrounding the Reagan administration's attempt to reinterpret the 1972 Anti-Ballistic Missile (ABM) treaty, which may prompt senators to spend too much time scrupulously examining each provision of the 200-page INF agreement to meet the target date (see p. 40).

But the main obstacle to rapid Senate approval centers on the question of treaty compliance and verification. The INF treaty introduces the most invasive techniques for verifying compliance in the history of arms control (see box, p. 31). But these very innovations are drawing the loudest complaints from conservatives who claim the INF treaty leaves ample room for Soviet cheating. Led by Sen. Jesse Helms, R-N.C., treaty opponents are even more concerned about U.S.-Soviet plans to conclude a sweeping agreement later this year to halve both superpowers' arsenals of intercontinental ballistic missiles. By preventing the rapid approval of the INF agreement, they could effectively stymie progress toward this strategic arms control accord as well.

There are several ways the INF treaty could be derailed. The first is outright rejection. This is considered unlikely. Since the first treaty was submitted for approval in 1789, the Senate has approved more than 1,500 treaties and rejected only 17 (see box, p. 34). [12]

Still, the near-rejection of the 1979 SALT II treaty is fresh in the minds of INF supporters. The second phase of the strategic arms limitation talks defined numerical limits on U.S. and Soviet intercontinental ballistic missiles. Senate debate over the treaty, which centered on the issue of treaty compliance and verification, dragged on for nearly six months until Jan. 3, 1980, when Carter finally withdrew it from consideration in retaliation for the Soviet incursion into Afghanistan the month before. Although the Senate did not formally reject SALT II, there was little doubt that the treaty did not have the support of the required two-thirds majority.

Few observers predict the INF treaty will suffer the same fate. The new agreement appears to enjoy the wide bipartisan support that has proved so critical in the past. But although the Senate is unlikely to reject the INF agreement outright, there is a real possibility that opponents will either delay the vote on the treaty or alter its provisions. Either tactic could effectively kill the treaty's prospects for ratification. Gorbachev warned senators during his Washington visit that the Soviet Union would not tolerate a delay in the ratification much beyond the April target date and would reject the document if it was significantly amended during the Senate proceedings.

INF agreement could be hurt by delaying tactics and amendments

By delaying action on a treaty, the Senate can kill it as effectively as it can by rejecting it outright. The Senate has often resorted to delaying tactics as a convenient means of tabling controversial agreements. The most blatant example is the U.N. Genocide Convention, which was signed in 1949 but not approved by the Senate until Feb. 19, 1986. Opponents feared that the treaty, which set up a system to monitor and punish the crime of genocide, would allow the United Nations to interfere with the internal affairs of the United States. Unwilling to reject an agreement of unquestionably lofty aims, the Senate delayed action on it for over 35 years. But even though it approved the genocide treaty in 1986, the Senate extended its delaying tactics by conditioning ratification on the passage of implementing legislation. Congress has yet to act, and the treaty remains unratified.

Conservative opponents to the INF treaty have already launched their efforts to convince the Senate to treat the agreement in the same way it did the Genocide Convention. Eugene Rostow, chairman of the Committee on the Present Danger, a Washington, D.C., organization that has often criticized arms control efforts, proposes that the Senate defer action on the INF treaty until the United States and the Soviet Union agree on equal levels of offensive intercontinental nuclear weapons and defensive systems such as those envisioned in Reagan's strategic defense initiative, commonly known as Star Wars. [13] Because both the administration and the Soviet Union have stated clearly their intention to seek agreement on these two areas only after the INF treaty is ratified, Rostow's proposal that "the United States should not ratify the INF agreement . . . until sound agreements on the other two elements of the nuclear equation are in hand," amounts

Continued on page 38

The Ratification Process

After the 100th Congress reconvened Jan. 25 for its second session, the signed INF treaty was delivered to the Senate parliamentarian, acting for the president of the Senate. The parliamentarian delivered the treaty to the Senate executive clerk, who placed it in a safe. After the Senate voted to lift the injunction of secrecy that kept its contents from being known, the clerk had copies of the treaty printed. These were referred to the Foreign Relations Committee, which has jurisdiction over treaties and which began hearings on it Jan. 25. As in the case of other arms control treaties, the Armed Services and Select Intelligence committees also are holding hearings on the treaty.

The committees will make their recommendations on the treaty and send them to the floor of the Senate. The full Senate may amend or change the treaty by simple majority vote. The treaty then is left to "lie over" one day. A resolution of ratification is then presented to the Senate, reflecting everything it has done to the treaty. It is this resolution that the Senate must approve by a two-thirds margin before the treaty can be ratified.

If the Senate adopts the resolution, the executive clerk sends it and the original treaty back to the White House. If the president doesn't like what the Senate has said in its resolution, he sends a message to that effect to the Foreign Relations Committee. Any change to the resolution would require a two-thirds vote by the full Senate.

If the president accepts the resolution, the White House will send it and the treaty to the State Department's Office of Treaty Affairs. That office will draft a one- or two-page instrument of ratification, which it will send to the White House for Reagan's signature. The signed instrument of ratification will then be returned to the State Department. After the Soviets complete their ratification process, the State Department will set a time and place for the two sides to exchange their instruments of ratification. Normally, if a treaty is signed in one capital, the instruments are exchanged in the other. The exchange will probably be carried out by the Soviet foreign minister and the U.S. secretary of state or the ambassadors. When the treaty takes effect, the president will issue a proclamation to that effect. The State Department keeps all the documents — treaty, Senate resolution, instrument of ratification and the president's proclamation — until they are printed. It then sends them to a special section in the National Archives where all the treaties signed by the United States are stored. ■

Executive
■ U.S. president and foreign head of state sign treaty.

Senate
■ Treaty referred to Foreign Relations Committee, and other committees, if necessary, which hold hearings and make recommendations.
■ Full Senate considers treaty and may make amendments or other changes by simple majority vote. A resolution of ratification reflecting any changes must be approved by a two-thirds majority.

■ The resolution of ratification fails to receive a two-thirds majority and the treaty is rejected.

Executive
■ President accepts the resolution and sends it to State Department's Office of Treaty Affairs. The office drafts an instrument of ratification, which the president signs.

■ President rejects Senate's changes and sends treaty back to Senate for reconsideration; a two-thirds vote is required to adopt a new resolution.
■ President can reject the new resolution and refuse to ratify the treaty.

■ Treaty parties exchange instruments of ratification. When the treaty takes effect, the president issues a proclamation.

Continued from page 36
to a call for the Senate to kill the agreement by delay.

Popular support for the INF treaty may make delaying tactics politically unattractive. Opponents will probably turn instead to the use of amendments and other changes to the treaty's text. The Senate first asserted its right to amend treaties that have already been signed in 1794, when it demanded the deletion of a clause that restricted U.S. trade with the West Indies from the U.S.-British Jay Treaty. The precedent gained further weight in 1868, when the Senate wrote rules granting itself the right to amend treaties by a simple majority.

On two occasions the Supreme Court has sustained the power of the Senate to amend treaties. In 1869, in the case of *Haver v. Yaker*, the court stated: "In this country a treaty is something more than a contract, for the federal Constitution declared it to be the law of the land. If so, before it can become a law, the Senate, in whom rests the power to ratify it (*see box, p. 32*), must agree to it. But the Senate is not required to adopt or reject it as a whole, but

may modify or amend it." In the 1901 case of *Fourteen Diamond Rings v. the U.S.*, the Court said: "The Senate may refuse its ratification or make it conditional upon adoption of amendments to the treaty."

A Senate reservation limits only the treaty obligation of the United States, although a reservation may be so significant that the other parties to the treaty may file similar reservations or refuse to ratify the treaty.

Senate alteration of treaties may take several forms. "Declarations," which do not change the treaty's language, often are included in the Senate's resolution of ratification and serve to notify the signatories of its views on related policy matters. The Senate could, for example, make a declaration in support of a conventional arms buildup in Western Europe to compensate for the loss of nuclear weapons that would result from the INF treaty. When it wants to clarify vaguely worded provisions, the Senate can also include in its resolution of ratification "common understandings" or "agreed statements" spelling out its interpretation of these provisions. The unratified SALT II

Soviet Ratification Process

Article XVII of the INF treaty states that the document "shall be subject to ratification in accordance with the constitutional procedures of each Party." The Soviet Constitution, or Fundamental Law, which was adopted Oct. 7, 1977, is no less vague than the U.S. Constitution on the procedures of treaty ratification. Article 121 states simply that "the Presidium of the Supreme Soviet of the USSR shall . . . ratify and denounce international treaties of the USSR. . . ."

According to a statement issued by the Soviet Embassy in Washington, the INF treaty will be referred by the government to the 39-member Presidium, which exercises state authority between sessions of the Supreme Soviet, or parliament, and has sole authority to "decide whether to ratify an international treaty concluded on behalf of the USSR or not."

When it receives "an important treaty" such as the INF agreement, the Presidium submits it to the foreign affairs commissions of the two houses of parliament, the Soviet of the Union and the Soviet of Nationalities, which are briefed by Foreign Affairs Minister Eduard A. Shevardnadze and "a panel of experts." The commissions formulate "their attitude to it and refer their recommendation and conclusion" to the Presidium. Gorbachev "or his deputies" report to the Presidium on the treaty. "If the Presidium members have no observations concerning the treaty or objections to it, a decision is taken." The chairman of the Presidium, former Foreign Minister Andrei A. Gromyko, would then "immediately sign a decree of ratification."

The statement goes on to predict that the INF treaty "will be ratified in the Soviet Union approximately at the same time as it will be done in the United States," but cautions that these procedures apply only "if a treaty raises no doubts." It quotes a government official who says, "We want the treaty to be ratified as soon as possible, for the treaty signed in Washington by Gorbachev and Reagan meets the interests of all people and the interests of peace." Translation: The Soviet Union is waiting to see how the INF treaty emerges from the U.S. Senate.

treaty, for example, contained an agreed statement specifying the Senate's definition of a multiple independently targetable re-entry vehicle (MIRV) that was far more precise than that provided by the treaty's original language.

The Senate can use "reservations" and "amendments" to make more binding changes to treaties. Before it approved ratification of the Genocide Convention, for example, the Senate added a reservation that placed the United States outside the jurisdiction of the World Court in any dispute arising from its adherence to the treaty. Sen. Malcolm Wallop, R-Wyo., a frequent critic of arms control and influential conservative voice on the Arms Control Committee, has said he will offer a reservation to the INF treaty "that will force a reconsideration of our commitment to that agreement if the Soviet Union violates it. It may also require the president to certify that the Soviet Union has stopped cheating on existing agreements before the treaty comes into force." [14]

Because it alters the language of the treaty itself and thus requires the signatories' approval before the agreement can take effect, an amendment is the strongest tool the Senate has at its disposal to change a treaty. Amendments have often been used to alter a treaty's language and can assume a significance that transcends the treaties to which they are attached. Sen. Henry M. Jackson, D-Wash., sponsored an amendment to the 1972 ABM treaty requesting that any future permanent treaty on offensive nuclear weapons "not limit the United States to levels of intercontinental strategic forces inferior to" those of the Soviet Union. Unlike the ABM treaty, which expired in 1977, the Jackson amendment is of unlimited duration and established numerical equality as the basic premise of the U.S. position in future arms control negotiations. The concept was included in the 1979 SALT II treaty and presumably would apply to the strategic-arms-reduction (START) agreement currently under negotiation in Geneva.

If, upon examination of the treaty text and evidence produced at the committee hearings, INF critics continue to oppose the treaty as written, they may introduce several amendments to the articles of ratification. Sen. Larry Pressler, R-S.D., has already said he would support two amendments that would address the critics' main concerns: one calling for closer on-site inspection of Soviet missile production facilities than the treaty stipulates, another linking the treaty's implementation to a cutback in Soviet conventional forces in Europe. Other conservatives support the addition of an amendment linking the treaty's ratification to Soviet withdrawal from Afghanistan or cessation of military support for Third World governments. Because the Soviets would undoubtedly reject this language as unwarranted interference in Soviet affairs and force the parties back to the negotiating table, these would constitute "killer" amendments.

Several influential senators support the INF agreement in principle but have reservations about its effects on the balance of military power in Europe. Their task will be to shepherd the agreement through the Senate proceedings and protect it from "killer" amendments while assuring that it contains language that reflects these concerns. Sen.

Sam Nunn, D-Ga., who is chairman of the Armed Services Committee and a leading congressional expert in defense matters, will examine the treaty's impact on NATO defense capabilities in the course of his committee's hearings on the treaty. According to Scott Maxwell, the senator's press assistant, Nunn is likely to support an amendment to the treaty "letting it be known that if we are not making progress" in reducing the conventional imbalance six months or a year after the INF agreement goes into effect, the United States reserves the right to pull out of the treaty. In Nunn's view, Maxwell says, such a "supreme national interest" clause constitutes a "psychological link" that is preferable to a killer amendment because it would allow the treaty to go into effect while ensuring the United States' right to withdraw from it if certain conditions are not met.

After the Senate vote: waiting for president and Soviets to respond

While it appears unlikely that the INF treaty will make it through the Senate proceedings unchanged, most observers predict the agreement's supporters will muster the 67 "yea" votes necessary for approval. After the three committees that are examining the treaty's provisions conclude their hearings, the Foreign Relations Committee will issue recommendations to the full Senate to approve or reject it, probably by mid-February. Unless conservative opponents undertake delaying tactics as a way to prevent the treaty's implementation, Sen. Robert C. Byrd, D-W.Va., the majority leader, expects to bring it to the vote by mid-April.

If the Senate approves the treaty, it will adopt and send to the White House a resolution of ratification reflecting all the amendments, reservations and other changes it has made. If the president does not accept these changes, he must send the resolution back to the Senate with a request to remove the objectionable clauses. Their deletion would require a two-thirds vote by the full Senate. If it is still unacceptable, the president may refuse to ratify the treaty at all; otherwise, he will sign the instrument of ratification, and the treaty will enter into effect as soon as the Soviets complete their own ratification process (see box, p. 38).

It is here that the treaty may encounter further difficulty. The Soviet leadership will await Senate action before deciding whether or not to accept the INF agreement and send it on to the 39-member Presidium for formal approval. Although Article XVI of the INF agreement stipulates that "each Party may propose amendments to this treaty," the Soviets have warned that they will not accept significant changes in the document. While the Presidium has already expressed approval of the treaty, explains Soviet Embassy spokesman Alexander Malushkin, "they ratify what was signed, not quite a different treaty having differences in principle brought about by so-called killer amendments."

Thus far in the ratification process, the House of Representatives has been nothing more than a bystander. But although the House has no constitutionally authorized role in the treaty-making process, it will be called on to approve the funding to implement the agreement. Shultz has predicted that it could cost as much as $7 billion to $9 billion to destroy the missiles as called for by the INF treaty. Whether the House therefore has the power to "repeal" a treaty by withholding the funds necessary to implement it is not addressed in the Constitution and remains an issue of some debate.

> *"Insisting upon a 'thorough examination' of 'the record' would be an ideal tactic for Senate opponents of an INF treaty, who could use the uncertainties inherent in such a record to create debilitating — and probably fatal — delay in the ratification process," writes Sen. Arlen Specter.*

The issue arose as early as the Jay Treaty, whose implementing legislation was approved only after a bitter debate over the House's authority to deny its support. It flared again when legislation was needed to implement the Panama Canal treaties. But the Constitution, in Article VI, section 2, defines treaties as "the Supreme Law of the Land," and Congress has never failed to pass implementing legislation once a treaty has been ratified. "I don't think Congress has the right not to appropriate the money," says Louis Henkin, a professor at Columbia University Law School and a noted constitutional scholar. "When the president makes a treaty with the consent of the Senate,

then the Congress is obligated to do what is necessary to implement it."

Although Article XV of the INF treaty stipulates that it "shall be of unlimited duration," it also concedes the right of each signatory to withdraw from the treaty "if it decides that extraordinary events related to the subject matter of this Treaty have jeopardized its supreme interests." The parties agree to give six months' notice of such a decision. In addition, international law recognizes the right of either party to withdraw from the agreement if the other side commits a serious breach of its terms.

But while few would deny the government's power to terminate treaties, the Constitution is silent on the issue, leaving open to question which of the treaty-makers has the authority to do so. Presidents have cited their power as commander in chief and chief executive to terminate treaties without consulting the Senate. Franklin D. Roosevelt, for example, unilaterally denounced a treaty of commerce with Japan in 1939. In 1979, Congress failed to prevent President Carter from abrogating the 1954 Mutual Defense Treaty with Taiwan when he recognized the People's Republic of China as the sole legitimate government of China. The Supreme Court also refrained from challenging the president's authority to terminate treaties on his own. If Congress "chooses not to confront the President, it is not our task to do so," commented Justice Lewis F. Powell Jr. when the Taiwan case was brought before the court.[15]

ABM reinterpretation debate could delay Senate vote on INF

A more recent controversy that has potentially more damaging implications for the future of arms control treaties concerns the president's authority to unilaterally reinterpret the terms of ratified treaties. The issue arose in October 1985, when the Reagan administration presented a new interpretation of the 1972 ABM treaty that would allow the United States to test components of its Star Wars program. Under the "narrow" interpretation of the treaty, which bans anti-ballistic defensive systems, the administration would be prohibited from proceeding beyond initial research and development of land- and space-based ABM weaponry. The "broad" interpretation issued by Abraham D. Sofaer, legal adviser to the State Department, would allow testing of these weapons, bringing the controversial program that much closer to implementation.

In the ensuing debate, which pitted Sofaer against Sen. Nunn and other congressional supporters of the traditional interpretation, both sides have repeatedly referred to clarifications contained in the ABM negotiating record to lend credence to their arguments (see p. 41). Unless the administration renounces the "Sofaer doctrine," Nunn has said, he will request Senate access to the entire INF negotiating record — a volume likely to total thousands of
Continued on page 42

AT ISSUE
Can the president unilaterally reinterpret the terms of ratified treaties?

YES says **ABRAHAM D. SOFAER,** State Department legal adviser.

"The executive is empowered to interpret, or to reinterpret, treaties as long as the interpretation reached is reasonable and consistent with the expressed intent of Congress. Not every executive branch statement to the Senate of a treaty's meaning is binding. Rather, the evidence relevant to the Senate's intent must be evaluated by the standards applied in construing treaties and statutes. Far more weight would be given, for example, to a clearly expressed condition or understanding of the Senate, than to questioning in committees that reflect an understanding reached by a few senators on an issue of marginal importance at the time. . . .

The Senate has enormous power over the meaning of a treaty, but that power is most effectively exercised by the adoption of amendments, conditions, reservations, or understandings. When such actions are communicated by the president to the other party to a treaty, they become part of the treaty itself, or of the context in which a treaty is construed. Absent such action, the ratification process has little if any significance as to the treaty's meaning under international law. The Senate has repeatedly evidenced awareness of this principle by qualifying its grant of advice and consent in appropriate and formal measures. . . .

Sen. Nunn places great emphasis on the Senate's power of advice and consent, contending that the ratification record binds the president as a matter of domestic law. The administration recognizes that executive branch statements to the Senate concerning the meaning of a treaty are significant events and must be carefully weighed. But Sen. Nunn's absolute bar on the president's discretion to depart from a record as ambiguous as the ABM treaty's would create a radically new restrictive principle on the president's established authority. . . .

The Senate's role in treaty review is already as broad as its interest in each treaty it considers; it is unlikely to be affected by the president's decision on the ABM treaty's meaning. This is . . . a case in which the Senate failed to evidence an intent, in any form, to bind the president to the restrictive interpretation. It is therefore no precedent for a departure from such an expression of intent. . . ."

From "The ABM Treaty: Legal Analysis in the Political Cauldron," The Washington Quarterly, *autumn 1987, pp. 59-75.*

NO says **SEN. SAM NUNN**, D-Ga., chairman of the Armed Services Committee.

"For the past two years, the United States has been embroiled in a contentious and arcane internal dispute over the correct interpretation of those portions of the 1972 Anti-Ballistic Missile (ABM) Treaty which pertain to the development and testing of futuristic or so-called exotic ABM systems. This controversy was precipitated in October 1985, when the Reagan administration announced with no advance notice or congressional consultations that the interpretation of the treaty which successive U.S. administrations had upheld since 1972 was incorrect. . . .

To defend his conclusions, Sofaer resorts to a new and profoundly worrisome new doctrine with regard to Senate ratification, one which risks serious constitutional confrontation between the executive and legislative branches. He argues that when the Senate gives its advice and consent to a treaty, it is to the treaty that was negotiated, 'irrespective of the explanations it is provided.' This doctrine is totally unacceptable. If adopted, it would inflict serious long-term damage on the institutional relationship between the president and the Congress and have destructive consequences for the conduct of U.S. foreign policy. It is contrary to the long-term interests of the United States to assert that statements made to the Senate have no standing with other parties to a treaty.

Unless this doctrine is modified, a reasonably prudent Senate would have to take the following steps. First, the Senate would have to obtain the negotiating record for each treaty it reviews, since the Senate certainly could not trust executive branch witnesses. This would require the otherwise undesirable step of making public all confidential materials associated with the record. Second, the Senate would have to record each and every understanding it has as to the meaning of a treaty in its resolution of ratification. Obviously, Senate resolutions of ratification prepared under this doctrine would be so laden as to sink under their own weight. More fundamentally, they would effectively precipitate a renegotiation with all states party to the treaty since they might well object to the wording employed in stating the Senate's interpretation."

From "The ABM Reinterpretation Issue," The Washington Quarterly, *autumn 1987, pp. 45-57.*

Past Coverage

■ **Defending Europe** addresses one of the main issues the Senate will take up in its consideration of the INF treaty, the state of NATO's defense capabilities in the absence of the intermediate-range nuclear forces the treaty would eliminate. By Mary H. Cooper, E.R.R., 1987 Vol. II, pp. 673-689.

■ **Making Foreign Policy** reviews the continuing struggle between Congress and the president for dominance in the conduct of foreign policy. The report focuses on the debate over the president's war powers, which was revived because of the Iran-contra controversy. By Sarah Glazer, E.R.R., 1987 Vol. I, pp. 313-328.

■ **Euromissile Negotiations** describes the course of U.S.-Soviet negotiations that produced the INF treaty, as well as Western European concerns over "nuclear nakedness" that might result from the Euromissile withdrawal. By Mary H. Cooper, E.R.R., 1987 Vol. I, pp. 193-208.

■ **Strategic Arms Debate** reviews the course of U.S.-Soviet arms control negotiations in the postwar period and examines the issue of treaty verification and compliance, as great a concern today as it was at the time of the SALT II ratification debate. By William Sweet, E.R.R., 1979 Vol. I, pp. 402-420.

■ **Treaty Ratification** traces the development of the treaty-making powers of the president and the Senate through the 1972 ratification debate over the SALT I treaties. By Leo Adde, E.R.R., 1972 Vol. II, pp. 519-538.

Continued from page 40
pages — during his committee's consideration of the treaty. Only in this way, he says, can the Senate be sure of the negotiators' intent behind the treaty's provisions and so be certain that it will not be vulnerable to similar reinterpretation by future administrations.

If the issue remains unresolved, Nunn's request could well derail Senate approval of the INF treaty. "Insisting upon a 'thorough examination' of the record would be an ideal tactic for Senate opponents of the INF treaty, who could use the uncertainties inherent in such a record to create debilitating — and probably fatal — delay in the ratification process," wrote Sen. Arlen Specter, R-Pa., a supporter of the treaty.[16] Other critics challenge the president's right to reinterpret treaties on constitutional grounds. House Foreign Affairs Chairman Dante B. Fascell, D-Fla., contends that the administration's attempts to reinterpret the ABM treaty "encroach on the Senate's constitutional responsibility to approve only one text of a treaty as the law of the land. The executive branch has no constitutional power to unilaterally reinterpret treaties."[17]

But the administration's desire to ratify the INF treaty appears to outweigh its determination to reinterpret the ABM treaty. According to Rhinelander, who calls the Sofaer doctrine "unfounded as a legal matter and dumb policy," the State Department may now be prepared to repudiate the Sofaer doctrine's applicability to all future treaties. "If the administration wants this treaty, it is going to have to come up with something which minimally satisfies Nunn," Rhinelander says. Otherwise, "there is no way a treaty can be ratified."

NOTES

[1] Televised address by President Reagan, Dec. 10, 1987.

[2] Under Senate rules, all treaties, regardless of subject matter, are referred to the Foreign Relations Committee. In cases where there are military or intelligence aspects to the accords, the Armed Services and Intelligence committees also may hold hearings on the treaty.

[3] *Youngstown Sheet & Tube Co. v. Sawyer*, 343 U.S. 579 (1952).

[4] Maclay's memoirs were cited by Edward S. Corwin, in *The President* (1957), pp. 209-210.

[5] *U.S. v. Curtiss-Wright Export Corp.*, 299 U.S. 304 (1936).

[6] Cited in Corwin, *op. cit.*, p. 443.

[7] See Marjorie Ann Browne, "Executive Agreements and the Congress," Congressional Research Service, May 1, 1975; updated Feb. 27, 1981.

[8] See Walter F. Mondale, *Toward a Responsible Presidency* (1975), p. 114.

[9] Arthur M. Schlesinger Jr., *The Imperial Presidency* (1973), p. 313.

[10] President Nixon and Soviet Chairman Leonid I. Brezhnev signed two strategic arms limitations pacts in Moscow on May 26, 1972. One was the Treaty on the Limitation of Anti-Ballistic Missile Systems (ABMs) and the other was technically an executive agreement placing a numerical freeze on U.S. and Soviet missile launchers for five years at roughly existing levels.

[11] Writing in *The Washington Post*, Dec. 13, 1987.

[12] Congressional Research Service, "U.S. Senate Rejection of Treaties," March 30, 1987.

[13] Writing in *The New York Times*, Jan. 5, 1988.

[14] Writing in *The Wall Street Journal*, Dec. 18, 1987.

[15] *Goldwater v. Carter*, 444 U.S. 996, 998 (1981).

[16] Arlen Specter, "The Threat to the INF Treaty," *The New York Review of Books*, Feb. 4, 1988, p. 23.

[17] Dante B. Fascell, "Congress and Arms Control," *Foreign Affairs*, spring 1987, p. 736.

Graphics: cover, p. 37, S. Dmitri Lipczenko.

RECOMMENDED READING

BOOKS

Edward S. Corwin, *The President: Office and Powers, 1787-1957*, New York University Press, 1957.

This book, a classic history of the president's role in making foreign policy, contains a brief but comprehensive overview of the ways chief executives have sought to circumvent the Senate in making agreements with other nations. In distinguishing between treaties and executive agreements, Corwin concludes that critics of the executive branch often ignore "the essential question, which is not whether the President can constitutionally enter into executive agreements with other governments — a point universally conceded — but what scope these may today validly take."

Louis Henkin, *Foreign Affairs and the Constitution*, W. W. Norton & Co., 1972.

Henkin, another leading authority on the struggle between the executive and legislative branches in making foreign policy, devotes a chapter to treaties and the treaty power. Of particular interest is his consideration of the treaty-makers — the president and the Senate — as a "fourth branch of government" that is as frequently at odds with Congress as a whole as with itself.

Lawrence Margolis, *Executive Agreements and Presidential Power in Foreign Policy*, Praeger Publishers, 1986.

The author, a professor of politics at Illinois State University, poses the question whether presidents have abused their constitutional authority by implementing executive agreements in place of treaties. After tracing the frequency of their use as well as the significance of the deals to which they have been applied, he concludes that "with all of its imperfections, this solution [the executive agreement] seems to allow for speed and secrecy without sacrificing democracy."

Arthur M. Schlesinger Jr., *The Imperial Presidency*, Houghton Mifflin Co., 1973.

Schlesinger, a historian and former assistant to President John F. Kennedy, traces the course of presidential power throughout the nation's history, culminating in the "imperial presidency" of Richard M. Nixon, when "the constitutional separation of powers began to disappear in the middle

distance." In discussing the treaty-making power, the author focuses on the increasing use of executive agreements in the postwar period.

ARTICLES

Henkin, Louis, "Foreign Affairs and the Constitution," *Foreign Affairs*, winter 1987/88.

In this article commemorating the 200th anniversary of the U.S. Constitution, Henkin re-examines the separation of powers in foreign affairs that was the subject of his earlier book of the same title. "The constitutional bifurcation of the treaty power is inefficient," Henkin writes. But the burden is on the president to improve the treaty process, he adds, by refraining from such actions as the ABM reinterpretation which "invite the Senate in the future to probe ambiguities and to express understandings with nearly paranoid scrupulousness, from fear not only of what other states may make of a treaty but of what a future executive branch will make of it."

Specter, Arlen, "The Threat to the INF Treaty," *The New York Review of Books*, Feb. 4, 1988.

The junior senator from Pennsylvania calls on his colleagues to abandon plans to demand access to the 1972 ABM treaty's negotiating record as a means of resolving an ongoing dispute over that agreement's intent. A Republican who supports the INF treaty, Specter says: "Insisting upon a 'thorough examination' of the record would be an ideal tactic for Senate opponents of the INF treaty, who could use the uncertainties inherent in such a record to create debilitating — and probably fatal — delay in the ratification process."

REPORTS AND STUDIES

Browne, Marjorie Ann, "Executive Agreements and the Congress," Congressional Research Service, May 1, 1975 (updated Feb. 27, 1981).

The author traces the growing use of executive agreements as alternatives to treaties, as well as proposals to increase congressional control over their use.

Collier, Ellen, "U.S. Senate Rejection of Treaties," Congressional Research Service, March 30, 1987.

The study reviews the Senate's record as partner in the treaty-making process. It finds that between 1789 and 1986, the Senate gave its consent to more than 1,500 treaties, and voted to reject only 17.

U.S. Senate Foreign Relations Committee, "Treaties and Other International Agreements: The Role of the United States Senate," June 1984.

Compiled by the Congressional Research Service, this comprehensive study of Senate action in treaty-making traces changes in the treaty process that have occurred over the years as well as the controversy over the use of executive agreements.

DECEMBER 24, 1987

DEFENDING EUROPE

DEFENDING EUROPE

Now that the United States and the Soviet Union have agreed to remove intermediate-range nuclear missiles from Europe, attention is turning to talks aimed at reducing conventional forces deployed on the continent. The United States and its NATO allies could be at a disadvantage in these talks unless they settle differences over military strategy, defense spending and Europe's role in the alliance.

by Mary H. Cooper

For all the fanfare that accompanied the signing of the first U.S.-Soviet arms control agreement in eight years, the treaty to ban intermediate-range nuclear forces (INF) has posed as many questions about the defense of Europe as it has resolved. By reducing the nuclear component of the superpowers' arsenals on the continent, the INF agreement has focused attention on conventional, or non-nuclear, forces. While all 15 U.S. allies in the North Atlantic Treaty Organization (NATO) endorse the treaty, which was signed Dec. 8 in Washington, they also agree that the withdrawal of 2,800 "Euromissiles" and the prospect of deep cuts in the superpowers' strategic nuclear forces make adequate conventional strength more urgent than ever. [1]

By nearly all accounts, the seven-nation Warsaw Pact [2] enjoys a substantial numerical advantage over NATO in conventional forces. At the same time, budgetary constraints in the United States and in Europe will make it more difficult to correct that imbalance. For this reason, support is growing for a new set of negotiations aimed at reducing the level of conventional forces deployed in Europe by NATO and the East bloc. "We and the Soviet Union are pretty much agreed to start conventional stability talks sometime early next year," says Matthew Murphy, a spokesman for the U.S. Arms Control and Disarmament Agency, which advises the president on arms control policy. Unlike the negotiations over nuclear weapons, which have been conducted between the superpowers alone, the conventional weapons talks will involve all 23 members of the two alliances. "We will consult with our NATO allies and be sure all are agreed on specific proposals to be presented to the Soviets," Murphy says.

U.S. forces in West Germany during 1987 exercise "Certain Strike."

But there are obstacles to reaching such a consensus that make the official timetable uncertain. Some of the West European allies fear that the removal of U.S. medium-range nuclear weapons from their territory is the first phase of a reduction in America's defense commitment to Europe.

Article V of the 1949 North Atlantic Treaty stipulates that "an armed attack against one or more of [the allies] in Europe or North America shall be considered an attack against them all," and requires them to defend one another from aggression. Because of America's preponderant military clout within the alliance, however, this notion of collective security has in effect meant U.S. protection of Western Europe through the threat of nuclear retaliation for any attack by the Soviet Union and its East European allies. But some Europeans now fear that the United States, increasingly preoccupied with economic problems at home and security concerns in the Far East and Latin America, is loosening its traditional bonds with Europe.

European jitters over America's commitment to the defense of Western Europe took on new urgency after President Reagan met with Soviet leader Mikhail S. Gorbachev in Reykjavik, Iceland, in October 1986. During that meeting the two leaders came close to agreeing to eliminate all nuclear weapons, a prospect many West European governments found appalling. In their view, the nuclear deterrent is responsible for keeping the peace in Europe for the last 40 years. In addition, two European powers, Britain and France, have developed nuclear arsenals

of their own, which would be jeopardized by a super-power agreement to eliminate nuclear weapons. "It is the loose talk like what we heard at Reykjavik that is devastating to the Europeans, more than the INF agreement," says Stanley Hoffmann, a professor of government and chairman of Harvard University's Center for European Studies.

Jolted by Reagan's apparent willingness to conclude arms agreements that might not serve their interests, the European allies have called for a strengthening of the "European pillar" of NATO. They have taken steps in recent months to increase the frequency and depth of consultations on strategic issues and to cooperate more closely in military planning and maneuvers, as well as arms production and procurement (*see p. 56*).

To European complaints about America's potential "decoupling" of its security interests from those of Europe, American critics respond with their own list of grievances over Europe's perceived shortcomings in the defense effort. "My definition of collective security is that Europe does the collecting and we do the securing," says Melvyn Krauss, a professor of economics at New York University and a senior fellow at the Hoover Institution, a conservative think tank affiliated with Stanford University.

Krauss' remark reflects growing impatience among U.S. academics and lawmakers with the European allies' continuing dependence on U.S. military might even as their economic power grows, often at America's expense. While most critics in the United States stop short of

Krauss' suggestion that America pull out of NATO, there is growing support in Congress for proposals that would force the allies to shoulder a greater share of the burden of defending Europe, especially those that enjoy sizeable trade surpluses with the United States (see p. 57). Rep. Patricia Schroeder, D-Colo. author of one such bill, chides Europeans for worrying about America's defense commitment while continuing to rely on U.S. might. "Guys, it's grow-up time," she tells them. "If you had better conventional forces, decoupling would not be a problem."

Difficulties in measuring conventional arms balance

Assessing the conventional arms balance between East and West is more difficult than measuring the nuclear balance. The statistics vary among different sources, in part because the vast array of conventional weaponry and frequent improvements make these weapons harder to classify and quantify than nuclear armaments. In addition, conventional forces have not been subjected to the careful quantitative analysis that decades of arms control negotiations have imposed upon nuclear weaponry.

Despite the wide discrepancy in numbers, however, nearly all accounts show that the Warsaw Pact enjoys a quantitative superiority over NATO in both manpower and most components of conventional weaponry (see chart, p. 49). NATO says it has about 942,000 ground and air forces in central Europe and estimates there are 1,180,000 East bloc personnel similarly deployed. These figures exclude 50,000 French troops deployed in West Germany because France, while a member of NATO, keeps its forces outside the alliance's integrated command.[3] The figures are further complicated by Warsaw Pact claims that it fields fewer troops, 997,000, than NATO reports.

The London-based International Institute for Strategic Studies, widely considered the most authoritative source of military statistics available to the public, confirms the conventional force imbalance. Last year, the institute reports, the East bloc held an advantage of nearly 6-to-1 over the West in surface-to-air missiles and more than 2-to-1 in main battle tanks, essential defensive and offensive ground-force equipment in the event of a conventional war. The Warsaw Pact has more land-based combat aircraft, including about six times as many fighters and almost twice as many bombers as the West. The two blocs' naval forces are more evenly matched. While the East has more submarines, NATO outnumbers its adversary in destroyers, carriers and other ships. The West also holds the upper hand in most types of naval aircraft.

But the numbers alone can be misleading, the institute points out, and cannot by themselves "answer basic questions about the relative capabilities of each side's forces to perform their required mission."[4] They do not, for example, take into account the quality of equipment and the training and morale of troops, categories in which NATO holds the upper hand. For this reason, Western forces are considered to be more mobile than their Eastern counterparts. For all their numerical superiority in tanks, on which any invasion would depend, Warsaw Pact tanks are technologically inferior to such Western equivalents as the German Leopard-2, judged to be the fastest and best armed tank in the world. "While I was chancellor," former West German leader Helmut Schmidt has written, "I never seriously worried about the undeniably greater numbers of Soviet conventional troops, because I was — and still am — convinced of the high combat effectiveness that would be demonstrated by the West German military in the event of an attack from the East."[5]

The statistics also understate NATO's inherent strength as a defensive force. According to military analysts, an aggressor must have a three-to-one numerical advantage over its adversary to ensure a successful offensive break through existing defensive lines, a greater edge than the East bloc currently enjoys. In terms of logistics — the supplying and movement of troops — and backup support that would be crucial to front-line forces, NATO has another important advantage. Although North American reserves and aircraft must travel much further than Soviet backup support to reach the central front that divides Eastern and Western Europe, the West's superior road and telecommunications networks would facilitate their mobility once they reached the European theater. More importantly, for all the well-publicized bickering over NATO defense policy, the civilian populations in Western Europe could be counted on to support NATO's military efforts to repulse an attack. The populations of Eastern Europe — whose territory has been occupied by Soviet forces since the end of World War II — would be a far less reliable source of support for a Soviet-led invasion of Western Europe.

But the story behind the force-balance statistics is not all in favor of NATO. The Center for Defense Information, a Washington-based organization that supports arms control and generally disputes the notion of Warsaw Pact superiority in conventional armaments, says the East bloc enjoys several qualitative advantages over the West. An unpublished paper issued by the center contends that logistics are less crucial for the East. Soviet soldiers, it says, "are not issued sleeping bags and are taught to make their beds in their coats even in the coldest weather. In addition, Soviet commanders would not hesitate to let their soldiers go for a couple of days without food, something that would not be tolerated with the Western traditions."

In virtually all plausible scenarios of East-West conventional warfare, time is of the essence. The prospects for a successful invasion of Western Europe rest on the Warsaw Pact's ability to move quickly and decisively to overrun NATO defenses before Western reserves can move to the front. The Eastern alliance, composed of fewer nations than NATO and far more strictly dominated by its superpower leader, is better suited for such quick decision-

Continued on page 50

Arms in Europe: The Atlantic to the Urals

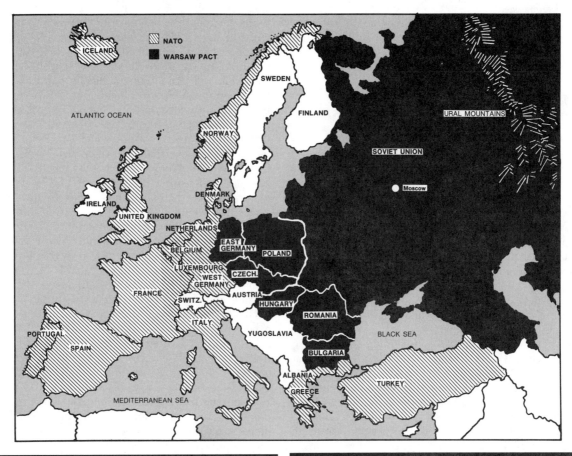

Short-Range Nuclear Forces

Nuclear weapons not covered by the Intermediate-range Nuclear Force (INF) Treaty

	RANGE (miles)	NATO	WARSAW PACT
Ballistic missiles			
Lance	68	93	—
Pluton (France) °	74	32	—
Scud	186	—	630
FROG and SS-21	43-74	—	749
Ground-launched cruise missiles	279	—	100
Artillery pieces		2,700	6,260
Land-based aircraft		1,543	2,348

° *French forces are not part of NATO's integrated military command.*
Source: International Institute for Strategic Studies

Conventional Forces

	NATO *	WARSAW PACT	WARSAW PACT ADVANTAGE
Ground Forces			
Active ground forces	2,385,000	2,292,000	1 : 1
Main battle tanks	22,200	52,200	2.4 : 1
Mechanized infantry combat vehicles	4,200	25,800	6.1 : 1
Artillery/mortars	13,700	46,500	3.4 : 1
Antitank guided weapons	10,570	17,650	1.7 : 1
Antiaircraft guns	7,400	12,000	1.6 : 1
Surface-to-air missiles	2,250	12,850	5.7 : 1
Air Forces			
Bombers	285	450	1.6 : 1
Armed helicopters	780	1,630	2.1 : 1
Attack aircraft	2,108	2,144	1 : 1
Interceptors/fighters	899	4,930	5.5 : 1
Navies			
Submarines	196	231	1.2 : 1
Aircraft carriers	24	4	−6 : 1
Major surface ships	358	244	−1.6 : 1

° *French and Spanish forces are not part of NATO's integrated military command, but are included insofar as they are deployed in the relevant geographical area.*
Source: International Institute for Strategic Studies

Continued from page 48
making than the Western alliance, which could lose precious time while forging a consensus for military action.

Support for NATO military buildup before treaty signing

Because these qualitative considerations color numerical assessments of the military balance in Europe, it is not surprising that judgments about NATO's ability to defend itself vary immensely. When he retired after eight years as Supreme Allied Commander in Europe (SACEUR) last June, U.S. Gen. Bernard W. Rogers decried the proposed INF treaty as a step toward denuclearization, a step he said would make "Western Europe safe again for conventional war."[6] Rogers had long called for improved conventional forces in Europe, saying that in case of attack NATO could hold out only for a matter of days before being either overrun or retaliating with a nuclear strike against the Soviet Union.

Other critics of the INF treaty, including former Secretary of State Henry Kissinger and Alexander M. Haig Jr., Reagan's first secretary of state and currently a contender for the Republican presidential nomination, say the United States should condition the removal of U.S. Pershing II and ground-launched cruise missiles called for by the treaty on improvements in NATO's conventional forces or progress in negotiations on conventional arms control.[7]

Other analysts say the INF treaty's impact on NATO's military strength is overblown. They point out that NATO will still have 4,300 nuclear weapons at its disposal after the accord is implemented. These include 1,070 nuclear-capable aircraft, more than 1,000 tactical nuclear artillery shells and more than 400 missile warheads deployed on U.S. Poseidon submarines, which gradually will be replaced by more accurate Trident D-5 missiles. These numbers do not include the independent nuclear arsenals of Britain and France, both of which are currently being modernized. Nevertheless, former Defense Secretary Caspar W. Weinberger, at a NATO meeting in November, hastened to reassure the European allies of U.S. intentions to correct what he called the "maldeployment" of nuclear forces that would result from the Euromissile withdrawal. Among his suggestions for nuclear-force modernization were a newer version of the short-range Lance surface-to-surface missile, currently deployed in five European countries, improvements in aircraft capable of carrying both conventional and nuclear warheads, new air-launched cruise missiles and new nuclear artillery shells.[8]

On the conventional side, many analysts point to the need for stronger armored forces to counter Soviet superiority in tank deployments. In response to warnings by Gen. Rogers and others that the West was becoming increasingly unprepared to sustain a conventional war in Europe beyond the first few days of combat, NATO in December 1984 initiated a program to increase stocks of ammunition and spare parts and cooperate more closely on armaments production and procurement. Beyond these measures, military analysts say additional aircraft, communications equipment and artillery also are needed. The

The INF Treaty

The Intermediate-Range Nuclear Forces (INF) agreement President Reagan and Soviet leader Gorbachev signed in Washington Dec. 8 calls for the elimination of all U.S. and Soviet land-based nuclear missiles with ranges of between 300 and 3,400 miles. The treaty would eliminate several types of U.S. and Soviet missiles with ranges of more than 600 miles, including 112 single-warhead Soviet SS-4 missiles, 441 triple-warhead Soviet SS-20s, and America's 108 Pershing IIs and 256 ground-launched cruise missiles, both of which carry one warhead. Only the Soviet Union possesses the shorter-range missiles covered by the treaty. The agreement requires the Soviets to eliminate 110 SS-12/22 Scaleboards and 20 SS-23s, both single-warhead missiles with ranges of 300-600 miles.

The treaty calls for the most intrusive verification measures ever included in a nuclear arms agreement. U.S. inspectors will be based at a Soviet missile production facility in Votkinsk for 13 years, while Soviet inspectors will be based at a facility in Utah for the same period. Representatives of both sides also will be allowed to inspect missile production factories on short notice.

United States, which is committed to transporting as many as 10 divisions to Western Europe in 10 days in the event of war, still lacks the airlift capability to do so.

The Pentagon has continued to modernize its conventional forces, introducing new surface ships, fighter planes, tanks and helicopters. But Frank C. Carlucci, who succeeded Weinberger as defense secretary in late November, has stressed the need to be "more creative" in approaching the problem of force modernization in NATO because of budget constraints. Instead of dedicating the shrinking defense budget to new weapons systems, he advocates less costly means of upgrading NATO's defense, such as improved cooperation among allied forces.

NATO defense ministers have not yet reached a consensus on what kinds of improvements in either nuclear or conventional forces will be needed in the wake of the INF treaty. U.S. spokesmen have repeatedly assured the European allies that the accord in no way reduces the U.S. commitment to defend their territory. If the INF treaty is ratified, said Gen. John Galvin after he succeeded Rogers as European commander, "the level of risk will go up and we must take steps to counteract this." [9]

Optimism over prospects for conventional stability talks

Modernization of conventional forces alone is not a realistic solution to NATO's problems. While all the allies call for force improvements, none is in a position to assume the financial burden that an all-out campaign to match the Warsaw Pact tank for tank and man for man would impose on their budgets. The International Institute for Strategic Studies reports that the NATO allies spent $420 billion last year for defense, compared to the $300 billion spent by the Warsaw Pact. Gorbachev, whose ambitious economic reforms at home depend on reducing defense spending, has for some time supported the idea of conventional arms control. Likewise, the continuing budget deficit in the United States has made it clear that the Reagan administration's campaign to "rearm America" must be curtailed. For their part, the European allies are unwilling or unable to fill in the gap in funding required for a significant force buildup. For this reason, Western leaders are finding the notion of arms control talks aimed at reducing troop levels and conventional weapons in Europe an increasingly attractive alternative to a military buildup on the continent.

History provides little promise of success for conventional force negotiations. The Mutual and Balanced Force Reduction (MBFR) talks in Vienna between the two alliances have dragged on since 1973 without progress. The aim of these talks has been to reduce the number of troops deployed by the East bloc in East Germany, Poland and Czechoslovakia, and by NATO in West Germany, Belgium, Luxembourg and the Netherlands. But after 467 meetings over 14 years, the two sides have never even agreed on current troop levels.

Events over the past 18 months appear to have broken the stalemate. On April 18, 1986, Gorbachev proposed in East Berlin that the reduction of all land forces and tactical nuclear weapons — shorter-range weapons not included in the INF agreement — be the subject of talks that would cover all of Europe including Soviet territory — "from the Atlantic to the Urals." The Warsaw Pact endorsed the proposal and on June 11 issued its version, called the "Budapest appeal," to its NATO counterparts. Specifically, the appeal called for demobilizing troops and their equipment by entire combat units, beginning with 100,000 - 150,000 troops from both sides. Each alliance would remove an additional half million troops in the early 1990s, followed by further force reductions that would also include the armed forces of neutral powers such as Finland and Austria.

The Budapest appeal set off a dispute within NATO over the proper forum in which the new talks would take place. France, which has long supported the notion of greater European participation in East-West arms negotiations, wanted them to come under the umbrella of the Conference on Confidence- and Security-Building Measures and Disarmament in Europe (CDE). This 35-nation forum was set up in 1984 under the auspices of the Conference on Security and Cooperation in Europe (CSCE), which produced the 1975 Helsinki Accords and includes the members of both alliances as well as the neutral and non-aligned countries of Europe.[10] Unlike the MBFR talks, the CDE has produced an agreement, which was signed Sept. 22, 1986, in Stockholm. Under the agreement, designed to reduce the risk of surprise attack and miscalculation during crises, both alliances agreed to notify each other before undertaking large-scale troop movements and allow representatives to observe military exercises. So far, the agreement has been a success. Since August of this year, NATO observers have overseen two troop maneuvers in Eastern Europe and Warsaw Pact representatives have been present at two NATO exercises. In at least two cases, East bloc exercises near the Soviet city of Minsk and NATO troop maneuvers in Scotland, the observers were allowed to mingle with the troops. "The exercises went smoothly," Murphy says. "To my knowledge, there have been no complaints."

Despite the CDE's successful record, the United States and most other NATO allies balked at the French proposal to extend its authority to East-West arms control negotiations. They say the neutral and nonaligned states should not have a say in NATO-Warsaw Pact arms reduction. NATO consequently adopted a compromise position that would limit participation in the "conventional stability talks" dealing with weaponry to the 23 members of the two alliances while proceeding separately with follow-up discussions on new confidence- and security-building measures that will include all 35 nations taking part in the Conference on Security and Cooperation in Europe. The CSCE is also being used as the forum for preliminary negotiations in the conventional arms talks.

NATO Ambivalence Over U.S. Military Presence

O f the 525,600 U.S. troops stationed abroad, 354,000 are assigned to Europe. Most of our NATO allies support this heavy military presence as concrete proof of America's commitment to Europe's defense. But in several southern European countries, the desire for U.S. protection is tempered by resentment over the superpower's military presence that has its roots in a variety of local concerns. These are resurfacing in talks over U.S. base agreements that by coincidence are up for renewal just as the INF treaty focuses concern on the state of NATO conventional forces. Although these talks are overshadowed by negotiations over two key U.S. bases in the Philippines, they may become more controversial as East-West conventional arms talks draw near.

Spain   The government of socialist Prime Minister Felipe Gonzalez announced in November that it would not renew the agreement that allows the United States to maintain four bases and other military posts in Spain which, while a member of NATO since 1982, remains with France outside the alliance's military command. Opinion polls show widespread opposition to the bases as symbols of U.S. support for the despised dictatorship of Generalissimo Francisco Franco, under whose regime they were set up. If a new base agreement is not reached by May, the United States will have one year to withdraw more than 12,500 troops. Of particular concern is the fate of 72 F-16 fighter-bombers stationed at Torrejon near Madrid, the largest American air unit in the Mediterranean area and deemed essential for the defense of NATO's southern flank.

Portugal   The United States' sole base here, located in the Azores, is a logical alternative location for the F-16s. Although the base agreement does not expire until 1991, the government has suggested it may call for early talks because it wants to receive more American military aid, which totaled $80 million in fiscal 1987. There are fewer than 1,500 U.S. troops stationed at Lajes air base, which serves as a mid-Atlantic refueling facility and staging area for NATO anti-submarine warfare operations.

Greece   The four main American bases and 3,500 U.S. troops have long been a source of controversy. Socialist Prime Minister Andreas Papandreou rose to power largely on his promise to rid the country of the U.S. presence, widely considered to be symbolic — as in Spain — of American support for a previous military regime. The current base agreement expires in December 1988, and talks on a new pact began in November. Like Portugal, Greece wants more U.S. aid, which in 1987 totaled $343 million.

Turkey   The Turks, too, have been pressing for more American military aid, although it receives more — $490 million in 1987 — than its traditional enemy but ally in NATO, Greece. Turkey hosts two U.S. air bases, but because of its location bordering on the Soviet Union, the five American intelligence-gathering posts there are considered to be especially important for NATO security. A recent base agreement that assures U.S. access until 1990 has not been ratified by the Turkish government.

In recent months, Polish leader Gen. Wojciech Jaruzelski, who heads the Warsaw Pact's second-largest conventional force after the Soviet Union, has served as spokesman for the East bloc's emerging position on conventional force negotiations. Among his proposals is the application of "asymmetry" to conventional force reductions in much the same way it was used to achieve the INF agreement. Just as the Euromissile accord calls on the Soviet Union to destroy four times as many missiles as NATO in order to arrive at an equitable result, Jaruzelski called Nov. 11 for a cut in Warsaw Pact tank forces in exchange for reductions in NATO's bomber aircraft deployed in Europe.

Although the United States disputes the claim that NATO in fact has more bombers than the East bloc, the Reagan administration welcomed the proposal in the context of the new talks expected to begin next spring. To the extent that the Warsaw Pact enjoys superiority in most types of conventional forces, asymmetrical reductions would work to NATO's advantage.

The two alliances are expected to open the conventional stability talks in Vienna sometime between next March and July. Although NATO has not yet formulated a specific set of proposals in answer to Jaruzelski's, the new negotiations will depart substantially from past conventional force negotiations. Unlike the MBFR talks, which will be discontinued when the new talks begin, the negotiations will no longer deal with manpower alone, but will concentrate instead on equipment. Although the problem of quantification will remain, the shift in focus from troops to equipment will allow the negotiators to sidestep troop counts, the principal roadblock to progress in the MBFR. In addition, expansion of the force reduction area is likely to make these talks more appealing to the European public. By including the European portion of the Soviet Union, the talks could produce an agreement to push heavy force concentrations more than 1,500 miles away from Western Europe, a prospect that would be especially appealing to West Germany, the most likely battlefield in a conventional war in Europe.

Jaruzelski has made a first step in this direction by proposing the talks begin with force reductions in a limited area along the central front, a so-called "thin-out zone" 100 to 150 kilometers (62 to 93 miles) wide. The initial focus on such a limited area — what military analyst Jonathan Dean calls the "Polish contribution to arms control" — is aimed at arriving quickly at force reductions that could be applied to incrementally larger areas later in the negotiating process. "Both sides are focusing on armament reduction," says Dean, arms control adviser of the Union of Concerned Scientists and a former U.S. representative to the MBFR talks.[11] Although NATO has not yet formulated a specific position, he predicts the alliance will aim first for cuts in ground forces in the central European zone.

But the Polish proposal has already generated controversy. "There is likely to be some haggling over the thin-out zone," Dean says. The first stumbling block is likely to concern the issue of whether or not to include parts of the Soviet Union, a prospect Moscow may rebuff. More importantly, NATO as a whole may balk at this incremental approach to arms reduction and press instead for inclusion of the entire Atlantic-to-the-Urals reduction area from the outset. In particular, Dean says "the West Germans don't like it because they feel it may signal the beginning of a pullback of allied forces from full participation in forward defense." Such a pullback, in the German view, would leave that country more vulnerable to attack.

Divisions among European allies over tactical nuclear weapons

NATO is even more deeply divided over the question of whether to include short-range nuclear weapons in the conventional stability talks. These include a variety of nuclear arms having ranges of less than 300 miles, which were excluded from the INF agreement. They comprise short-range missiles, such as the Soviet Scuds and SS-21s, as well as bombs and artillery shells intended for use on the battlefield — so-called tactical nuclear weapons (see chart, p. 49).

In theory, "tac-nukes" offer an important advantage over conventional artillery because a single shot could wipe out a large column of invading tank forces. For this reason, their very presence serves to discourage the Warsaw Pact from concentrating its forces along the central front, a necessary first step under most invasion scenarios.

The Soviet Union has long advocated including short-range and tactical nuclear weapons in conventional arms talks as a follow-on to the "zero-zero" option to eliminate both superpowers' intermediate-range nuclear arms from Europe. West Germany also supports adopting the "third zero" to do away with tactical nuclear weapons, which former West German Chancellor Schmidt calls "lethal and deadly weapons for the German and Polish populations living on the battleground." Indeed, he challenges the common reference to these weapons as merely "tactical" as "a belittling term for a category of weapons that if used in great numbers, will kill or cripple the greater part of the central European peoples." [12]

But other NATO members, who fear the INF agreement may signal the beginning of a U.S. nuclear pullback from Europe, balk at including short-range nuclear weapons in the conventional arms negotiations. They worry that removal of tactical weapons would make Western Europe even more vulnerable to a conventional attack from the East. "Britain and France are highly opposed to the third option," says Hoffmann, "especially with the Soviets hinting they would go for it." The two European nuclear powers have another reason for wanting to keep tactical nuclear weapons off the agenda. Both are eager to hang on to their independent nuclear arsenals.

The United States has stated its intention to exclude short-range nuclear weapons from the talks, at least for now. But NATO ministers are still disputing the impact of the INF agreement on the East-West nuclear balance, a discussion that can be expected to become more heated if the United States and the Soviet Union proceed rapidly toward a major reduction in strategic nuclear weaponry as Reagan and Gorbachev promised during their Washington summit. "I think that sooner or later there will be some nuclear add-in in the conventional stability talks," Dean predicts. "The problem is that there too the Warsaw Pact has a large numerical superiority. I urge we offer to go to a low number of tactical weapons as part of these talks."

Gorbachev's 'peace' offensive: rethinking military strategies

In the view of many military analysts, the most innovative aspect of Gorbachev's two-year-old "peace offensive" toward the West and a key ingredient in the Polish proposals leading up to conventional arms talks is to be found in the field of military doctrine. Beginning with the June 1986 Budapest appeal, the Warsaw Pact has called on the West to join in negotiations aimed at reconsidering the basic strategies that both alliances use to justify the levels of troops and armaments in Europe.

Until the mid-1970s, the Soviets' stated goal in nuclear weaponry was one of supremacy over the West. Soviet leaders replaced this strategy, which set the stage for an open-ended arms race, with one calling for nuclear parity. But since he rose to the Kremlin leadership in March 1985, Gorbachev has called for a more drastic turn-about in Soviet military thinking. Addressing the 27th Communist Party Congress in February 1986, he declared that "reasonable sufficiency" was the official goal of Soviet nuclear strategy.

Since that address, the doctrine of reasonable sufficiency has been extended to conventional weaponry as well, and has cropped up in several Warsaw Pact proposals. A communique issued in May, for instance, states that the East bloc would "strictly comply with the limits of sufficiency for defense, for repelling possible aggression," and invited NATO to participate in talks to discuss this and other doctrinal issues separating the two alliances.[13] The current Soviet position marks a clear departure from its previous reliance on the ability to stage a massive and sudden non-nuclear offensive against the West in case of war. After breaking through NATO defenses along the central front, Warsaw Pact strategy has until now called for the East bloc's superior reserve forces to quickly move in before the West could respond with a counteroffensive led by U.S. reinforcements from across the Atlantic.

The East bloc's call for a doctrinal shift has important implications for the West as well. Although it is officially a defensive alliance, NATO strategy has long called for early offensive action against enemy territory to repel an attack. In recognition of its geographic disadvantage, NATO early adopted the "trip-wire" strategy, which called for a minimal U.S. troop presence along the central front. The first American casualties on the battlefield, the East bloc was told, would lead to all-out nuclear retaliation against the Soviet Union by America's home-based intercontinental ballistic missiles. When France withdrew its forces from NATO's command structure and closed alliance military bases in the country in 1967, West Germany became the dominant member of the alliance on the continent. Under its influence, NATO abandoned the "trip-wire" strategy, which exposed German territory to massive destruction at the outbreak of hostilities. "To accept such a military strategy for Europe may be easy for someone who lives in California or Georgia," wrote Schmidt. "It is not so easy — it is almost impossible — to accept it if you are living in the center of Europe."[14]

In its place, NATO adopted the "forward defense, flexible response" strategy that still holds today. This strategy calls for greater allied force concentrations along the central front, which would be more capable of stopping an invasion with conventional means, while keeping the option to use nuclear weapons as a last resort. But NATO strategy increasingly relies on offensive elements as well. Since the late 1970s, the West has planned for and developed electronically guided weapons to conduct what it calls a "follow-on force attack" (FOFA). This would entail artillery and bombing strikes with nuclear and conventional weapons from behind the lines against airfields and other targets well within Warsaw Pact territory to disrupt the arrival at the front of Soviet reinforcements soon after an invasion of NATO territory.

Discussions of military doctrine in the context of next year's conventional arms negotiations challenge the operating strategies of both alliances. Of particular interest is the question of what the doctrine of "reasonable sufficiency" will mean for Warsaw Pact conventional force levels. In particular, analysts wonder if this new doctrinal twist might be a step toward the notion of "non-offensive defense," long advocated by the West European peace movement. If adopted, this doctrine would require both alliances to withdraw or dismantle all weapons, such as tanks and missiles, that could be used to launch an offensive strike. If both sides possessed only the kinds of arms and levels of forces suitable to defend themselves from attack, this doctrine holds, they could abandon the frustrating efforts of attaining a military balance. "What a nation or alliance needs for security at the nonnuclear level is that the *defensive* capability of its nonnuclear forces be superior to its potential opponent's nonnuclear *offensive* capability," write Robert Neild and Anders Boserup, European analysts who call on both alliances to restructure their forces with the aim of attaining "mutual defensive superiority." "To achieve this, a new and more constructive form of dialogue is needed, for which the Warsaw Pact proposals appear to offer an opening that the West should seize."[15]

But the conventional arms talks are unlikely to produce a switch to an exclusively defensive posture in Europe, at

Continued on page 56

Chemical Weapons

Although they have not been used on a large scale since World War I, chemical weapons remain a particularly lethal ingredient of both alliances' non-nuclear arsenals. Citing the Warsaw Pact's growing stockpile of nerve gas, President Reagan has promised to modernize NATO's chemical arsenal in the absence of an agreement banning the weapons, which thus far has eluded U.S. and Soviet negotiators. It is uncertain whether chemical weapons will appear on the agenda of the talks on reducing conventional arms in Europe. Meanwhile, the administration is living up to its promise: On Dec. 16, 1987, the day an 18-year moratorium on U.S. production of chemical weapons expired, the Army began to rebuild its stockpile of deadly nerve gas.

AT ISSUE

Do our European allies shoulder their fair share of the defense burden?

YES says former Defense Secretary **CASPAR W. WEINBERGER**.

"Our allies continue to make a very substantial contribution to the common defense — considerably more than they are often given credit for. While the United States by certain measures is doing more than almost all its partners, other valid measures of performance convey a much more positive picture of the allied contribution. . . .

Any assessment of burden-sharing must include an examination of the political environment in which allied governments operate. We continue to share with our allies a common perception of the serious threat that the Soviet Union and its military buildup poses to Alliance security. However, there are understandable differences among the allies as to the most appropriate way to meet the Soviet challenge. These differences arise not only by virtue of history and culture, but also because of geography.

Because their homeland is the potential battlefield, the Europeans' sense of the risks of conflict is more immediate than our own or the Japanese, and the public desire for an easing of East-West tensions is more wide-spread. Families divided by the East-West border have different perceptions and different priorities for an East-West rapprochement. And Europe generally tends to attach greater importance to expanding East-West trade.

With these factors in mind, we must regard the leadership that European governments have provided, and their successes in support of Alliance defense policies, as very real contributions to burden-sharing. Differences in perspective that sometimes lead the allies to take independent positions have not marred a record of cooperation that is, on the whole, remarkably good (and surely the envy of any other Alliance system).

Moreover, for some important quantitative defense measures our NATO allies and Japan compare well with the United States. For example, our NATO allies field roughly the same active duty military manpower as a percent of population as the United States and substantially more Division Equivalent Firepower (DEF) and tactical combat air forces aircraft in relation to their economic strength. . . .

Unilateral pronouncements by the United States on the extent to which our allies are or are not sharing the burden are not an effective formula for encouraging improved allied efforts. Our positive leadership has always been, and will remain, a better means to ensure the adequacy of our common defense effort."

From "Report on Allied Contributions to the Common Defense: A Report to the United States Congress," April 1987.

NO says **REP. PATRICIA SCHROEDER**, D-Colo.

"The fact is that in 1971, West Germany spent 3.4 percent of its Gross Domestic Product on defense, and by 1985 the figure had dropped to 3.2 percent. U.S. spending stayed about the same, at 6.9 percent. About eight out of every 1,000 Germans are in uniform; 9.5 out of every 1,000 Americans are in uniform. And more than a half million of these Americans are stationed in Europe.

How about the question of conscription? The reason the Pentagon is not interested in going back to drafting soldiers is because the all-volunteer peacetime military has been a success. We are attracting high-quality, dedicated men and women who will serve long enough to master the incredibly complicated weapons we deploy. Our readiness would plummet if we had to rely on an army of short-time draftees. . . .

The fact is that we are in two global conflicts. In one — the dangerous competition between the superpowers — Germany and our other NATO allies, as well as Japan, South Korea and other Asian nations, are our allies. We need them and they need us. In the other — the trade war — Germany, Japan and South Korea are some of our most successful rivals. And we are being taken to the cleaners.

The link between the security and trade is clear. Japanese goods can enter the United States cheaply because we deploy the massive Navy which keeps the Pacific sea lanes open. German manufacturing can concentrate on building top-quality consumer products because the majority of German R&D marks are not going into defense, as a majority of our dollars are.

Of the $300 billion the United States spends on defense, something over half — say, $150 billion — goes for NATO obligations. Our trade deficit is running at about $175 billion a year. What we are spending to protect our allies is nearly the same amount by which we are losing the trade war. . . .

I would no sooner cede West Germany to Soviet expansion that I would give up Florida. We have spilled too much American blood in Western Europe to relinquish our interests now. Our security interests require a strong Western Europe. . . .

Clearly, the administration's feeble attempts to beg a little additional defense spending from our allies have not worked. Between 1979 and 1984, while real U.S. defense spending went up 42 percent, our European NATO allies' real defense spending went up only 10 percent — far, far less than the 3 percent real annual growth they committed to in 1979."

From an op-ed article in The Washington Post, *Oct. 13, 1987.*

Continued from page 54

least in the short run. While the Warsaw Pact has dropped hints of its interest in such a doctrinal about-face, it has made no changes in conventional force composition to reflect its application in practice. As for NATO, all movement in recent years has been toward strengthening its offensive capability, and European fears of nuclear nakedness in the wake of the INF treaty have accentuated this trend. Although the United States faces severe budget constraints that are sure to curtail defense spending in coming years, force modernization remains a top priority among U.S. lawmakers. A $15 million program to develop a system of underground pipes containing explosives to be deployed along the central front — a strictly defensive weapon system designed to stop a tank offensive from the East — was dropped from the defense budget for fiscal 1988. At the same time, a $111 million program to develop a missile able to carry antitank warheads up to 100 miles behind enemy lines — a key component of FOFA doctrine — has received congressional approval.[16]

As the tentative deadline for conventional stability talks grows nearer, some analysts fear that the NATO allies — which have yet to develop a consensus on the issue — will not be adequately prepared to bargain effectively with their more cohesive counterparts in the Warsaw Pact. "The worst outcome would be to slide into a post-nuclear world with nuclear forces that are largely irrelevant and non-nuclear forces that are structurally inadequate," writes Edward Luttwak of the Center for Strategic and International Studies in Washington, D.C. "A fundamental decision at the level of grand strategy is thus required to determine whether the strategic decline of nuclear weapons is to be resisted or accelerated. Only then can congruent arms-control and military policies be formulated. At this stage, however, even the nature of the problem has yet to be recognized in its full strategic implications."[17]

Signs of movement toward greater cooperation in European defense

Because the upcoming conventional stability talks are to be conducted between the two alliances, NATO's 16 member nations must reach an unprecedented degree of consensus before it can formulate the "congruent policies" of which Luttwak speaks. In particular, the Western alliance's four dominant powers — the United States, Britain, France and West Germany — must overcome longstanding differences in defense priorities that have undermined NATO cohesion over the past 40 years.

Events of recent months provide some cause for optimism. Spurred by the fear that the INF treaty might signal a broader dissipation of the U.S. defense commitment to Europe, the allies have shown signs of willingness to increase defense cooperation within the "European pillar" of NATO and shoulder a greater part of the defense burden until now carried by the United States. The movement

toward greater European defense cooperation has been building since March, when British Foreign Secretary Geoffrey Howe called for a closer "partnership" between Britain and France, in the belief "that we should recognize a greater responsibility on the part of Europeans for the defense of Western Europe — in other words for a more truly equal second pillar of the alliance." Such a gesture represented a departure for Britain, which historically has kept its distance from the other European members of NATO, often supporting the United States in times of transatlantic policy disputes.

But the most dramatic changes in defense posture have come from France. Since 1966, when President Charles de Gaulle pulled the country out of NATO's military command structure, France had until recently stressed its independence in military matters. Under President François Mitterrand, however, the country has shown a greater willingness to participate more fully in European defense efforts. At the end of September, following joint maneuvers in Bavaria of 20,000 French and 55,000 West German troops, Mitterrand and Chancellor Helmut Kohl announced their intention to create a joint military council to "coordinate and harmonize" questions related to arms procurement and deployment that would be open to participation by other European countries as well. The two countries have also announced plans to create a joint French-German brigade to be stationed on German territory, another sign of French willingness to commit its independent forces to help its neighbor in case of attack.

Some critics dismiss these steps as mere cosmetic cover-ups of lingering policy differences between the two continental powers. "What the Germans want the most from the French is the commitment of more conventional forces, and the French won't give them," Hoffmann says. "They also won't extend a guarantee of nuclear protection to Germany or grant Germany any say in the use of French nuclear forces." He explained that this is an important aim, from Germany's viewpoint, of the bilateral effort because "French tactical weapons can only hit German territory."

Aside from these bilateral moves toward European cooperation on defense matters, the seven members of the long-dormant Western European Union (WEU) in late October issued a platform on defense that could form the basis of a multilateral European defense effort within NATO. Acting on an appeal launched last year by French Premier Jacques Chirac to use the 40-year-old organization as a vehicle for strengthening NATO's European pillar, the defense and foreign ministers of Britain, France, West Germany, Italy, Belgium, the Netherlands and Luxembourg called for strengthening the continent's military forces. Spain, Portugal and Greece have since asked to join the WEU, originally set up in 1948 by Britain, France and the Benelux nations to monitor West Germany's postwar rearmament. Other organizations, including NATO's Eurogroup and the Independent European Program Group, set up outside NATO to foster European arms production and procurement, have also been mentioned as possible vehicles the European allies could use to coordinate their defense efforts.

To many American observers, NATO rumblings about restructuring in order to strengthen the alliance's European pillar are nothing new. "It's all words, words, words," Hoffmann says. "You can put the Europeans together, but they don't agree on what to do. It's just the same ballet, the same crisis atmosphere. The alliance continues to just stumble along."

U.S. economic woes and support for sharing the defense burden

Pressure is building to force the allies' hand. "Surely, 374 million Europeans with an aggregate economy of $3.5 trillion — faced with an opponent with 275 million people and a GNP of only $1.9 trillion — should not need to depend for their defense as heavily as they do on 241 million Americans with a $4.2 trillion economy," wrote former National Security Advisor Zbigniew Brzezinski, sounding a frequent refrain of NATO critics.[18]

The Reagan administration rejects such numerical comparisons as simplistic and points to the European allies' less quantifiable contributions to NATO (see p. 55). "Any burden-sharing calculus cannot ignore the less tangible but nonetheless very real burdens imposed on some of our allies by the concentration of military forces and activities on their soil," writes Richard Burt, U.S. ambassador to West Germany. "Each year, nearly 5,000 military exercises are held throughout West Germany — more than in any other Allied country — while the air forces of seven nations fly more than half a million sorties annually in German air space. . . . Moreover, the West German government provides some 4,000 military installations and training areas for the use of Allied forces at no cost. . . . One must question whether American voters would be willing . . . to make the same kind of nonfinancial sacrifices for defense that the Germans and many other Europeans have made."[19]

Such contributions, as well as indications that the European allies may be willing to shoulder more of NATO's defense burden, do not impress some members of Congress. "There's been some talk," says Rep. Schroeder, "but we haven't seen anything yet that is at all concrete."

Such resentment at what is considered to be European freeloading at America's expense is a longstanding ingredient of the transatlantic dialogue. Former Sen. Mike Mansfield, D.-Mont., introduced several measures in the late 1960s and early 1970s aimed at reducing the U.S. military presence in Europe and thus requiring the allies to take greater responsibility for their own defense. In 1984, Sen. Sam Nunn, D.-Ga., also gained substantial support for a measure that threatened to withdraw forces from Europe unless the allies honored a NATO commitment to increase their defense spending by 3 percent annually.

Although these efforts failed to win congressional approval, the U.S. federal budget deficit and this country's growing trade deficit with many of its allies are fueling

NATO Allies' Defense Budgets

	Total Defense Budget (millions)	Percent GDP
United States	208,811	6.9
Britain	30,171	5.2
France	27,984	4.1
West Germany	26,666	3.2
Italy	11,403	2.7
Canada	6,178	2.2
Netherlands	5,289	3.1
Spain	4,850	2.2
Belgium	3,446	2.9
Turkey	3,178	4.5
Greece	2,952	7.1
Norway	2,028	3.1
Denmark	1,617	2.2
Portugal	783	3.2
Luxembourg	55	0.9

Note: Data are for 1985 in 1980 dollars at 1980 exchange rates. GDP is Gross Domestic Product, the total of that country's domestically produced goods and services.

Source: International Institute for Strategic Studies

similar calls today. Schroeder's measure (HR 2620), for example, would impose a fee on goods the NATO allies and Japan export to the United States, calculated by subtracting their defense spending as a percentage of gross domestic product — in many cases less than 3 percent — from that of the United States, which spends 7 percent of gross domestic product on defense (see chart, above). The result, what Schroeder calls a "defense protection fee," would be a kind of tariff imposed on the exports of countries whose contribution to defense is especially low. Schroeder concedes that the bill is a product of frustration. "Let's face it," she says, "the defense protection fee is like operating with a hatchet, but there really isn't anything else you can do as a member of Congress. What we're seeing is the Europeans becoming more independent while we're still paying, and I think that is troublesome."

Schroeder is pinning hopes for gaining support for her initiative on the budget deficit. Since the Oct. 19 stock market crash, blamed in part on investors' loss of confidence in the government's ability to reduce the federal budget deficit and avert a recession, lawmakers have searched for new ways to stem the flow of red ink.[20] A prime target is the defense budget, including programs to modernize U.S. forces and maintain some 300,000 troops in Europe. Defense Secretary Carlucci already has ordered a $33 billion cut in the Pentagon's proposed fiscal 1989

Past Coverage

■ **Euromissile Negotiations** examines the NATO allies' ambivalence toward U.S.-Soviet talks aimed at removing intermediate-range nuclear forces (INF) from Europe in the period leading up to the Washington summit. By Mary H. Cooper, E.R.R. 1987 Vol. I, pp. 193-208.

■ **Science Wars over Star Wars** assesses the feasibility of the Strategic Defense Initiative, Reagan's ambitious plan to set up a space-based defense against nuclear attack that has proved the biggest stumbling block to arms control in recent years. By William Sweet, E.R.R. 1986 Vol. II, pp. 685-708.

■ **Chemical Weapons** reviews the use of chemical weapons in past conflicts as well as current U.S. and Soviet stockpiles and stalled negotiations over their elimination. By Harrison Donnelly, E.R.R. 1986 Vol. II, pp. 513-532.

■ **Gorbachev's Challenge**, written a year after Mikhail S. Gorbachev rose to power, analyzes the Soviet leader's apparent shift in priorities from the superpower arms race to the domestic economy and its implications for U.S. policy. By Mary H. Cooper, E.R.R. 1986 Vol. I, pp. 105-124.

■ **Arms Control Negotiations** reviews the superpowers' efforts to constrain the quest for nuclear supremacy. It appeared just before bilateral negotiations, which had been suspended for more than a year, were resumed in early 1985. By Mary H. Cooper, E.R.R. 1985 Vol. I, pp. 145-167.

■ **West Germany's 'Missile' Election** looks at the impact the 1979 NATO decision to deploy INF forces in Europe had on the political landscape in the country that would probably serve as the battlefield in any NATO-Warsaw Pact conflict. By William Sweet, E.R.R. 1983 Vol. I, pp. 149-168.

to keep military personnel at current levels. Countries whose armies make up the bulk of NATO troops are facing a growing shortage of potential conscripts because of declining birth rates.

The Bundeswehr, the West German army, which Sloan calls "the heart of NATO defenses," is a case in point. Although West Germany has extended the military draft from 15 to 18 months and made conscientious objection more difficult to obtain, Sloan predicts there will be a decline in German troops by 30,000 men over the next four years. Whatever increases in defense spending the West Germans introduce, "they will have to spend as incentives for non-commissioned officers to re-enlist," he says. Because other European nations, especially the Netherlands and Britain, are affected by the same problem, Sloan concludes, "there is no way that there will be a noticeable increase in European burden-sharing in the foreseeable future."

NOTES

[1] U.S. allies in NATO are Belgium, Britain, Canada, Denmark, France, Greece, Iceland, Italy, Luxembourg, the Netherlands, Norway, Portugal, Spain, Turkey and West Germany.

[2] The members of the Warsaw Pact are Bulgaria, Czechoslovakia, East Germany, Hungary, Poland, Romania and the Soviet Union.

[3] French President Charles de Gaulle withdrew his country from NATO's integrated military structure on July 1, 1966, saying it was dominated by the United States. The decision ended the participation of France's military forces in the alliance and forced the removal of all NATO facilities from the country by April 1, 1967.

[4] International Institute for Strategic Studies, "The Military Balance 1987-1988," p. 230.

[5] Writing in the West German newspaper *Die Zeit*, May 8, 1987; cited by the Center for Defense Information, unpublished material.

[6] Rogers made his comments on June 27, 1987, in Mons, Belgium.

[7] See article by Kissinger in *The Washington Post*, April 5, 1987, and article on Haig in *The Wall Street Journal*, Nov. 17, 1987.

[8] Weinberger spoke at a news conference following a meeting of NATO's High-Level Group of senior defense officials in Monterey, Calif., Nov. 2, 1987.

[9] Quoted in *Jane's Defense Weekly*, Sept. 26, 1987, p. 648.

[10] The Helsinki Accords called for advance notification of troop maneuvers in Europe. Signatories also agreed to allow freer movement of people and information across national boundaries.

[11] The Union of Concerned Scientists is an independent group based in Cambridge, Mass., that is concerned with U.S. nuclear policy.

[12] Helmut Schmidt, "Defense: A European Viewpoint," *Europe*, November 1986, p. 15.

[13] The Warsaw Pact issued the statement, entitled "Military Doctrine," in Berlin on May 29, 1987.

[14] Schmidt, *op. cit.*, p. 15.

[15] Robert Neild and Anders Boserup, "Beyond INF: A New Approach to Nonnuclear Forces," *World Policy Journal*, fall 1987, p. 606.

[16] See *Congressional Quarterly Weekly Report*, Nov. 7, 1987, p. 2727.

[17] Writing in *The Washington Post*, Nov. 29, 1987.

[18] Writing in *The Washington Post*, Sept. 27, 1987.

[19] Writing in *The Washington Post*, Oct. 8, 1987.

[20] For background on the stock market crash, see "Spotlight on Wall Street," E.R.R., 1987 Vol. II, pp. 657-672.

Graphics: cover, p. 46, U.S. Army.

budget, bringing down projected defense spending for the year beginning Oct. 1 from $332 billion to $299 billion.

Even if the European allies wanted to assume a greater portion of NATO's defense burden, they could face substantial opposition from constitutents who support popular social programs over military spending amid a widespread perception that the danger of Warsaw Pact aggression is waning under Gorbachev's tenure. "There will be a steady pattern of slow growth in defense spending in Europe of about 1 to 2 percent," predicts Stanley R. Sloan, a specialist in U.S.-NATO relations for the Congressional Research Service. These increases are likely to be consumed by efforts

RECOMMENDED READING

BOOKS

Calleo, David P., *Beyond American Hegemony: The Future of the Western Alliance*, Basic Books, Inc., 1987.

Calleo, director of European Studies at the Johns Hopkins School of Advanced International Studies, challenges the United States to cede some of its military power to its economically advanced allies. He concludes: "The United States has become a hegemon in decay, set on a course that points to an ignominious end. If there is a way out, it lies through Europe. History has come full circle: the Old World is needed to restore balance to the New."

Kelleher, Catherine M., and Gale A. Mattox, *Evolving European Defense Policies*, Lexington Books, 1987.

A collection of articles by defense analysts that studies the divergent policies among NATO allies on defense priorities and on the alliance's role. West German, French and British policy differences are emphasized, and special focus is given to such issues as burden-sharing, conventional weaponry and strengthening of the European pillar of NATO.

Sloan, Stanley R., *NATO's Future: Toward a New Transatlantic Bargain*, National Defense University Press, 1985.

The author, a defense expert at the Congressional Research Service, reviews the history of the Atlantic alliance and puts forward his formula for its survival: "The new bargain must bring greater European responsibility and leadership to the deal; it must ensure continued American involvement in European defense while at the same time constructing a new European 'pillar' inside, not outside, the broad framework of the Western alliance."

ARTICLES

Dean, Jonathan, "Military Security in Europe," *Foreign Affairs*, fall 1987.

The author assesses Western Europe's position in the wake of Soviet leader Mikhail S. Gorbachev's "peace offensive" and the INF treaty. He focuses on the conventional stability talks aimed at reducing non-nuclear forces on the continent.

Ehmke, Horst, "A Second Phase of Detente," *World Policy Journal*, summer 1987.

Ehmke, deputy chairman of the Social Democrats in the West German parliament, presents the widespread conviction among West Germans that the next step in arms control should focus on the elimination of short-range and battle-field nuclear weapons, which were excluded from the INF agreement. He also supports the definition of a "nuclear-free corridor" along the border between the two Germanys in the context of new talks on conventional weaponry.

Moreau-Defarges, Philippe, "Anti-American Feeling in Europe: Between Fear of War and Obsession with Abandonment," *NATO Review*, April 1987.

The author, a professor at the Institute of Political Studies in Paris, describes West Europeans' ambivalent attitudes toward the U.S. defense policies. "On the one hand, Europe cannot contemplate a system of relations other than that which has been in force since the end of the 1940s (American troops on European soil, the nuclear umbrella)," he writes. "On the other, Europe makes ill-defined claims to its own independent destiny. . . . Europe fears abandonment, while at the same time dreading involvement."

"NATO's Central Front," *The Economist*, Aug. 30, 1986.

A detailed analysis of conventional and nuclear defenses in Europe, including a breakdown of forces and manpower units as well as an analysis of military doctrine and possible scenarios for conflict between NATO and the Warsaw Pact. While acknowledging the East bloc's superiority in conventional weaponry, the article concludes that "it is a fair guess that if the NATO's conventional forces could hold out for two weeks they could hold out for ever."

REPORTS AND STUDIES

"The Military Balance 1987-1988," International Institute for Strategic Studies, autumn 1987.

The London-based research institute, set up in 1958, has become the leading source of non-classified statistical data on the world's military arsenals, with special focus on U.S. and Soviet nuclear and conventional forces. In light of the INF agreement and the prospect of upcoming talks on conventional forces between NATO and the Warsaw Pact, this year's edition emphasizes the need to take into account qualitative differences between the two sides that the raw data may conceal.

Sloan, Stanley R., "Defense Burden Sharing: U.S. Relations with NATO Allies and Japan," Congressional Research Service, July 8, 1983 (updated April 10, 1985).

Sloan provides a detailed account of the transatlantic dispute over who should pay more for Western Europe's defense that dates back to NATO's creation in 1949. "The simple fact," he concludes, "is that, by almost any quantitative measure, the United States devotes more resources to defense than do any of its allies."

"Soviet Military Power," Department of Defense, March 1987.

The Pentagon's annual report, issued since 1981, describes the weapon systems, both nuclear and conventional, of the Soviet Union and its allies, as well as Warsaw Pact strategies. A short concluding chapter also addresses U.S. and NATO strategies and weapon systems.

ERR

APRIL 24, 1987

EUROMISSILE NEGOTIATIONS

Western Europe
is taking a cautious
attitude toward

EUROMISSILE NEGOTIATIONS

between the superpowers.
Europe's independence
may signal shifting
NATO allegiancies.

by Mary H. Cooper

The fate of the most promising superpower arms
control negotiations in years may depend as much on
London, Paris and Bonn as on Washington and Moscow.
The three-day talks in Moscow between Secretary of State
George P. Shultz and Foreign Minister Eduard A.
Shevardnadze and Shultz' meeting with Soviet leader
Mikhail S. Gorbachev ended April 15 with optimistic
predictions on both sides of an early agreement on the
removal of medium-range nuclear missiles from Europe.
Tass, the official Soviet news agency, called the talks
"timely and useful," while Shultz said that "very consid-
erable headway" had been made, adding that "it should be
possible to work out an agreement."

But the secretary of state stressed that acceptance of a
new Soviet proposal to eliminate short-range nuclear missiles
would depend on the consent of America's West European allies. "We are a member of a strong alliance and on
matters of this importance, of course, we don't respond
immediately," he said. "We consult carefully with our
allies." Shultz went directly to Brussels to discuss the
proposal with America's increasingly skittish European allies, who are concerned that a reduction in U.S. nuclear
weapons in Europe would leave it vulnerable to Soviet
conventional forces and weaken nuclear deterrence.

Indeed, the vision of a nuclear-free world is sending
shock waves through the continent. Fearful that the United
States may decouple its strategic interests from those of
Europe, British Prime Minister Margaret Thatcher dis-
missed that vision as "a dream" when she visited Moscow
several weeks ago. "You cannot base a sure defense on
dreams," she told Gorbachev, who has proposed that all
nuclear weapons be eliminated within the next 10-15 years.

(See p. 68.) President Reagan, who
initially welcomed Gorbachev's proposal
during their October 1986 summit in
Reykjavik, Iceland, has since backed away
from the idea.

But the leaders of America's strongest
European allies aren't leaving it to America to press their case. Although the
official parties to these talks are the United
States and the Soviet Union, Western
Europe is emerging as a highly visible
third party intent upon impressing its
interests on any agreement between the superpowers. In
taking Western Europe's case to Moscow, Thatcher signaled a widespread concern that the Reagan administration
— eager to put behind it the debilitating scandal over the
secret Iran-contra arms deal — will rush into an arms
agreement that fundamentally alters traditional military
strategy in Europe.

The European allies are playing a greater part in these
East-West talks than they did during negotiations that led to
the SALT (Strategic Arms Limitation
Talks) agreements limiting long-range nuclear weapons, test ban treaties and
other nuclear arms pacts. These were made
between Moscow and Washington
largely over the heads of their allies.

Thatcher has become Europe's chief
broker in the U.S.-Soviet negotiations over
the removal of Soviet and U.S. medium-
and short-range nuclear missiles, known as
"Euromissiles," that are deployed in or
within range of Europe. Britain and
France are the only members of the 16-nation North
Atlantic Treaty Organization (NATO) besides the United
States that possess their own nuclear weapons, while West
Germany, as NATO's front-line state, hosts the greatest
number of U.S. medium-range nuclear weapons aimed at
the Soviet Union and its Eastern European allies of the
Warsaw Pact.[1] Before her highly publicized trip to
Moscow, Thatcher conferred with France's President Fran-
çois Mitterrand and West Germany's Chancellor Helmut

Kohl. In Moscow, she presented Gorbachev with their consensus that any Euromissile agreement should include NATO's right to deploy short-range nuclear missiles, a class of weapons currently deployed by the Warsaw Pact alone.

In retrospect, Thatcher's message to Gorbachev may have heralded the touchiest aspect of the negotiations on the Euromissiles, which were set to resume on April 23 in Geneva. When Gorbachev announced the surprise Soviet offer to remove the short-range missiles, it was widely viewed as so attractive the United States would have to say yes. But as Thatcher made plain to Gorbachev, Europe has misgivings. Even if NATO ultimately endorses a Euromissile deal, the current divergence between Europe and America may bring to the surface other differing interests within the alliance.

The United States will face the budgetary issue of who will pay the NATO bill for the increased cost of strengthening Western Europe's conventional defenses if the nuclear missiles are removed. As a cost-conscious Congress searches for ways to reduce the federal budget deficit and chafes under the country's growing trade deficit with Western Europe, it can be expected to press its allies to pay their own way in conventional defense.

Western European countries may be less reluctant than in the past to increase defense spending if the missiles are removed. They have already taken steps to coordinate conventional arms production, and there is talk of closer defense policy consultation among the 14 European members of the alliance — all except the United States and Canada. While this may be welcomed by congressional budget-cutters, it poses a threat to trans-Atlantic cohesion. A splintered alliance would give Gorbachev far more than a missile agreement.

U.S. 'nuclear umbrella' over Europe

Since its creation as a defensive alliance in 1949, NATO has based its strategy on maintaining a combination of conventional and nuclear forces. While the U.S. nuclear umbrella has been the foundation of NATO's deterrent from the beginning, since 1967 the alliance has relied to a greater degree than previously on conventional forces. This "flexible response" strategy is to deter an attack by making the Soviet Union unsure whether NATO would respond with a limited conventional defense or all-out nuclear retaliation.

The medium-range missiles that are the main object of the current negotiations are relatively recent ingredients in the nuclear arsenals of both sides. The Soviets began deploying their SS-20 missile in 1977 as a longer-range, more accurate alternative to older, fixed-based SS-4 and SS-5 missiles. The SS-20 is mounted on a mobile launcher, so that it is less vulnerable than its fixed-based predecessors. It is armed with three warheads that can be aimed at separate targets up to 3,100 miles away. Thus the 441 SS-20s deployed in the European region of the Soviet Union — west of the Ural Mountains — and in the Soviet Far East, where the mobile missiles could easily be transported within range of Europe, carry a total of 1,323 nuclear warheads. In addition, 112 single-warhead SS-4s are still deployed in the western Soviet Union, within range of Europe.

The United States began developing the medium-range Pershing II and ground-launched cruise missiles as early as 1972. But the impetus for their deployment in Western Europe came initially from America's European allies in response to the Soviets' SS-20 deployment. The Europeans were concerned that the rough parity in U.S. and Soviet strategic nuclear forces that was codified in SALT I in 1972 and refined in talks leading up to the unratified SALT II agreement left the allies exposed to an imbalance in battlefield nuclear weapons and conventional forces in Europe. In 1977, then-West German Chancellor Helmut Schmidt warned that the SALT process would inevitably impair Western Europe's security if disparities in Soviet and European military power were not removed.

In 1979, NATO announced that it would begin deploying 108 Pershing II and 464 cruise missiles in Europe beginning in late 1983 unless a negotiated withdrawal of the Soviet SS-20s and SS-4s was obtained before that time. To date, 316 single-warhead missiles — 108 Pershing IIs and 208 cruise missiles — have been placed there.

The Pershings are all based in West Germany, where they replaced a similar number of shorter-range Pershing IA nuclear missiles. Although its range of about 1,100 miles is shorter than that of opposing Soviet missiles, the Pershing II can reach the Soviet Union from European positions. Its handicap of a single warhead is overcome by far-greater accuracy than the SS-20 achieves.[2]

The ground-launched cruise missiles have a range of 1,600 miles, longer than the Pershing's. For that reason, and because West Germany insisted that it not be the only NATO nation to deploy Euromissiles, cruise missiles have been based farther from the Eastern European border, in Belgium, Britain and Italy, as well as West Germany. If the negotiations fail to produce agreement removing medium-range missiles from Europe, 256 more cruise missiles are due to be installed in Britain, West Germany, Belgium and the Netherlands by the end of 1988.

Negotiations between the United States and the Soviet Union over reducing medium-range nuclear weapons in Europe began in 1980 in Geneva. But until the Iceland summit, the talks were essentially deadlocked over how many missiles should be allowed on both sides and where they should be deployed.

The United States sought equal global limits on U.S. and Soviet medium-range missiles, no matter where they are based. The ceiling would apply to Pershing IIs and ground-launched cruise missiles in Europe, but not to the separate nuclear forces of Britain and France. These, the American negotiators argued, are not under U.S. control. On the Soviet side, the United States wanted the ceiling to apply to all SS-20 and SS-4 missiles, including those in the Soviet Far East and on the eastern slopes of the Urals, which could be moved to positions that would threaten NATO. The American position also included a temporary freeze at equal levels on short-range missiles, whose fate would be determined later along with that of medium-range aircraft capable of carrying nuclear warheads.

The Soviet Union wanted to set equal limits on European-based missiles, but wanted to exclude missiles based elsewhere. The limits thus would not apply to the mobile SS-20s outside Europe. In addition, the Soviets wanted the agreement to apply to the nuclear forces of Britain and France.

So far, the Geneva negotiations have failed to reconcile these opposing positions. They were suspended for 16 months when the Soviet delegation walked out in November 1983, protesting the deployment of the Pershing II and cruise missiles that had just begun. But in January 1986, Soviet negotiatiors made the first of several major concessions. They changed their position on medium-range missiles in Asia, putting these forces on the negotiating table for the first time and offering to freeze their number.

At the Iceland summit, when Reagan and Gorbachev moved closer to breaking the Euromissile deadlock. They agreed to eliminate all medium-range missiles from Europe except those of the British and French forces. However, the agreement fell apart over the strategic defense initiative, when Reagan refused to meet the Soviet demand that the United States agree to give up testing the planned U.S. space-based ballistic missile defense.

Gorbachev's offer on Feb. 28 of this year to separate the Euromissile negotiations from talks on long-range strategic nuclear weapons and from the strategic defense initiative lifted another major obstacle. At the same time, he made his "zero option" offer to remove from Europe all U.S. and Soviet nuclear missiles with ranges of 600-3,000 miles. The proposal — actually a reformulation of one advanced by Reagan in 1981 — called for the removal over five years of all Soviet SS-20 and SS-4 missiles and all U.S. Pershing II and ground-launched cruise missiles from Europe.

Under the agreement, each superpower would be allowed to keep 100 medium-range warheads in home territory outside Europe, though their deployment sites remain uncertain. The Soviet Union has proposed basing its 100 missiles on the eastern slopes of the Ural Mountains, while the United States has insisted they be stationed 1,000 miles farther east, well out of range of Europe. The U.S. suggestion to base its 100 missiles in Alaska, just across the Bering Strait from Siberia, is unlikely to be accepted by Soviet negotiators.

Because the Soviet Union currently has 1,435 warheads, and the United States only 316, an agreement to eliminate all but 100 on each side would appear to benefit NATO at Soviet expense. Indeed, when Reagan first proposed the zero option, the Soviets rejected it out of hand. Many observers say that the Reagan administration knew the Soviets would dismiss the proposal and made it only to counter criticism that it was uninterested in arms control.

SPEAKING OF MISSILES

BALLISTIC MISSILES Rocket-launched missiles that approach their targets as free-falling projectiles after the rocket thrust is terminated. Long-range ballistic missiles travel outside the Earth's atmosphere in the middle portion of their trajectory. The U.S. Pershing IIs and the Soviet SS-20s and SS-4s that are being discussed in the Euromissile negotiations are medium-range ballistic missiles. In contrast, U.S. ground-launched cruise missiles are self-propelled guided missiles that fly inside the earth's atmosphere on the way to their targets.

EUROMISSILES A catchall term describing the medium- and short-range nuclear missiles based within range of Eastern and Western Europe over the past decade. In the current negotiations between the United States and the Soviet Union, Euromissiles include medium and short-range missiles based in Europe and in both the Asian and European parts of the Soviet Union. The Soviet missiles are in range of Europe or could quickly be moved within range. Until 1981, Euromissiles were known officially as "theater nuclear forces." Now they are officially designated as intermediate-range nuclear forces.

INTERMEDIATE-RANGE NUCLEAR FORCES (INF) The medium-range nuclear missiles in the current Euromissile negotiations — the U.S. Pershing II and ground-launched cruise missiles and the Soviet SS-20s and SS-4s — are referred to in ongoing Geneva arms control negotiations between the superpowers as long-range INF missiles (LRINFs). These have ranges of about 1,500-3,000 miles (1,800-5,500 kilometers). So-called short-range INF missiles (SRINFs) — which include the Soviet SS-12/22 and SS-23 missiles that are part of the Euromissile negotiations— have ranges of about 300-600 miles (500-1,000 kilometers).

STRATEGIC FORCES Long-range nuclear missiles that enable the United States and the Soviet Union to attack each other's territory directly. Stratetgic missiles — which were the subject of the Strategic Arms Limitation Talks (SALT) I and II — include Soviet and U.S. submarine-launched ballistic missiles and bombers as well as intercontinental ballistic missiles such as the MX or the Soviet SS-18. Currently, strategic missiles are the focus of separate talks in Geneva and are excluded from the Euromissile negotiations.

But whatever reservations the administration might have over the zero option, it was hard to refuse when Gorbachev dropped his demand that America give up testing of its planned space-based anti-ballistic missile defense. Four days later, U.S. negotiators presented a counterproposal at Geneva, and expressed confidence that an agreement could be reached in time for a treaty-signing summit between Reagan and Gorbachev in the United States before the end of the year. When Shultz traveled to Moscow and the Soviets unveiled their offer to remove their short-range missiles, the deal became more interesting from America's standpoint. However, the reaction in Western Europe was decidedly cooler toward the proposed pact.

'Nuclear nakedness' worries Europe

Gorbachev's offer to open new talks on missiles in Europe on the eve of Shultz' arrival in Moscow was clearly made for Western European consumption. Fears among the European NATO allies that a reduction in nuclear forces would leave them vulnerable to attack by Warsaw Pact conventional forces and the friction those fears have created within the Western alliance constitute powerful leverage for Moscow because of the potential for divisiveness with NATO. The offer served to put Europe on notice that lack of progress in Moscow would not be for any lack of Soviet good will.

The Soviet leader's call upon "Paris, London and Bonn also to contribute" to the arms control process underscored Moscow's awareness of the trans-Atlantic debate over the consequences of a Euromissile agreement. In acknowledging that "there naturally is an asymmetry in the armed forces of the two sides in Europe" and offering to reduce "the numbers on the side which has a superiority in them," Gorbachev played to Western Europe's concern over the Warsaw Pact's numerical superiority in conventional forces.

Until recent years, the disparity was offset by NATO's better weaponry, as well as its nuclear deterrent. But technological advances in Soviet weaponry and the Eastern alliance's 2-to-1 advantage in troop strength have shifted the balance. According to U.S. Defense Department figures, the Warsaw Pact has 133 divisions in Europe or capable of being deployed there rapidly, against NATO's combined troop strength of 90 divisions. The Soviet Union and its allies field 32,000 battle tanks, compared with NATO's 19,600. NATO has only 13,370 anti-tank guided weapon launchers to combat this larger number of tanks, while the Warsaw Pact has 18,000. In the air, too, the Warsaw Pact holds a more than 2-to-1 advantage, with 8,000 combat aircraft and attack helicopters compared with NATO's 3,700.

Conventional weapons would become more significant

Nuclear Weaponry Not Being Negotiated

WEST

US/NATO

Nuclear-capable aircraft	1,500
Sub-launched warheads	400
Ship-launched cruise missiles	166
Battlefield missiles	163
Nuclear-capable cannons	3,032

BRITAIN

Sub-launched warheads	64

FRANCE

Sub-launched warheads	176
Land-based missiles	18
Battlefield missiles	44
Nuclear-capable aircraft	18

GERMANY

Short-range missiles	72

EAST

USSR/WARSAW PACT

Nuclear-capable aircraft	2,000
Sub-launched cruise missiles	24
Ship-launched cruise missiles	446
Battlefield missiles	1,778
Nuclear-capable cannons	3,884

Sources: International Institute for Strategic Studies, Arms Control Association

to Europe's defense if short-range nuclear weapons were out of the picture. That is why Europe looks askance at the Soviet offer to remove its 130 short-range missiles. America's European allies had strongly supported the earlier U.S. position that would have equalized short-range missiles by allowing NATO to build up its force to a level equal with the Soviet force. That position was reiterated by Thatcher in Moscow. "We would like the right to match" the number of Soviet short-range weapons, she said, adding that the issue "might hold up complete agreement" on medium-range missiles. Labeling Gorbachev's goal of a nuclear-free world a "dream," she said, "Conventional weapons have never been enough to deter a war."

For weeks prior to Shultz' visit to Moscow, Soviet rejection of this demand was the main stumbling block to an agreement. Then Gorbachev's surprise offer to remove the Soviet short-range missiles, which have ranges from 300-600 miles, presented a new possibility for equalizing the short-range forces. But it wasn't the option many Europeans would have preferred.

The United States has no missiles in this category. The Soviet Union has about 110 launchers for its 540-mile-range SS-12/22s based in Eastern Europe and the western

Continued on page 70

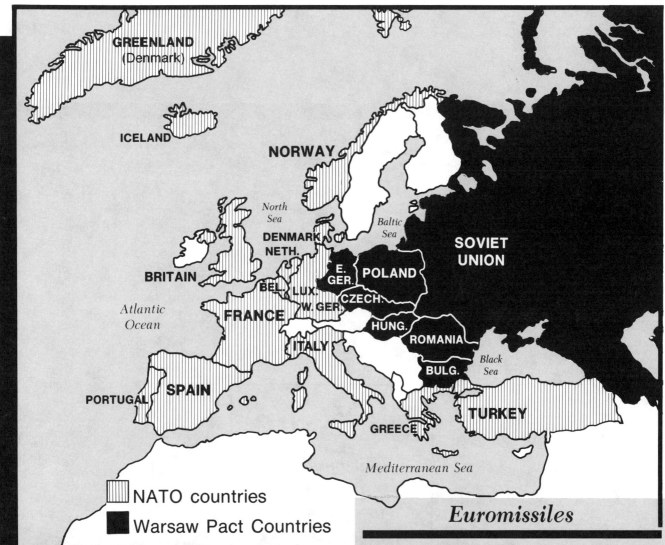

GREENLAND
(Denmark)

ICELAND

NORWAY

North Sea

DENMARK

Baltic Sea

SOVIET UNION

NETH.

BRITAIN

BEL. LUX.

E. GER. POLAND

CZECH.

Atlantic Ocean

FRANCE W.GER.

HUNG.

ROMANIA

ITALY

Black Sea

BULG.

PORTUGAL SPAIN

TURKEY

GREECE

Mediterranean Sea

NATO countries

Warsaw Pact Countries

Conventional Weapons

	NATO	WARSAW PACT
Combat aircraft and attack helicopters	3,700	8,000
Troop divisions	90	133
Battle tanks	19,600	32,000
Antitank weapons launchers	13,370	18,000

Source: Defense Department

Euromissiles

Medium-range

	Launchers	Warheads
U.S./NATO		
Pershing II	108	108
Ground-launched cruise missiles	52	208
		316
USSR/Warsaw Pact		
SS-20	441	1323
SS-4	112	112
		1435

Short-range

	Launchers	Warheads
U.S./NATO	0	0
USSR/Warsaw Pact		
SS-23	20+	20+
SS-12/22	110	110
		130+

Note: Data includes 171 Soviet SS-20s based in Soviet Asia and 80+ short range missiles kept in the Soviet Union. NATO plans to deploy an additional 256 ground-launched cruise missiles by the end of 1988.

Source: Arms Control Association.

YES, says Soviet leader **MIKHAIL S. GORBACHEV**. A "number of major foreign policy actions . . . are prompted by the need to overcome the negative, confrontational trends that have been growing in recent years and to clear the ways toward curbing the nuclear arms race on Earth and preventing it in outer space. . . .

Our most important action is a concrete program aimed at the complete elimination of nuclear weapons throughout the world and covering a precisely defined period of time.

The Soviet Union is proposing a step-by-step and consistent process of ridding the Earth of nuclear weapons, to be implemented and completed within the next 15 years, before the end of this century. . . .

What is required here is rising above national selfishness, tactical calculations, differences and disputes, whose significance is nothing compared to the preservation of what is most valuable — peace and a safe future.

Our proposals can be summarized as follows.

Stage One. Within the next five to eight years the USSR and the USA will reduce by one half the nuclear arms that can reach each other's territory. On the remaining delivery vehicles of this kind each side will retain no more than 6,000 warheads.

It stands to reason that such a reduction is possible only if the USSR and the USA mutually renounce the development, testing and deployment of space strike weapons. As the Soviet Union has repeatedly warned, the development of space strike weapons will dash the hopes for a reduction of nuclear weapons on Earth.

The first stage will include the adoption and implementation of the decision on the complete elimination of intermediate range missiles of the USSR and the USA in the European zone . . . as a first step toward ridding the European continent of nuclear weapons.

At the same time the United States should undertake not to transfer its strategic and medium-range missiles to other countries, while Great Britain and France should pledge not to build up their respective nuclear arms.

The USSR and the USA should from the very beginning agree to stop any nuclear explosions, and call upon other states to join in such a moratorium as soon as possible.

Stage Two. At this stage, which should start no later than 1990 and last for five to seven years, the other nuclear powers will begin to engage in nuclear disarmament. . . .

In this period the USSR and the USA will go on with the reductions agreed upon during the first stage and also carry out further measures designed to eliminate their medium-range nuclear weapons and freeze their tactical nuclear systems.

Following the completion by the USSR and the USA of the 50 percent reduction in their relevant arms at the second stage, another radical step is taken: All nuclear powers eliminate their tactical nuclear arms, namely the weapons having a range . . . of up to 1,000 kilometers.

All nuclear powers would stop nuclear-weapons tests.

There would be a ban on the development of nonnuclear weapons based on new physical principles, whose destructive capacity is close to that of nuclear arms or other weapons of mass destruction.

Stage Three will begin no later than 1995. At this stage the elimination of all remaining nuclear weapons will be completed. By the end of 1999 there will be no nuclear weapons on Earth. A universal accord will be drawn up that such weapons should never again come into being. . . .

We have in mind that special procedures will be worked out for the destruction of nuclear weapons as well as the dismantling, re-equipment or destruction of delivery vehicles. In the process, agreement will be reached on the numbers of weapons to be destroyed at each stage, the sites of their destruction and so on.

Verification with regard to the weapons that are destroyed or limited would be carried out both by national technical means and through on-site inspections. The USSR is ready to reach agreement on any other additional verification measures. . . .

In summary, we propose that we should enter the Third Millennium without nuclear weapons, on the basis of mutually acceptable and strictly verifiable agreements. If the United States administration is indeed committed to the goal of the complete elimination of nuclear weapons everywhere, as it has repeatedly stated, it is being offered a practical opportunity to begin this in practice. Instead of wasting the next 10 to 15 years by developing new, extremely dangerous weapons in space, allegedly designed to make nuclear arms useless, would it not be more sensible to start eliminating those arms and finally bring them down to zero?"

From a speech on Jan. 15, 1986, before the Central Committee of the Communist Party of the Soviet Union.

At Issue

Is it possible or wise to eliminate nuclear weapons from the planet beginning now?

No, says **KENNETH L. ADELMAN**, director of the U.S. Arms Control and Disarmament Agency. "I think it would be useful to remind ourselves of some of the problems [complete nuclear disarmament] would entail. . . .

[W]e would face . . . Soviet superiority in conventional arms. In Europe right now there is a serious imbalance in conventional forces between [the North Atlantic Treaty Organization] NATO and the Warsaw Pact. . . .

The second problem we would face is that of verifying a total ban on nuclear weapons. The verification problems posed by such an agreement would be truly monumental. . . .

Elimination of nuclear weapons would require the most extensive and intrusive system of on-site inspections anyone could imagine. It is hard to think of a major military or even industrial installation that could be legally exempted from inspection on demand. That would mean, in turn, unprecedented openness to foreign intrusion on the part of all nations. Thus far the Soviet Union has raised objections to even the most limited inspection arrangements. . . .

[W]ithout a comprehensive and thoroughly intrusive inspection system, a treaty eliminating nuclear weapons would simply be impractical. . . .

[W]e can't put the nuclear genie back in the bottle. While it may someday be possible to return to a non-nuclear world, it is utterly impossible to return to a prenuclear world. . . . The knowledge for creating atomic bombs exists and will remain. The knowledge is widely disseminated. It cannot be unlearned. . . .

The most basic reason that eliminating nuclear weapons will not solve our problem is that nuclear weapons are not the cause of our problem. They are merely the symptom. The cause of tension, the cause of fear, and the cause of danger are not weapons but aggressive intentions and aggressive policies. Nobody in the United States loses any sleep over the British nuclear arsenal. The source of tension is not the possession of nuclear weapons but the presence of aggressive intentions. . . .

But what about the possibility . . . of eliminating ballistic missiles? . . . It's a job we would have to go about very carefully, with a clear understanding of the complexities and problems involved. But a world without ballistic missiles would offer great advantages over our present situation, provided we had some form of insurance like the strategic defense initiative (SDI) coming on stream to cope with potential cheating.

[B]allistic missiles are weapons *par excellence* of surprise attack and nuclear blackmail. . . . [T]hey are the weapon system most likely to prompt a 'use it or lose it' type of response in a crisis. . . .

If both sides' weapons are vulnerable, temptation on both sides to use them in a crisis increases. So ballistic missiles, in addition to being very threatening weapons, can be destabilizing. . . .

But what about the problems of a world without ballistic missiles? There is no use pretending that such a world would be problem free. . . . [N]uclear deterrence would still operate. But now we would be talking about slower flying, air-breathing delivery vehicles. . . .

If deterrence is no longer going to rely on ballistic missiles, then we need to think seriously about improving our ability to penetrate Soviet air defenses. And we would probably have to think seriously also about strengthening conventional forces. . . .

In a world without ballistic missiles and without strategic defense, there would always be a tremendous temptation for a potential aggressor to produce a clandestine force of ballistic missiles. Such a force would give its possessor enormous power. . . .

In addition, clandestine production, storage, and deployment of missiles would be very hard to detect. . . .

In a world without ballistic missiles, we would have to worry about not just Soviet noncompliance. We would also have to worry about third countries. These are all very serious problems. . . .

If we were to couple elimination of ballistic missiles with deployment of strategic defenses against ballistic missiles, we would have a critical hedge against cheating. We would also create a powerful disincentive against cheating, since in the presence of effective defenses, ballistic missiles would tend to lose the overwhelming military value they now have.

That is what President Reagan proposed to General Secretary Gorbachev in Reykjavik — a plan for elimination of ballistic missiles coupled with deployment of strategic defenses. . . . It is a vision of a world in which the most menacing weapons, ballistic missiles, had been eliminated by arms control and simultaneously rendered obsolete by defenses. . . ."

From a speech on Nov. 13, 1986, before the Woodrow Wilson School of Public and International Affairs.

Continued from page 66
Soviet Union. More than 20 launchers for the 300-mile-range SS-23s are also based in the western Soviet Union.

Of course, the actual balance of military power that would exist under Gorbachev's proposal is not so heavily skewed toward the Soviet bloc as might appear at first glance. Even under the most sweeping Euromissile proposal, eliminating both medium- and short-range missiles, Europe would not be free of nuclear weapons or denuded of the deterrent value they represent. In addition to the independent nuclear forces of Britain and France, there are 400 U.S. submarine-launched missiles available to NATO, and 116 U.S. F-111 bombers based in Britain for NATO. These aircraft can be armed with as many as three nuclear gravity bombs each and have a greater range than the Pershing missiles. *(See p. 66.)*

Europeans ask whether Washington would risk Chicago to save Bonn. Many suspect it would not. And they point to repeated instances of ambivalent U.S. statements and actions.

Also, Western Europe has hundreds of battlefield nuclear weapons, with ranges of less than 300 miles, which would not be limited by current the Euromissile proposal. In all, there are about 207 such missiles in Western Europe. Some 108 U.S. Lance missiles with a range of 66 miles are based in West Germany, and an additional 55 are controlled by West Germany, Italy, Belgium, the Netherlands and Britain. When Shultz met with Western European officials in Brussels, he emphasized that battlefield nuclear weapons were "not on the table" and "not part of these negotiations."

According to outgoing Assistant Secretary of Defense Richard N. Perle, there are now 4,600 U.S. nuclear weapons in Europe, and that number could be maintained following removal of medium- and short-range missiles by re-deploying to Europe warheads not covered under the agreement. "And that," he said, "is hardly leaving our allies naked in front of the Soviet Union."[3]

Paul H. Nitze, President Reagan's adviser on arms control, has said of the 400 submarine-launched nuclear ballistic missile warheads available to NATO: "Given these remaining systems, as well as our extensive conventional contribution to NATO's defense," talk of decoupling Europe's strategic interests from America's is "unjustified."[4] Finally, the United States is committed under the 1949 North Atlantic Treaty to the notion that "an armed attack" against any NATO ally "shall be considered an attack against them all" and therefore to calling into play its U.S.-based strategic ballistic missiles, if necessary, to defend its allies.

But Europeans ask whether Washington would risk Chicago to save Bonn. Many suspect it would not. And they point to repeated instances of ambivalent U.S. statements and actions to justify their less than total faith in America's nuclear umbrella.

For example, the Nixon administration's pronouncements in 1973 on the possibility of a limited nuclear war were seen by many Europeans as an alarming deviation from the postwar strategy of "mutual assured destruction." According to that strategy, any nuclear attack by either superpower would result in the annihilation of both. President Carter's support in 1977 for the idea of testing a neutron bomb produced a similar outcry. Especially in West Germany, where the enhanced radiation weapon would presumably have been deployed, popular condemnation of this "bomb to kill people but not buildings" was strong enough eventually to scuttle the project. When the Senate in 1979 balked at ratifying the nuclear arms limits of the SALT II agreement, Europe's hopes of easing East-West tensions and slowing the arms race received a blow, creating new suspicions about U.S. nuclear policy.

These suspicions have grown during the Reagan administration, which has been openly critical of the arms control process. France, Belgium, Sweden and the Netherlands deplored Reagan's decision last November to break out of the arms ceilings set by SALT II.[5] Although the treaty remained unratified, both sides observed its limits. Even such staunchly conservative Reagan supporters as Thatcher and Kohl have expressed doubts about the strategic defense initiative and criticized the administration's attempt to reinterpret the 1972 Antiballistic Missile (ABM) Treaty so as to allow the United States to proceed with testing components of the space-based missile defense system. According to the traditional interpretation of the treaty, which limits ABM weapons, testing of space-based weapons is prohibited.

But it was the stated agreement between Reagan and Gorbachev during their Iceland summit on the desirability of a nuclear-free world that has most alarmed America's Western European allies. Aghast at the prospect that Reagan would suddenly scrap the nuclear deterrent, Thatcher, speaking for the British, French and West German governments, rushed to Reagan's official retreat at Camp David, Md., where she obtained Reagan's agreement to seek limits on nuclear weapons rather than their elimination. Since that meeting last November, administration officials have backed away from the proposal to eliminate all nuclear weapons, conditioning this long-term goal on achieving parity in conventional forces, greater openness in Soviet society and a treaty on chemical weapons.

While a Euromissile agreement would not remove all nuclear weapons from Europe, America's NATO allies worry that it could be viewed by the Soviet Union and its allies as a decoupling of U.S. security interests from those of the Western Europeans. "They would be vulnerable, they could be pre-empted, they could be saturated," said Christoph Bertram, a West German military analyst. "Then you could think of limiting nuclear conflict to Europe. This is one of the nightmares of the Europeans: conflict in general, but [especially] *nuclear* conflict limited specifically to Europe." [6]

In America, former Secretary of State Henry A. Kissinger shares the European skepticism about the zero option. Although the Soviet Union would be forced to give up a greater number of warheads than the United States under the zero option, he writes, "what they give up in warheads they gain in political, psychological and diplomatic dissociation between the United States and Europe." [7] Kissinger has proposed making removal of the last Pershing II and cruise missiles conditional upon an agreement to achieve parity in short-range nuclear and conventional forces. John Deutch, Brent Scowcroft and R. James Woolsey, former Carter administration officials who are also critical of the zero option, favor leaving the 100 missiles allowed under the current proposal in Europe instead of withdrawing them to U.S. territory.

Another aspect of a Euromissile pact that is highly controversial in Europe is verification. The Soviet Union has long resisted U.S. attempts to include on-site inspection of weapons installations and production facilities as part of bilateral arms control agreements. Verification has been limited to information received via satellite and other information-gathering facilities outside the territories under surveillance. But this time it may be the Western alliance that will drag its feet on verification. It remains to be seen whether all five NATO allies involved in the Euromissile agreement — Belgium, Britain, Italy, the Netherlands and West Germany — will go along with the idea of Soviet military personnel inspecting their facilities.

The verification issue will be even murkier if limits on short-range missiles are included in the agreement. Most of these weapons are even smaller and more mobile than the Soviet SS-20s, so that on-site inspection of their deployment sites and production facilities would be even more critical. Some of these weapons, the SS-21 and SS-23 missiles, are also used as conventional weapons by arming them with nonnuclear warheads. Any ban on their use as nuclear weapons would complicate verification arrangements because it would be a simple matter to replace their conventional warheads with nuclear ones unless NATO inspectors were allowed frequent and sudden access to Warsaw Pact military installations.

The Euromissile talks have added a new and ironic twist to the verification issue. Whereas critics of arms control in the United States have long cited Soviet resistance to on-site verification to bolster their claims of

America will continue to help defend Europe with nuclear weapons such as this attack submarine.

Soviet non-compliance with existing treaties, there are signs that NATO may pose an obstacle to agreement on verification of a Euromissile pact. The United States would like to see highly intrusive inspection rights included in any agreement. Because the Pershing IIs and cruise missiles, as well as shorter-range weapons that may also be covered by an agreement, are produced in the United States, this would entail Soviet inspection of privately owned munitions factories as well as government-controlled storage areas.

The Soviets appear more willing to accept this arrangement than in the past. But in addition to a permanent Soviet presence in the United States, and an American presence in the Soviet Union, the United States also proposes the right to short-notice visits to any public or private site that either side suspects may be used to circumvent the agreement. The Soviets are not the only ones to say this may be taking verification too far.

U.S. negotiators were not able to include these proposals for verification arrangements in the draft proposal they took to Geneva in early March. It took another week before the Americans could persuade the five European allies to go along with their verification demands. Although they finally agreed, the five European nations,

which balk at the prospect of allowing Soviet inspectors on their military bases, continue to favor less intrusive verification measures.

Despite frictions within the NATO alliance, however, it seemed unlikely after Shultz' Moscow trip that Western Europe would stand in the way of Reagan's first nuclear arms control agreement. Shultz called the Soviet short-range missile offer "a great opportunity for the alliance," though he conditioned its acceptance on consultations with America's NATO allies. Following Shultz' his consultations with them in Brussels, the foreign ministers of Britain, West Germany and Italy all expressed positive opinions of the Soviet offer, although they deferred official endorsement to the completion of consultations, a process that is expected to take about three weeks.

Stronger European NATO pillar

The fear of nuclear nakedness has fostered the emergence of a common position on nuclear defense by Britain,

One Way to Make a Short-Range Missile

Gen. Maxwell R. Thurman, Army vice chief of staff, suggested in congressional testimony on March 12° that if a Euromissile agreement permitted the West to build up its short-range missile force to match the Soviet force, as was being discussed, then the United States might convert some of its long-range missiles in West Germany into short-range missiles as a cost-effective way to produce short-range missiles. The 1,120-mile-range Pershing II, he said, could be converted into a 460-mile Pershing IB simply by removing a stage from the missile's rocket.

Although Reagan administration officials said the United States had no intention to deploy short-range weapons in Europe, but only wanted to include the right to do so under a Euromissile pact, Thurman's comments sparked a vehement reaction in Moscow. If it is so simple to convert a Pershing II into the shorter-range Pershing IB, it was pointed out, how hard can it be to turn the missile back into a weapon capable of hitting Soviet targets? Indeed, Viktor Karpov, the chief Soviet arms negotiator, called U.S. support for a Euromissile agreement a "bluff," and said the conversion idea proved Washington's bad faith at the negotiating table. Some U.S. observers agreed. James P. Rubin, assistant director for research for the Arms Control Association, called the conversion issue "an absurdity." He said proposals had been advanced to convert U.S. medium-range missiles into short-range weapons. Ground-launched cruise missiles are very similar to submarine-launched cruise missiles, and could easily be redeployed aboard U.S. submarines. Conversion, Rubin said, "makes a mockery of eliminating a class of weapons, which is how the . . . [medium-range] program has been sold to the public."

° He testified before the Senate Armed Services Conventional Forces Subcommittee.

West Germany and France. United in the concern that Reagan might enter into an unwise agreement with his Soviet counterpart, the three biggest Western European powers have forged a stronger European pillar of NATO. Sometimes it appears less a component of the Western side than a third party to negotiations between the super-powers.

Britain's emergence as enunciator of the European position on medium-range missiles underlines this trend. Long characterized as Reagan's best friend in Europe, Thatcher has been accused by her opponents — for example, in her defense of the U.S. military attack on Libya last April — of being "Reagan's lap dog." But Britain's special relationship with the United States, based on the two countries' historical and cultural ties, has not prevented it from leading Europe's more independent stance on nuclear defense policy.

Britain maintains an independent nuclear force comprising 64 U.S.-made Polaris submarine-launched ballistic missiles, which the Thatcher government plans to replace with the same number of more modern Trident II missiles beginning early in the 1990s. Both of these long-range missiles are capable of striking targets in the Soviet Union, and Thatcher has made it clear Britain would not want to give up this force. "It is vital that we continue to have an independent nuclear force," she told Reagan during their meeting last year at Camp David.

However, anti-nuclear sentiment, focused on the basing of U.S. F-111s and submarines, both capable of carrying nuclear weapons, grew during the deployment of cruise missiles in Britain beginning in 1983. It has strengthened more recently during the Labor Party's challenge to Thatcher's leadership over the Trident modernization program. Labor leader Neil Kinnock, who may face Thatcher in elections expected to be held this year, has pledged to rid Britain of both its nuclear forces and U.S. forces deployed there as part of NATO's nuclear defense.

France, the only other Western European country with an independent nuclear force, has played an ambivalent role in the Western alliance ever since President Charles de Gaulle withdrew his country from NATO's integrated military command in 1966. Unlike the other European members of NATO, France hosts no allied military forces or military headquarters. Its defense posture has depended increasingly on its nuclear arsenal, which comprises land-based missiles and air-launched weapons as well as submarine-based missiles, all of which can strike targets in the Soviet Union. Unlike Britain, France has built its nuclear deterrent relatively independently, and plans to strengthen it under a modernization plan now under way.

Although Moscow has dropped its insistence that Euromissile limits apply to the nuclear forces of Britain and France, both countries fear that their arsenals may be considered as bargaining chips in future U.S.-Soviet negotiations. Their interest in preventing such a development has encouraged the forging of a new agreement between the two European nuclear powers. Britain and France in March announced plans to cooperate more closely on de-

fense issues, including arrangements to co-produce conventional weapons. France, in particular, has been divided over the prospects of any Euromissile agreement. Its defense minister, Andre Giraud, warned darkly that agreement to remove the Pershing II and cruise missiles would constitute a "nuclear Munich," an act of appeasement that could pave the way for Soviet aggression in the same way Britain and France acquiesced to Hitler's demands before World War II. Mitterrand, a Socialist, and Conservative Prime Minister Jacques Chirac recognize France's ultimate dependence on the NATO military structure de Gaulle repudiated two decades ago. Meeting March 31 with Reagan in Washington, just as Thatcher was presenting Britain's position to Gorbachev in Moscow, Chirac reiterated his government's concern that any removal of medium-range missiles take place over a long enough period to ensure that the Warsaw Pact does not maintain its advantage in short-range weapons.

While Moscow has dropped its insistence that missile limits apply to the separate nuclear forces of Britain and France, both fear their arsenals may become bargaining chips in the future.

This concern is shared by West Germany, which hosts the largest contingent of NATO troops and conventional weaponry, and would stand to bear the heaviest losses in the initial phase of a conventional attack against NATO. Germany's longstanding support for détente stems largely from its desire to smooth relations with East Germany, from which it was split in the wake of World War II. But German enthusiasm for arms control is tempered by an acute awareness of being a front-line state between the two alliances. Because of its location and vulnerability to the Warsaw Pact's superior numbers in conventional forces, Bonn has insisted that NATO retain a short-range nuclear deterrent.

Some Europeans want the informal cooperation among Europe's NATO allies that has grown in the wake of the Iceland summit to be formalized. Chirac has presented a plan for a European defense charter as part of the Western

PAST COVERAGE

"Science Wars Over Star Wars" describes opposition within the scientific community to Reagan's "Star Wars" strategic defense initiative to build a space-based ballistic missile defense system. The report also looks at attempts by a budget-conscious Congress to cut back the Reagan administration's requests to finance the program. By William Sweet. E.R.R. 1986 Vol. II, pp. 685-708.

"Chemical Weapons: Push for Control" examines the development of chemical weapons stockpiles by the United States and the Soviet Union. It also looks at obstacles to a bilateral agreement to limit them. By Harrison Donnelly. E.R.R. 1986 Vol. II, pp. 513-32.

"German Reconciliation," written on the eve of Reagan's May 1985 trip to West Germany, reviews relations between the two Germanys and their place in Europe and in the context of superpower relations. By David Fouquet. E.R.R. 1985 Vol. I, pp. 293-312.

"Arms Control Negotiations" discusses U.S.-Soviet negotiations in Geneva on strategic nuclear weapons, intermediate-range nuclear weapons and space weapons, and how they differ from past arms control talks. By Mary H. Cooper. E.R.R. 1985 Vol. I, pp. 145-68.

European Union, a little-known organization within the European Economic Community. Composed of Britain, France, West Germany, Italy, Belgium, the Netherlands and Luxembourg, the group's current role is limited to that of a debating forum on defense issues. British Foreign Secretary Sir Geoffrey Howe supported this idea in a March 16 address before the Royal Institute of International Relations in Brussels. Emphasizing that Europeans provide the vast majority of NATO's European-based troops and conventional weapons, he called on Europe to "get its own ideas straight" in order to become "a far more rewarding partner for the United States and far more likely to have its views taken seriously than a Europe which speaks with a multitude of voices."

U.S. budget-cutters eye NATO spending

But strengthening Europe's say in matters of the common defense is a delicate task. European criticism of U.S. nuclear policy has long struck a sour note in some quarters in the United States, where the European allies are accused of freeloading at America's expense. While the United States spends 6.7 percent of its gross national product on defense, NATO's European members spend on average less than 4 percent.

A large part of U.S. defense expenditures go to Europe, where 330,000 U.S. military personnel are stationed as part of the allied NATO force. Members of Congress who are eager to find ways to cut the growing federal budget deficit are looking more boldly at defense authorizations, which have grown from $180 billion in fiscal 1981, when Reagan came to office, to $290 billion in fiscal 1987. The administration has requested $312 billion for the next fiscal year, which begins Oct. 1.

In their search for ways to cut defense spending, members of Congress are finding U.S. troop presence in Europe a tempting target, especially as the trade deficit with Western European countries continues to grow. "We spend about $150 billion in defense now going to our overseas commitments, and more is in store as the dollar falls in value," Rep. Patricia Schroeder, D-Colo., told reporters on April 6. "Our allies must know that the party is over," she said. "They can do more." Schroeder supports bringing about 200,000 U.S. troops home from Europe over five years. If the Europeans want them to stay, she suggests, the United States should impose a service charge on the countries where they are stationed, equal to the tariffs those countries impose on American imports.

European allies say this argument understates their contribution to NATO. "Of the allied forces stationed in Europe in peacetime, Europeans provide 90 percent of the manpower, 95 percent of the divisions, 85 percent of the tanks, 95 percent of the artillery and 80 percent of the combat aircraft," according to Dutch Foreign Minister Hans van den Broek.[7] Europeans also emphasize the contributions they make to NATO defense that are less easily calculable than defense expenditures, such as the land where troops and weapons are based.

Some American observers also dispute the calls for troop withdrawals from Europe, saying they are not only self-defeating but dangerous. In the view of Richard Burt, the American ambassador to West Germany, "Demobilization of the U.S. forces currently in Europe would leave the United States an army of half a million men. It would turn the U.S. from a superpower into a military and political dwarf."[8]

NOTES

[1] The Soviet Union's allies in Eastern Europe, signers of the Treaty of Warsaw in 1955, are Bulgaria, Czechoslovakia, East Germany, Hungary, Poland and Romania.

[2] See Raymond L. Garthoff, *Détente and Confrontation* (1985), p. 799.

[3] Perle was interviewed in a CBS News television broadcast on April 17.

[4] Writing in *The Washington Post*, March 30, 1987.

[5] On Nov. 28, 1986, the United States exceeded the 1,320 limit on nuclear warhead delivery systems when the Air Force deployed a B-52 bomber capable of carrying cruise missiles.

[6] Bertram was interviewed in *Arms Control Today*, January/February 1987, p.17.

[7] Writing in *Europe*, November 1986, p. 47.

[8] Writing in *The Washington Post*, March 22, 1987.

Graphics: cover, p. 63, p. 69, Defense Department; p. 63 (left), United Press International/Bettmann Newsphotos; p. 63 (right) Reuters/Bettmann Newsphotos.

RECOMMENDED READING

BOOKS

Blacker, Coit D., *Reluctant Warriors*, W. H. Freeman and Co., 1987.

The associate director of Stanford University's Center for International Security and Arms Control examines the interplay between the arms race and political competition between Washington and Moscow since World War II. ". . .Americans must learn to be patient with the process and to assess whatever agreements are forthcoming not against some absolute standard — such as whether this will achieve disarmament — but against present-day realities," Blacker says.

Garthoff, Raymond L., *Détente and Confrontation*, Brookings Institution, 1985.

A chapter entitled "European Theater Nuclear Forces, 1977-80" describes the events leading up to the installation of Euromissiles and contrasts U.S. and Soviet perceptions of the threat they pose. He writes: "The existence of fears on both sides compounded the issue, as each side took steps to ensure its own security which the other in turn perceived as threatening to its security." Garthoff, a senior fellow at Brookings who was involved in negotiations that led to the 1972 SALT I agreement, also has chapters on European reactions to Euromissile deployment and on the Reagan administration's arms control policy.

Krauss, Melvin, *How NATO Weakens the West*, Simon & Schuster, 1986.

Krauss, of New York University and the Hoover Institution on War, Revolution and Peace, a conservative think tank affiliated with Stanford University, arrives at an extreme solution to the country's difficulties with its allies: "The United States must abandon NATO." Only then, he argues, will the Western Europeans assume responsibility for their own defense, freeing the United States of some $150 billion in annual defense expenditures.

McNamara, Robert S., *Blundering Into Disaster: Surviving the First Century of the Nuclear Age*, Pantheon Books, 1986.

McNamara, defense secretary for Presidents Kennedy and Johnson, would reduce nuclear armaments and use the savings to strengthen conventional forces. "Most Americans are simply unaware that Western strategy calls for early initiation of the use of nuclear weapons in a conflict with the Soviets. Eighty percent believe the United States would not use such weapons unless the Soviet Union used them first. They would be shocked to learn they are mistaken. And they would be horrified to be told that senior military commanders themselves believe that to carry out our present strategy would lead to destruction of our society. But those are the facts. In truth, the Emperor has no clothes. Our present nuclear policy is bankrupt."

Scribner, Richard A., Theodore J. Ralston and William D. Metz, *The Verification Challenge*, American Association for the Advancement of Science, Birkhauser, 1985.

The authors describe different methods of verifying arms control agreements. They question the value of on-site verification, a U.S. demand in the Euromissile talks, which may "have to be too intrusive for either the U.S. or the U.S.S.R. to accept."

Talbott, Strobe, *Deadly Gambits*, Alfred A. Knopf, 1984.

Time magazine's Washington bureau chief and former diplomatic correspondent devotes the first half of his book on Reagan's arms control policy to a detailed account of the ongoing talks on medium-range nuclear missiles, which began in 1980. ". . .Reagan and his administration came into office not really wanting to pursue arms control at all," Talbot says. "But two key constituencies wanted them to pursue it anyway: the Western Europeans and, speaking for the American public, Congress."

ARTICLES

"A World Without Nuclear Weapons?" *The New York Times Magazine*, April 5, 1987, pp. 45-54, 65.

Six experts present their views on the main question coming out of the October 1986 summit in Reykjavik between President Reagan and Soviet leader Mikhail S. Gorbachev. They range from the assessment of Zbigniew Brzezinski, President Carter's national security adviser, that such a world is "an illusion," to Massachusetts Institute of Technology Professor Emma Rothschild, who writes: "If we cannot imagine a world without nuclear weapons, then we have already lost. The nuclear weapons will have killed our imagination, and our power to invent a different world."

Schlesinger, James, "Reykjavik and Revelations: A Turn of the Tide?" *Foreign Affairs*, No. 3, 1987.

Schlesinger, President Ford's defense secretary, calls the Reykjavik summit "a near disaster from which we were fortunate to have escaped." Echoing the concerns of many NATO allies, Schlesinger calls nuclear weapons "the indispensable ingredient in Western deterrence strategy" and faults U.S. negotiators for being "little informed either on the exigencies imposed by Western deterrence strategy or on several decades of discussion and debate regarding both the possibilities and the limitations of nuclear disarmament."

Schmidt, Helmut, "Defense: A European Viewpoint," *Europe*, November 1986, pp. 13-15, 45.

The former chancellor of West Germany calls for a greater European role in its own defense. He writes: "If France would bring its conventional forces and reserves into the joint framework of Western defense, it would be easy to achieve a satisfactory equilibrium in conventional forces between Western Europe and the Soviet Union."

REPORTS AND STUDIES

Central Intelligence Agency and Defense Intelligence Agency, "Gorbachev's Modernization Program: A Status Report," March 19, 1987.

Prepared for Congress' Joint Economic Subcommittee on National Security Economics, this paper found a 4 percent growth in the Soviet economy last year, contradicting many less upbeat assessments following the introduction of economic reforms under Mikhail S. Gorbachev. The authors found no evidence that Gorbachev has changed policy on defense spending, which absorbs "about 15-17 percent" of Soviet gross national product. Available from the committee, Room SD-G01, Dirksen Building, Washington, D.C. 20510.

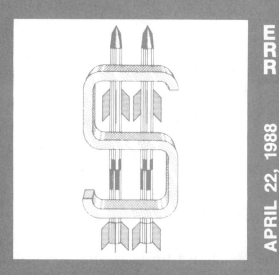

APRIL 22, 1988

THE MILITARY BUILD-DOWN IN THE 1990s

THE MILITARY BUILD-DOWN IN THE 1990s

by Mary H. Cooper

The Reagan administration's campaign to "rearm America" is at an end, and now the armed services face immediate cutbacks and even deeper ones ahead. With "austerity" as a watchword for the 1990s, the nagging question is whether these budget cuts require strategic changes as well.

The next occupant of the White House will inherit a far different kind of defense crisis than the one that propelled Ronald Reagan to the presidency. In 1980, Reagan was elected largely on the basis of his promise to "make America strong again." He vowed to close the "window of vulnerability" he claimed his predecessors had opened by allowing the Soviet Union to catch up with and then surpass the United States in weapons development and deployment. Together with Defense Secretary Caspar W. Weinberger, Reagan launched his campaign to "rearm America." They enjoyed broad bipartisan support for their effort: Congress approved $2 trillion in defense spending over the next seven years. This enormous expenditure, the highest peacetime military budget in the post-World War II era, amounted to $21,000 for each American household.[1]

The Reagan defense buildup is at an end. Since he replaced Weinberger last November, Defense Secretary Frank C. Carlucci has called for a new approach to meeting the nation's defense needs. Presenting a revised defense spending request in February, Carlucci took the unusual step of asking Congress for less money — a $33 billion cut — than the administration had previously requested for fiscal 1989.* He called for the elimination of several weapons programs as well as cuts in manpower while stressing the need to improve the readiness of the shrunken forces. "Simply put," he told Congress, "the priorities reflected in this budget are people, training, and no artificial program stretches," by which he meant the deferral of weapons production to later years, a technique the Pentagon frequently uses to meet budget targets.[2]

---

*Budgetary figures refer to fiscal years. Fiscal 1989 begins Oct. 1, 1988.

President Reagan revived the controversial B-1 bomber as part of his defense buildup.

Carlucci's comments were welcomed on Capitol Hill, where lawmakers have been looking for ways to reduce the federal budget deficit, which topped $150 billion last year. But the search for a new national consensus on defense spending will not be easy. Carlucci's cuts for 1989 alone produced a flurry of protest at the Pentagon. Navy Secretary James H. Webb Jr. resigned abruptly upon hearing that Carlucci, in the name of fiscal restraint, had scrapped Reagan's plan for a 600-ship Navy. Webb's reaction was only the most visible sign of turmoil that is bound to grow as the military services struggle to save their pet programs from the budget ax in coming years.

For as Carlucci pointed out, this year's fiscal constraints are just the beginning. In addition to the $33 billion cut he called for in his revised budget request, Carlucci said another $200 billion would have to be carved from current spending plans over the next three years if Congress approves his proposal to limit Pentagon spending increases to 2 percent a year. Carlucci has said he intends this summer to restructure the Pentagon's current five-year plan to reflect the ceiling. But most observers say lawmakers are likely to pare the Pentagon's budget requests even more, possibly forcing an actual decline in spending. In fact, if inflation is taken into account, 1989 would be the fourth consecutive year defense spending has declined *(see graph, p. 80).*

The need to cut defense spending may become even more urgent if the economy weakens over the next few months. Under the 1985 Gramm-Rudman-Hollings anti-deficit law, across-the-board cuts will be made in all federal spending, including defense, if the budget deficit exceeds $146 billion in fiscal 1989.* The administration predicts the deficit will be only $134 billion, but its forecast is based on optimistic economic assumptions. The deficit forecast must be revised in August, by which time the economy could have slowed, which would force the administration to revise it upwards. In that case, the administration will have to enact spending cuts with or without tax increases, allow the automatic cuts to occur or ignore the law. The hard choices, of course, will fall to the next president.

No matter what the outcome, defense spending, which accounts for 27 percent of the federal budget, will continue to be a top priority for the foreseeable future. But even a slowdown of projected increases in the defense budget means that billions of dollars Pentagon planners had counted on to fund projects in coming years will no longer be available.

Just how U.S. military forces will adjust to the new austerity remains to be seen. Entire weapons programs launched during the Reagan buildup may be scrapped, and the defense contractors that make them are already gearing up for battle to save their lucrative government contracts. Alternatively, there may be changes in the basic strategy that has defined U.S. military policy in the postwar period. The sense of austerity has already height-

*The law (PL 99-177) set deficit targets over a five-year period, leading to a balanced budget by 1991.

ened calls for America's allies to pay more for the defense of Western Europe and for a reduction in the number of American troops stationed overseas. In the words of a State Department official: "Nobody thinks expenditures for defense are irrelevant, but I think the United States as a country has to think more carefully about what expenditures are most cost-effective for security."

At the same time, there is a widening public debate over the military role of the United States, whose economic power relative to other industrial nations is shrinking. Some analysts predict that unless the country's military mission is scaled back to reflect its waning economic clout, the United States will find itself in the position that Yale historian Paul Kennedy calls "imperial overstretch," a progressive imbalance between military might and economic strength that has led to the downfall of other world powers.[3]

"The American public is redefining what national security means to them," said Ann Lewis, former political director of the Democratic National Committee and now a consultant to Democratic presidential candidate Jesse Jackson. While people expect better performance from the military, she said, they are less willing to spend so much on new weaponry. In her view, this shift reflects both a perception that the Soviet Union is less threatening under the leadership of Mikhail S. Gorbachev and a growing concern about "America's place in the world. This means that national security has a new economic component, our ability to remain competitive."

Reagan's defense buildup enjoyed wide public support

If Lewis is correct, the public mood is radically different from what it was at the beginning of the decade. After 1973, when the United States withdrew its forces from Vietnam, defense expenditures fell sharply. During the 1970s, defense spending fell by $62 billion, or 27 percent. From 1970 to 1980, defense spending shrank from 39 percent of all federal expenditures to 22.5 percent.[4]

Although President Carter began a defense buildup of his own, reflected in a $20 billion increase in defense spending his last year in office, he was widely considered to be "weak on defense" by the end of his term. Reagan tapped into the public's outrage at the Soviet incursion into Afghanistan in December 1979 and the inability of U.S. forces to free American hostages taken prisoner in Iran to build support for a massive weapons buildup as the basis of his military policy. As Weinberger made clear, cost was no obstacle: "America's defense budgets should be based on defense needs, not on political expediency or short-term fiscal goals. . . . Anyone who says we cannot afford to do whatever we must to keep our freedom is halfway along the road to losing it."[5] The administration succeeded in gaining congressional approval for much of the buildup. Between 1980 and 1987, real defense outlays grew by 52 percent while the proportion of the gross national product (GNP), the total output of goods and services, devoted to

Real Growth in Defense Budget Authority

The Reagan defense buildup ended in 1985. When inflation is taken into account, 1989 will be the fourth consecutive year defense spending has declined.

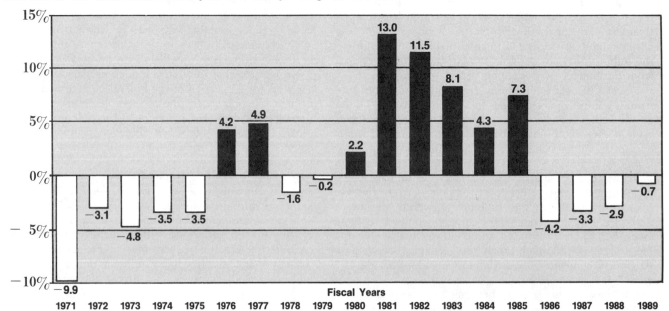

Fiscal Years

1971 1972 1973 1974 1975 1976 1977 1978 1979 1980 1981 1982 1983 1984 1985 1986 1987 1988 1989

Source: Defense Department

defense outlays rose from 5 to 6.2 percent.

Reagan's campaign to "rearm America" focused initially on strategic nuclear weaponry. Claiming Carter's emphasis on arms control had allowed the Soviet Union to surpass the United States in nuclear weaponry, the Reagan Pentagon undertook a program to modernize all three components of the U.S. "triad" of strategic nuclear weapons — weapons that are capable of striking Soviet territory from land, air or sea. These included the MX intercontinental ballistic missile, the B-1 and Stealth bombers, and Trident II submarines armed with D-5 missiles. Since 1980, the number of land-based ICBMs has fallen, from 1,052 in 1980 to an estimated 1,000 in 1988. The number of strategic bombers also has declined. But the other component of the strategic triad, submarine-launched ballistic missiles (SLBMs), has grown (*see table, p. 82*).

Reagan also planned to increase the overseas naval presence of the United States. To that end, he set the goal of building up the U.S. fleet — which had shrunk from 1,000 ships during the Vietnam War to about 480 in 1980 — to field a 600-ship Navy by 1988. While the Navy has fallen short of its 600-ship goal because of budget constraints, the number of deployable ships has grown from 479 in 1980 to an estimated 568 this year.

The Reagan buildup was not limited to weapons and equipment procurement. Troop levels, which had fallen from about 3,000,000 at the peak of the Vietnam War to fewer than 2,000,000 in the mid-1970s, were raised again. Since 1980, the number of active-duty military personnel has increased by 134,000 to 2,174,000. In addition, the Defense Department's civilian payroll, currently 1,049,000 employees, has increased by 133,000 since 1980. The Reagan buildup has also been credited with improving the quality of U.S. troops. The Center for Defense Information points out that the percentage of high school

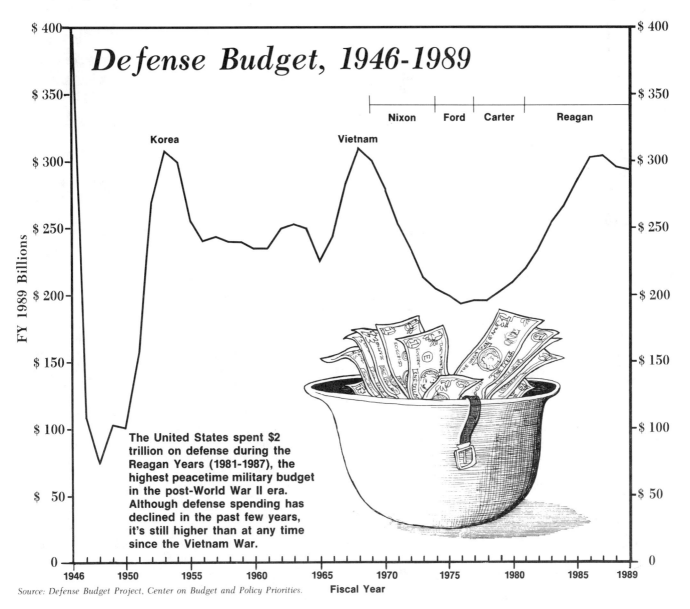

Defense Budget, 1946-1989

Nixon Ford Carter Reagan

Korea

Vietnam

FY 1989 Billions

Fiscal Year

The United States spent $2 trillion on defense during the Reagan Years (1981-1987), the highest peacetime military budget in the post-World War II era. Although defense spending has declined in the past few years, it's still higher than at any time since the Vietnam War.

Source: Defense Budget Project, Center on Budget and Policy Priorities.

America's Arsenal 1980 to 1987

Reagan's defense buildup bought more people, aircraft and ships, but fewer strategic weapons, with the exception of sea-launched missiles.

	FY 1980	FY 1987	Change
Personnel			
Active Duty Military	2,040,000	2,174,000	+134,000
Defense Dept. Civilian	916,000	1,049,000	+133,000
Strategic Forces			
Land-based ICBMs	1,052	1,000	−52
Strategic Bombers	372	344	−28
Submarine-Launched Ballistic Missiles	416	528	+112
General Purpose Forces			
Active Divisions			
Army	16	18	+2
Marine Corps	3	3	——
Tactical Air Forces			
Attack/Fighter Aircraft			
Air Force	1,608	1,812	+204
Navy	696	752	+56
Marine Corps	329	331	+2
Naval Forces			
Strategic Ships	48	43	−5
Battle Ships	384	445	+61
Support Ships	41	58	+17
Reserve Ships	6	22	+16
Total Deployable Battle Forces	479	568	+89

Source: Defense Department

graduates among the armed forces went from 68 percent in 1980 to 92 percent in 1986. The average level of expertise has also improved, as more enlisted personnel remained in service. They also tended to stay longer in the same unit than had been the practice.

In March 1983, Reagan announced a controversial program to build a space-based defense system to shield the United States from nuclear attack. The strategic defense initiative (SDI), popularly known as "star wars," called for the development of a high-technology defense system capable of destroying incoming ballistic missiles before they could reach their targets. In the past five years, $12 billion has been spent on SDI research and development.

What the buildup bought: Less bang for the buck

Critics contend that the defense buildup is far less impressive than the money spent would indicate. "Essen-tially, every weapon that has been started since the Carter administration is worse than the one it has replaced," said a former Pentagon planner and expert in combat aircraft design who asked not to be identified. "The B-1 is a worse bomber than the B-52 it is replacing, and the even newer Stealth bomber is every bit as bad as the B-1. Both are perfectly useless relative to the B-52, and the B-52 was not a great bomber." He also criticized the Navy's new A-6 attack aircraft, which he called "a big cumbersome truck for hauling radar that doesn't work particularly well for dropping bombs," and the latest version of the Army's M-1 tank, which he said was "less maneuverable and has less sustainable fire power than the first version . . . which in turn was poorer than the older M-48 and M-60 [tanks]."

Modern weaponry, with its high-technology compo-nents, is expensive. As a result, each additional defense dollar buys fewer weapons. William W. Kaufmann, a defense analyst and professor emeritus at the Massachusetts Institute of Technology, says the growing depreciation of the military dollar is particularly visible in the Navy's shipbuilding program. While budget authority for the Navy grew by 49 percent from 1980 to 1986, the total $550 billion Navy budget for that period bought only 105 major new ships, rather than the 150 originally budgeted.[6]

For many critics, the Navy's 600-ship goal came to symbolize military planning gone awry. The core elements of the new flotilla were to be 15 aircraft carriers, which cost about $18 billion each, if the planes and support vessels are taken into account. In addition to being among the most expensive items in the military budget, these large, relatively slow-moving ships are highly vulnerable to enemy attack. Because carriers accommodate about 90 aircraft, a single well-placed hit on one of them could deal a devastating blow. Funds would be better spent, critics said, by purchasing a larger number of less expensive, less vulnerable ships, such as submarines.

Also contributing to the loss of enthusiasm for the Reagan defense buildup were a series of scandals in the mid-1980s involving Pentagon procurement procedures, such as the payment of $7,400 for a coffee brewer installed in an Air Force transport plane. Defense contractors were charged with stealing the taxpayer's money, while the Pentagon came under fire for allowing the contractors a free ride in the name of national defense.

The scandals prompted the appointment of a presidential commission, the Blue-Ribbon Commission on Defense Management headed by David Packard, a former deputy secretary of defense. Reagan adopted several of the Packard commission's recommendations soon after they were issued in 1986. In an effort to coordinate procurement, the chairman of the Joint Chiefs of Staff was given greater power over the separate services, which compete among themselves for defense funds. Congress made other changes, such as the creation of a Pentagon procurement "czar" charged with making sure that the military got what it paid for from defense contractors. Lawmakers also attempted to reduce conflicts of interest in procurement by making it harder for Pentagon officials to work for defense contractors immediately after they leave the military.[7]

But these reform efforts were not enough to cure all the flaws in the procurement process. Contractors continue to defraud taxpayers. For example, TRW Inc. was fined $17 million last year after pleading guilty to fraud; last month Motorola Inc. was penalized $5 million after making a similar plea. Dina Rasor, director of the Project on Military Procurement in Washington, D.C., says waste and fraud in arms purchases will continue to boost the price of defense "as long as the Pentagon refuses to have an adversarial, buyer-customer relationship with the defense industry." Such a relationship is unlikely to develop, given the strong interests at stake in defense procurement.

For one thing, reform laws have not completely closed the "revolving door" through which Pentagon brass often pass upon retirement from the military to find lucrative jobs in the defense industry. Lawmakers, too, are under pressure to approve such programs; to oppose them would undercut their support among defense contractors and their employees at home. "The self-interested politics and economics of many parties — the armed services, Congress, the president, the defense industry, and large chunks of the American public — intrude into almost every aspect of a weapon system's conception, development, manufacture, and deployment," Nick Kotz wrote in his recently published book on the controversial B-1 strategic bomber, a weapon that Carter abandoned and that Reagan subsequently revived. "The total effect is to warp the defense process in ways that serve neither the defense needs nor the overall well-being of the nation."[8]

Worried about spending cuts? You ain't seen nothing yet

What years of reform efforts failed to accomplish may come about by the budget ax. After dedicating $2 trillion to the Reagan military buildup, Congress has made halting steps toward slowing the rise of the federal budget deficit, and the Pentagon is beginning to feel the pinch. Under the bipartisan "budget-summit" agreement struck last November between Congress and the White House, a cap of $299.5 billion was placed on defense spending for fiscal 1989. While slightly higher in nominal terms than this year's $291.4 billion military budget, this sum was less in real terms, that is when inflation is taken into account.

> *"The self-interested politics and economics of many parties intrude into every aspect of a weapon system's conception, development, manufacture and deployment," says Nick Kotz.*

In order to meet the new budget target, Carlucci had to cut $33 billion from the Pentagon's 1989 budget. In making the cuts, Carlucci said he based his decisions on the direction the military should take in the 1990s. He made slight reductions in the size of all three services while emphasizing the need to preserve their readiness for combat. "We cannot afford to return to the 'hollow' force structure of the 1970s," Carlucci explained in his Feb. 18 report to Congress. He also canceled several weapons

Defense Money: Where Does It Go?

Defense expenditures in fiscal year 1988 are less than last year's in most categories when inflation is taken into account. Defense Secretary Carlucci proposes further reductions for fiscal year 1989 by trimming personnel and by purchasing fewer weapons than the administration had originally requested.

	FY 88 Appropriations	Real Growth over FY '87	FY 89 Request (Jan. '87)	FY 89 Request (Feb. '88)	Real Growth of Feb. '88 Request over FY '88 Appropriations
Military Personnel	$ 76.1	−0.3%	$ 81.6	$ 78.4	−0.2%
Operations and Maintenance	80.7	−4.8%	91.5	85.6	2.4%
Procurement	81.0	−2.5%	94.6	80.0	−4.3%
Research and Development	36.7	−1.0%	44.3	38.2	0.3%
Military Construction	8.5	0.0%	10.7	9.0	2.5%
Other	0.2	0.0%	0.6	−0.4	0.0%
Total	$ 283.2	−2.9%	$ 323.3	$ 290.8	−0.7%

(Dollar amounts are in billions)

Source: Defense Department

programs altogether and delayed the production of others.

Manpower reductions will result in a net loss of about 36,000 military personnel. The Air Force is the biggest loser, with 31,000 fewer airmen, while the Army will cut 9,000 and the Marines 2,000. The Navy alone is slated to gain more recruits, but the 6,000 new sailors are fewer than it had requested. The troop reductions will be accompanied by the retirement of weapons and the elimination of combat units. The Army will drop two battalions it had planned for its new light infantry division in Alaska and retire 620 helicopters that had been in service since the Vietnam War, the first of some 2,000 helicopters slated to go over the next five years. The Navy will be forced to take out of service 16 1960s-vintage frigates. It was this cut, which will leave the Navy 20 vessels short of its 600-ship goal, that prompted Webb's sudden retirement as Navy secretary.* The Air Force is being asked to rely more heavily on reconnaissance satellites, which are cheaper to maintain than spy planes. The Air Force must also retire two tactical fighter wings, one in the United States and the other in Spain.

Carlucci eliminated 18 weapons programs, most of which had long been criticized as technically flawed, too expensive or both. But many other controversial weapons, including the Army's Bradley Fighting Vehicle, were retained. Critics call the Bradley, an armored personnel carrier, a "flaming coffin" because it rides so high off the ground that it exposes the troops on board to danger from enemy attack. The biggest cut Carlucci requested in strategic nuclear forces was the Midgetman single-warhead missile. The program, which would cost some $50 billion to deploy, would receive just enough funding — $200 million — to keep it alive long enough for the next administration to decide the weapon's fate.

Carlucci partially offset these cuts by requesting more

funds than are currently being spent for operations and maintenance, the segment of the defense budget that pays for training and the upkeep of ships, tanks and other weapons, and for military construction. He said these increases reflected the Pentagon's "resolve not to allow a return to the poor state of readiness that existed in the 1970s." Carlucci also requested a 4.3 percent pay increase for the nation's volunteer forces as an incentive to attract and keep high-quality personnel in the military *(see box, p. 89)*.

The defense secretary's revision of the 1989 budget marked the first time the Reagan Pentagon had ever taken the initiative in suggesting funding cuts; under Weinberger, the job was left entirely to Congress. Accordingly, Carlucci's stance has been welcomed on Capitol Hill as more realistic than that of his predecessor. But when examined in the context of current plans for weapons procurement in future years, Carlucci's revisions are far less impressive than they first appear and leave the most painful decisions about the direction of military spending and policy to the next administration.

For one thing, the revised defense budget assumes that Congress will approve a 2 percent increase in spending for the Pentagon. While this is down from Weinberger's original assumption that defense spending would grow by 3 percent, it is considered to be overly optimistic because Congress has reduced defense spending increases for the past two years. And that was before it became more serious about reducing the federal budget deficit, as shown in last November's budget agreement.

More importantly, the revised budget does not affect the backlog of funds appropriated during the Reagan buildup for research and development, procurement and military construction, but that have not yet been spent. According to the Defense Budget Project in Washington, D.C., these "obligated" funds will total about $271 billion by the end of fiscal 1989, by which time they will account for about 40 percent of the defense budget. Because

---

*Webb's successor, William L. Ball III, was confirmed by the Senate March 23. Ball was formerly the chief White House lobbyist on Capitol Hill.

these funds have already been committed, they make it harder for budget planners to control future defense outlays.

Carlucci has said he will review the Pentagon's plans for future outlays this summer, but some budget analysts say it is too late to do much about these funds. To retrieve them would require the cancellation of entire weapons programs, an almost impossible feat because of high termination penalties contractors charge when programs are dropped and because most programs are farmed out among numerous defense contractors. Defense manufacturers in 48 states are involved in the B-1 project alone. The Defense Budget Project says that as a result of the backlog of obligated funds, the next administration "will have to cope with high levels of peacetime defense spending, large amounts of which cannot be controlled, at a time when high federal budget deficits must, by law, be reduced." [9]

In the view of one Pentagon official who has prepared a detailed analysis of the defense budget, the budgetary crisis amounts to nothing less than a "meltdown" that will begin as soon as the next administration arrives in the White House. According to his study, the Pentagon's five-year plan for the period 1988-1992, drawn up under Weinberger, locks the federal government into spending between $250 billion and $400 billion more than Congress is likely to approve. The $250 billion difference would occur if defense spending remained at current levels. The $400 billion difference between what Congress will provide and what the Pentagon has committed itself to spend would

occur if across-the-board cuts mandated by the Gramm-Rudman law were to take effect.

Fighting the budget battle: trying to get more for less

Carlucci has acknowledged that the cuts he proposed in February would not be enough to meet budget targets if Congress fails to appropriate the requested 2 percent spending increase for fiscal 1989. If more cuts need to be made, he said, they would likely be in manpower. "Although force-structure reductions do not save a great deal of money in the near team," Carlucci told the congressional Appropriations panel Feb. 25, "they save money every year thereafter in increasing amounts as more infrastructure savings are identified."

The current defense budget calls for the removal of 36,000 men and women from the military payroll, but far more personnel would have to go if manpower is to bear the brunt of future defense spending cuts. This might force the United States to withdraw troops from Western Europe and the Far East that are there under formal treaty commitments. To give an idea of the magnitude of the problem, the Pentagon analyst, who asked not to be identified, estimated that all U.S. troops would have to be

The Military Reform Movement

As early as 1961 President Eisenhower warned against "the potential for the disastrous rise of misplaced power" on the part of the "military-industrial complex." But it was not until the beginning of the Reagan defense buildup that Pentagon critics made a concerted effort to reevaluate the way defense policy is made and the way weapons are chosen and procured.

The reformers' message was brought to public attention with the publication of James Fallows' book *National Defense* in 1981. Fallows, an editor of the *Atlantic Monthly*, described a faulty procurement process that produced inferior weapons at growing cost and warned that the defense buildup would fall short of its promise to "make America strong again."

Some members of the defense establishment agreed. Franklin C. Spinney, a Pentagon budget analyst, was pictured on the cover of *Time* magazine in 1983 for his persistent criticism of what he called the "plans-reality mismatch" between the Defense Department's procurement programs and the funds available to carry them to completion.

The reform movement took root in Congress as well with the creation in 1981 of the Congressional Military Reform Caucus. Co-founded by former Sen. Gary Hart, D-Colo., and Rep. G. William Whitehurst, R-Va., the caucus now has 140 members and emphasizes the need for more efficient use of defense funds.

withdrawn from their NATO positions by 1992 to meet budget requirements under his most optimistic scenario, in which $250 billion must be carved from the defense budget. If manpower were to bear the brunt of budget cuts under his worst-case scenario, which foresees reductions totaling $400 billion, those troops would have to go by 1990. If the savings were to be made by troop reductions in Asia, there would be no more U.S. forces in the Far East by next year, even under the more optimistic scenario.

Other analysts are considering ways the force structure might be changed to cope with the fiscal constraints. The Congressional Budget Office, a nonpartisan office that provides budgetary information to Congress, estimates that reducing the number of weapons and military personnel would save little money in the short term, but could save significant amounts later. "Future personnel costs would be lower because there would be fewer people to pay; operation and maintenance costs could be lower because there would be fewer people to train and less equipment to maintain; and procurement costs could be lower because the smaller forces would need less equipment," CBO concluded.[10]

Defense Spending and the Economy

As lawmakers contemplate reductions in the military budget as a means to bring federal spending under control, they must consider the effects of an eventual military build-down on the economy as a whole. Although the U.S. economy is enjoying one of the longest recession-free periods ever, the business cycle eventually will begin its downward swing. A sudden contraction in defense spending could speed its arrival.

But economists differ over the impact of defense spending on the rest of the economy. The traditional school of thought, espoused by the defense industry, says that military spending stimulates the economy. They point out that the United States' entry into World War II ended the Depression, as the demand for weapons boosted employment. In this view, defense spending also benefits the civilian economy, as the production of military hardware produces technological "spinoffs" such as aircraft and high-technology goods that find application in non-military manufactures. Commercial airplanes, which are spinoffs of military designs, are one of a dwindling number of successful American exports.

In anticipation of the build-down, defense contractors are already gearing up for battle. Three leading defense lobby groups commissioned a recent study that concluded the industry is already losing money be-

cause of tax law and regulatory changes that resulted in part from earlier reform efforts.† By forcing the contractors to pay a greater share of research and development costs, more business-related expenses and other charges previously billed to the Pentagon, the study concluded, the changes have cost the nine contractors examined $8.5 billion.

Equally compelling arguments are advanced by those who say military spending depletes the economy by diverting to essentially non-productive uses investment funds and expertise that could otherwise be used to boost the ailing civilian economy. In this vein, Rep. Patricia Schroeder, D-Colo., calls defense contractors "the welfare queens of the '80s." Paul Kennedy, a historian at Yale University, blames the United States' excessive emphasis on military spending for its economic decline. While the United States devotes over 6 percent of its wealth to defense spending, he points out, West Germany and Japan — this country's chief economic rivals — devote far less to defense. As military allies, they enjoy the United States' military protection while using their resources to outperform the United States in international trade.

Clearly, communities that depend heavily on large defense contractors or on military bases for their livelihood have benefited during the Reagan buildup. Employment Research Associates of Lansing, Mich., has esti-

mated that California enjoyed a net gain of more than 600,000 jobs from increased Pentagon spending from 1981-85, while 12 other states†† also added more than 10,000 jobs each during the first five years of the buildup. But the organization also concluded that 36 states lost jobs as a result because the diversion of investment funds into the military-industrial sector deprived other sectors of the economy of resources. The biggest losers, it found, were Texas and Illinois, with job losses exceeding 250,000 each, followed by New York, Michigan, Louisiana, North Carolina, Pennsylvania and Ohio, each of which lost more than 100,000 jobs. "The same states that gained heavily during the last seven years stand to suffer disproportionately with the build-down," said Michael Dee Oden, an economist and the author of a recent study published by Employment Research Associates. "If the build-down occurs, we might begin to see the negative effects three or four years from now." ‡

† "The Impact on Defense Industrial Capability of Changes in Procurement and Tax Policy, 1984-1987," February 1988. The study was conducted by the MAC Group, a management consulting firm, under commission by the Aerospace Industries Association, National Security Industrial Association and Electronic Industries Association.
†† Utah, Georgia, New Mexico, Washington, Nevada, Hawaii, Kansas, Connecticut, Missouri, Massachusetts, Maryland and Virginia.
‡ Michael Dee Oden, "A Military Dollar Really Is Different: The Economic Impacts of Military Spending Reconsidered," Employment Research Associates, 1988.

The Military Reform Caucus, a bipartisan group of about 140 lawmakers who support a more effective use of defense funds (*see box, p. 85*), recommends shrinking the officer corps as a way to save money. "There are three times as many officers now than there were during World War II," explained Scott Baker, a staffer for Rep. Tom Ridge, R-Pa., co-chairman of the caucus with Rep. Charles E. Bennett, D-Fla. "There are many bureaucrats in the officer corps, but few combat officers, because the people who tend to get promoted are those who are skilled at maneuvering themselves into higher ranks," Baker said.

Steven L. Canby, an adjunct professor of national security at Georgetown University, recommends more drastic changes in military manpower. Because of the same careerist tendencies Baker described, officers in search of rapid promotion try to gain experience in many fields of the military. But such "ticket-punching" involves rapid turnover and a consequent lack of expertise. This system takes its toll in many ways. "In Vietnam, they rotated officers in three jobs over a year's time so that everybody could have combat experience," Canby recalled. "Where company commanders stayed on the job for more than a few months, there was a dramatic fall in the casualty rates among conscripts." Under today's peacetime conditions, keeping officers at the same job for longer periods would save money, Canby said. "With people continually coming and going, people don't know their jobs, and that means the unit is never really ready. To make them ready, you have to have training exercises all the time, and that costs money." He also says $10 billion could be saved in training costs alone by lengthening enlistment terms from 3-4 years to 6-10 years.

Some analysts say manpower expenses could be cut by reverting to the draft. Since President Richard M. Nixon abandoned the draft in 1973, the armed forces have been manned by volunteers. The CBO estimates that a return to conscription, using the national lottery draft system of the early 1970s, could save as much as $1.7 billion in 1989, assuming that draftees would be paid less than volunteers. Opponents of conscription, including the Pentagon, point to the improved quality of the armed forces since the volunteer military went into effect (*see box, p. 89*).

Some military officials, including former Army Under Secretary James R. Ambrose, favor drastic reductions in manpower over the elimination of weapons programs initiated during the Reagan buildup. The Army, which accounts for the largest number of personnel among the military services, is scheduled to shrink from 781,000 to 772,600 soldiers in fiscal 1989, the lowest number in a decade and far below the 1.57 million level reached in 1968 during the Vietnam War. But Ambrose, who resigned his post in February, said he would rather lose 250,000 more troops than cut into the Army's procurement of tanks, planes and high-technology weapons that would reduce the need for soldiers on the battlefields of the future. "The idea is to keep people off the battlefield, to keep them alive," he said.[11]

Although Ambrose's views clash with those of other

Pentagon's Slice of the Dollar

President Reagan's campaign to "rearm America," which began in 1981, significantly increased the Defense Department's share of the federal budget. Although in constant dollars military spending has dropped over the last few years, the Pentagon's share of the public-spending pie has not fallen.

| | Defense Outlays as a Percent of | | |
Fiscal Year	Gross National Product	Federal Outlays	Net Public Spending
1950	4.4	27.5	18.5
1955	9.1	51.5	35.6
1960	8.2	45.0	30.3
1965	6.8	38.8	25.2
1970	7.8	39.4	25.5
1975	5.6	25.5	16.5
1980	5.0	22.5	15.3
1981	5.2	23.0	15.8
1982	5.8	24.5	16.7
1983	6.2	25.4	17.3
1984	6.0	25.9	17.5
1985	6.2	25.9	17.7
1986	6.3	26.8	18.1
1987	6.2	27.3	18.0
1988	5.9	26.2	17.5

Source: Defense Department

generals who say money should be spent to raise troop levels and improve their training, they agree with the findings of the Commission on Integrated Long-Term Strategy, a blue-ribbon panel of retired military and former government officials.

The commission's report, presented in January, recommends that emphasis be given over the next 20 years to high-technology, conventional weaponry. Stealth technology, which makes planes less visible to enemy radar, is among the commission's first priorities for future spending. Although current expenditures for stealth technology is classified, the Congressional Budget Office deduces from published reports that the top-secret program to build a Stealth B-2 bomber amounts to about $59 billion.

The commission also recommended the development of more "smart" weapons, precision-guided munitions that are highly accurate over long ranges. The problem is, these weapons also tend to be expensive. So far, programs to develop smart munitions have been plagued by technical problems, prolonging their development time and increasing their cost. For this reason, several, including the Army's 14-year program to develop a remotely piloted plane, fell victim to Carlucci's budget ax.

In presenting his revised budget request in February,

Continued on page 89

AT ISSUE   Did President Reagan's military buildup mask a decline in America's power?

YES says **PAUL KENNEDY,** professor of history at Yale University.

". . .[T]he United States today has roughly the same massive array of military obligations across the globe as it had a quarter-century ago, when its shares of world GNP, manufacturing production, military spending, and armed forces personnel were so much larger than they are now. Even in 1985, forty years after its triumphs of the Second World War and over a decade after its pull-out from Vietnam, the United States had 520,000 members of its armed forces abroad (including 65,000 afloat). That total is, incidentally, substantially more than the overseas deployments in peacetime of the military and naval forces of the British Empire at the height of its power. Nevertheless, in the strongly expressed opinion of the Joint Chiefs of Staff, and of many civilian experts, it is simply not enough. Despite a near-trebling of the American defense budget since the late 1970s, there has occurred a 'mere 5 percent increase in the numerical size of the armed forces on active duty.' As the British and French military found in their time, a nation with extensive overseas obligations will always have a more difficult 'manpower problem' than a state which keeps its armed forces solely for home defense. . . .

[T]he only answer to the question increasingly debated by the public of whether the United States can preserve its existing position is 'no' — for it simply has not been given to any one society to remain *permanently* ahead of all the others, because that would imply a freezing of the differentiated pattern of growth rates, technological advance, and military developments which has existed since time immemorial. . . .

[I]t may be argued that the geographical extent, population, and natural resources of the United States suggest that it ought to possess perhaps 16 or 18 percent of the world's wealth and power, but because of historical and technical circumstances favorable to it, that share rose to 40 percent or more by 1945; and what we are witnessing at the moment is the early decades of the ebbing away from that extraordinarily high figure to a more 'natural' share. That decline is being masked by the country's enormous military capabilities at present. . . .

The task facing American statesmen over the next decades, therefore, is to recognize that broad trends are under way, and that there is a need to 'manage' affairs so that the *relative* erosion of the United States' position takes place slowly and smoothly, and is not accelerated by policies which bring merely short-term advantage but longer-term disadvantages."

From The Rise and Fall of the Great Powers: Economic Change and Military Conflict from 1500 to 2000 *(1987).*

NO says **JEANE J. KIRKPATRICK**, U.S. representative to the United Nations, 1981-85.

"Though [Paul] Kennedy eschews 'crude economic determinism,' he concludes that 'productive economic forces' are finally crucial in determining the decline and fall of nations. 'To be a great power — by definition, a state capable of holding its own against any other nation — demands a flourishing economic base.'

This is both true and not true. The Soviet Union constitutes the strongest evidence against Kennedy's argument that a great power must be sustained by a comparably great industrial base, or that preeminent military power depends on technological preeminence or that defense expenditures must be kept in harmony with economic growth.

A very large share of Soviet GNP has been devoted to defense every year since the Bolshevik Revolution — that is, during the entire period in which the Soviets became a great world power and developed a global empire. The Soviet Union is, as the London Times noted, 'a Third World country with First World weapons.' And it is not the only example of a lack of correlation between economic and military power. Japan is a First World country with less military strength than China. The European community's economic strength far exceeds its relative military strength.

Kennedy seeks to explain too much by economic factors. In so doing he ignores or understates too many other dimensions in the rise and fall of nations — particularly including such political factors as will, skill and conquest and such moral factors as human purpose and human nature.

. . .Kennedy knows that none of the new industrial and trading nations constitutes a military threat to the United States or to each other. He also knows that the Soviet Union constitutes no economic threat to anyone.

But he ends by suggesting that we can best deal with the potential military threat of the Soviet Union by cutting defense expenditures and competing more effectively with the challenges of Japan and the new industrial countries.

The problem is that economic power and military power are related, but they are not fungible. Economic competition challenges the United States. It does not threaten us. And a positive trade balance with Japan cannot save us — or the Japanese — from Soviet missiles. Protection against missiles requires a defense against missiles. Even the Koreans have not yet invented consumer goods that can deter aggression."

Writing in The Washington Post, *March 7, 1988.*

Continued from page 87

Carlucci said he chose to terminate the plane, the AQUILA, as well as another "smart" weapon, the Copperhead projectile, because they were too expensive. The biggest savings, in fact, were made in the Pentagon's weapons procurement accounts, which total $80 billion, down $14.5 billion from the original 1989 defense spending request.

He said that other programs, including the Army's Anti-Tactical Missile, the Navy's A-6 attack aircraft and the Air Force's C-27 transport, were dropped because older systems could be upgraded to serve the same purpose. Terminating a total of 18 procurement programs, Carlucci said, will save almost $5 billion in fiscal 1989 and another $47 billion in the future. Deferring the development of others, such as the Army's armored vehicles, would bring further savings of $1.1 billion in 1989 alone.

Once again, however, procurement cuts outlined by Carlucci would do little to bring Pentagon spending plans into line with fiscal realities beyond 1989. The Pentagon official foresees a procurement "blood bath" in the early 1990s when programs in weapons procurement and research and development will have to be canceled. Under his most optimistic scenario, 157 programs, including the Trident submarine and the $2 billion rail system for the MX missile, would have to go if procurement accounts bear the brunt of spending cuts. Under the worst case, 169 programs, including SDI and the Air Force's F-16, would be eliminated.

The strategic implications of the new fiscal realities

At the same time such drastic adjustments are being discussed behind the scenes, defense spokesmen give little public sign of worry over the strategic implications of America's budget quandary. "We have not changed our basic strategy," Carlucci told reporters at a Feb. 18 news conference. "It is essentially a forward-based strategy, a strategy of deterrence, a strategy which requires control of sea lanes, close relationships with our allies." Carlucci acknowledged the risks entailed in maintaining such a strategy, which continues to count on a heavy U.S. military presence overseas, with the smaller force size his 1989 budget foresees. But he sidestepped the issue, concluding: "I frankly don't know how we can change a strategy that has successfully deterred major war for some 40 years. I'm not sure which part of the world we'd give up."

Many people would point to Western Europe and Japan in answer to Carlucci's query. "The United States is already spending 60 percent, or $171 billion, of our military budget on the defense of NATO and Japan," said Rep. Patricia Schroeder, D-Colo., chairwoman of the House Armed Services Committee's panel on burden-sharing. "Military spending as a percentage of the total output of goods and services for the United States is 6.2 percent, it drops to 5 percent for the United Kingdom, falls again to 3.1 percent for West Germany and goes as low

Life in the Volunteer Army

Budgetary concerns are bringing into question the future viability of the all-volunteer military. Since conscription was dropped 15 years ago, the armed forces have undergone changes that make some observers question their ability to weather severe spending cutbacks.

Proponents of the military draft originally questioned the forces' ability to attract enough educated young people to serve in the aftermath of the Vietnam War. But the Pentagon points out that for the past eight years it has either met or exceeded its recruiting goals without sacrificing educational standards. In fiscal 1987, 93 percent of new recruits had completed high school, marking the fifth consecutive year that at least 91 percent of recruits had diplomas. The educational preparation of military

recruits far exceeds that of the population as a whole — about a quarter of young people are high school dropouts — thus scrapping predictions that the volunteer force would be a ghetto of poor youth, unqualified to operate the military's increasingly complex weaponry.

The most striking change in the armed forces is the presence of women. Since the volunteer force began, the number of women in the military has jumped from about 50,000 to almost 225,000, or from 2.5 percent to more than 10 percent of all military personnel. Although women are prohibited from serving in positions that would place them in direct combat, sex-discrimination complaints have led all three services to stretch the rules. Women now fill many positions that could expose

them to enemy fire, for example as Air Force tanker pilots, Marine embassy guards or sailors aboard ships that run supplies to Navy warships.

Despite their success, the volunteer forces continue to come under fire from proponents of conscription, including Sen. Sam Nunn, D-Ga., chairman of the Armed Services Committee. He and other supporters for a reconstituted draft system say the "baby bust" of the 1970s will reduce the number of potential recruits in the 1990s. But Pentagon officials do not want to abandon the volunteer force. In spite of the shrinking defense dollar, Carlucci has proposed a 4.3 percent raise in military pay for fiscal 1989 in an effort to attract and retain quality recruits. ■

Past Coverage

■ **Defending Europe** examines the implications of arms control treaties on NATO strategy. The intermediate-range nuclear forces (INF) treaty, whose ratification is expected at the end of May, would remove nuclear weapons from Europe and has prompted calls to modernize the alliance's conventional forces. By Mary H. Cooper, E.R.R., 1987 Vol. II, pp. 673-688.

■ **Defense Economy,** an overview of the "military-industrial complex" President Eisenhower warned against upon leaving office in 1961, shows the difficulty of controlling the military budget and examines the economic impact of defense spending on states and localities. By Mary H. Cooper, E.R.R., 1985 Vol. I, pp. 357-376.

■ **Reagan's Defense Buildup** looks at the current administration's campaign to "rearm America" three years after it was launched. The author concentrates on military-reform efforts which were reaching their peak at the time. By William Sweet, E.R.R., 1984 Vol. I, pp. 309-328.

as 1 percent for Japan."[12] The allies respond that their contribution to the common defense is fair. West Germany, for example, is host to most U.S. military installations in Europe and would serve as the likely battleground in case of war with the Soviet Union. But as America's trade deficit with Japan and Western Europe widens, and concern for the federal budget deficit mounts, calls for a shift in the defense burden to the allies likely will grow louder.

The growing economic strength of America's allies, coupled with this country's entrenched fiscal dilemma, is prompting many military analysts to openly challenge the forward-based strategy and call for a limited withdrawal of U.S. forces from overseas. David P. Calleo of John Hopkins University's School of Advanced International Studies, for example, estimates that $67 billion could be saved by withdrawing half the American divisions assigned to NATO.[13] Tens of billions of dollars could also be saved if the United States reduced its presence in the western Pacific.

The recent progress in U.S.-Soviet arms control initiatives may provide greater leeway for the United States to shift part of the defense burden onto its allies. The intermediate-range nuclear forces (INF) treaty may win Senate approval in time for Reagan and Gorbachev to formally ratify the pact during their next summit, scheduled for the end of May. The treaty, which eliminates an entire class of nuclear weapons now deployed mostly in Europe, is expected to be followed by an even more ambitious agreement to halve both superpowers' strategic nuclear weapons. It also opens the way for a new set of negotiations to reduce conventional weapons. Because the Soviet Union and its Eastern European allies are widely considered to hold a numerical advantage over NATO in tanks and heavy artillery, a negotiated reduction of these weapons could allow the United States more easily to reduce its presence on the continent.

But other forces are at work that make potential candidates for defense-spending cuts harder to identify. The prospect of a U.S.-Soviet agreement to reduce nuclear arms has prompted calls for beefed-up conventional forces, especially by Europeans who fear the pact may signal the beginning of America's disengagement from Europe. In the absence of the intermediate-range nuclear deterrent, they say, NATO's conventional forces must be modernized. Because conventional weapons generally are costlier to develop and maintain than nuclear weapons, such a modernization program would pose an additional burden on the U.S. defense budget. "The INF treaty will not save us money," Carlucci told the Senate Armed Services Committee in January. "With or without an INF treaty, we need to remedy NATO's longstanding conventional shortcomings." The 1989 budget, in fact, calls for almost $240 million for the Balanced Technology Initiative, a research program aimed at developing the kind of "smart" conventional weapons called for by the Long-Term Strategy Commission.

But these ambitious plans once again ignore the growing pressure to reduce federal spending. "The abyss is growing between the Pentagon's grossly unreasonable expectations and the availability of funds to meet them," the former defense planner and aircraft designer concluded. The next president will be left with the problem of how to maintain a viable defense in the 1990s as the cost of weapons continues to increase.

NOTES

[1] The Center for Defense Information, *The Defense Monitor,* 1987 Vol. XVI, No. 7, p. 1. The center, based in Washington, D.C., says it supports a strong national defense but "opposes excessive expenditures for weapons and policies that increase the danger of nuclear war."
[2] Carlucci testified Feb. 25, 1988, before the House Defense Appropriations Subcommittee.
[3] See Paul Kennedy, *The Rise and Fall of the Great Powers: Economic Change and Military Conflict from 1500 to 2000* (1987).
[4] See Office of Management and Budget, *Budget of the United States Government, Fiscal Year 1989,* p. 2a-3.
[5] Writing in *The Washington Post,* Jan. 25, 1987.
[6] William W. Kaufmann, *A Thoroughly Efficient Navy* (1987).
[7] The fiscal 1986 defense authorization act barred certain Pentagon officials from working for defense contractors for two years after leaving government service.
[8] Nick Kotz, *Wild Blue Yonder: Money, Politics and the B-1 Bomber* (1988), p. 235.
[9] Stephen Alexis Cain, "The FY 1989 Defense Budget: Preliminary Analysis," Defense Budget Project, Center on Budget and Policy Priorities, Feb. 22, 1988, p.8.
[10] Congressional Budget Office, "Reducing the Deficit: Spending and Revenue Options," March 1988, p. 36.
[11] Quoted in *The Washington Post,* Feb. 11, 1988.
[12] Schroeder spoke at hearings her panel held March 3 on defense burden-sharing.
[13] See David P. Calleo, *Beyond American Hegemony* (1987).

Graphics: cover, p. 81, Robert Redding

RECOMMENDED READING

BOOKS

Fallows, James, *National Defense*, Random House, 1981.

Although it first appeared before the Reagan buildup took off, this book is still considered by many military reformers to be the best description of how defense industry and Pentagon interests determine procurement practices to the detriment of the national defense. Fallows closely examines two weapons — the Army's M-16 rifle and the Air Force's F-16 fighter — to illustrate how "the culture of procurement in the Pentagon" has produced inferior equipment.

Hart, Gary, and William S. Lind, *America Can Win: The Case for Military Reform*, Adler & Adler, 1986.

Hart, who as a Democratic senator from Colorado was a founder of the Congressional Military Reform Caucus, suggests several changes aimed at improving the country's ability to defend itself. More competition among contractors for weapons projects and the substitution of submarines for aircraft carriers as the Navy's main component are among the recommended structural reforms the authors say are needed to get better results from the defense dollar.

Kotz, Nick, *Wild Blue Yonder: Money, Politics, and the B-1 Bomber*, Pantheon Books, 1988.

Like Fallows, Kotz studies the development of weapons systems to illustrate the interests at work in defense procurement. In this case, the B-1 bomber, a weapon whose military significance four presidents questioned, was shepherded past critics by the Air Force to production as a key element of the Reagan buildup.

Luttwak, Edward N., *The Pentagon and the Art of War*, Simon & Schuster Inc., 1986.

The author, a scholar at the Center for Strategic and International Studies, argues that the Pentagon is dominated by a managerial establishment that lacks combat expertise. A defender of Reagan's buildup of strategic nuclear weapons, Luttwak blames the "officer surplus" for America's lack of combat preparedness.

ARTICLES

Chace, James, "A New Grand Strategy," *Foreign Policy*, spring 1988.

Chace, a senior associate of the Carnegie Endowment and co-author of *America Invulnerable: The Quest for Absolute Security from 1812 to Star Wars* (1988), calls on policy makers to shift their attention from Europe to the Far East, "where the economic stakes are greater than ever and a shifting balance of power creates new opportunities and new dangers for American security." He discounts Western European reluctance to see an American withdrawal from the continent as "a phantom fear" on the part of "rich and powerful" countries.

Morrison, David C., "And Now, the Guillotine," *National Journal*, Feb. 27, 1988.

The article analyzes the Pentagon's planning and budget-making procedures and describes how the Reagan administration's focus on expensive weaponry created "an irresistible 'bow wave' of expanded future spending requirements" that reduces the availability of funds needed to preserve combat-readiness.

Record, Jeffrey, and David B. Rivkin Jr., "Defending Post-INF Europe," *Foreign Affairs*, spring 1988.

The authors see the recently signed intermediate-range nuclear forces (INF) treaty as a "watershed" for Western Europe's defense, in which "the long-standing deficiencies in NATO's conventional force posture are no longer tolerable." But shrinking military budgets and a widespread perception that the Soviet Union poses less of a threat than before mean the alliance "has painted itself into a corner," and is "unwilling or unable to put its non-nuclear defenses in order."

REPORTS AND STUDIES

Cain, Stephen Alexis, "The FY 1989 Defense Budget: Preliminary Analysis," Center on Budget and Policy Priorities, Defense Budget Project, Feb. 22, 1988.

After analyzing the administration's most recent defense budget proposal, the author concludes that "there is a strong probability that in the coming decade too many programs will be competing for resources that did not grow at the rapid rates expected. The President's FY 1989 budget request neglects to make the choices that would alter this legacy."

Center for Defense Information, "Two Trillion Dollars in Seven Years," *The Defense Monitor*, 1987.

This analysis of the Reagan buildup found only "a modest increase in U.S. military weapons and personnel" when compared with the $2 trillion investment made in defense over the past seven years.

Congressional Budget Office, "Quality Soldiers: Costs of Manning the Active Army," June 1986.

While recognizing the improvement in the quality of active-duty enlisted recruits in recent years, CBO questions the Army's ability to continue to attract high-quality personnel. It concludes that "a downturn in recruit quality is likely to begin toward the end of the decade," forcing the Army to devote more funds to manpower at a time when available funds are growing scarcer.

ERR

OCTOBER 30, 1987

PERSIAN GULF OIL

As the industrial
nations continue
to depend on

PERSIAN GULF OIL

OPEC's vast reserves
favor the return
of a stronger cartel.

by Mary H. Cooper

Iran's attacks on an oil tanker and platform inside Kuwait's territorial waters have pulled outside powers deeper into the expanding "tanker war" between Iran and Iraq. The attacks in mid-October came just as U.S. warships completed their 11th mission escorting Kuwaiti oil tankers on the journey from the Gulf of Oman through the Strait of Hormuz to Kuwait's oil-loading terminals at the northern end of the Persian Gulf. Along the way, the U.S. convoy passed mine sweepers, frigates and destroyers of five European nations in what has become the biggest show of Western allied military force outside European territory since World War II.

Why the uncharacteristic show of force? Neither America nor any of the other countries whose navies are present in the gulf has a defense commitment in the region. All have carefully maintained a formal position of neutrality in the seven-year war of attrition between Iran and Iraq. However, the industrial nations look to the Middle East — in particular, the countries around the Persian Gulf — for much of their energy needs.

In the short run, the Western powers are concerned that either of the combatants in the war might halt the flow of oil through the Strait of Hormuz, the narrow passage at the southern end of the gulf. The construction of overland oil pipelines to the Red Sea and the Mediterranean Sea has only diminished, not eliminated, the strait's strategic importance. A sudden cutoff of tanker traffic would still reduce the worldwide supply of oil.

No one knows for sure what such a cutoff would mean for the world's economy. In today's glutted oil market, a cutoff might not even push prices above their current level of about $20 a barrel. But oil prices are as vulnerable to

An accidental attack on the U.S.S. Stark *by an Iraqi jet, May 17, 1987, tore a gaping hole in the warship and caused concern over the plan to provide U.S. military protection to reflagged Kuwaiti oil tankers.*

panic buying as to changes in actual supply and demand. Given the precarious state of the international economy, of which the recent gyrations on the world's stock exchanges are a symptom, a sudden rise in prices could trigger a recession. "We learned from the 1970s that severe dislocations in supplies and prices affect us immediately," said Energy Secretary John S. Herrington as he concluded a tour of Persian Gulf suppliers in mid-October.

The U.S.-led naval presence in the Persian Gulf also reflects a longer-term concern. Despite the development of oil fields outside the volatile Middle East and efforts by the major industrial nations to reduce oil consumption, they continue to depend on oil imports for much of their energy needs. Moreover, proven oil reserves in other parts of the world are diminishing, while those of the Persian Gulf region will become more important in coming years. In this sense, the naval presence of America and its European allies in and around the gulf is a statement of their stake in preventing a cutoff.

In the early years of the Iran-Iraq war, which broke out in September 1980, the conflict was largely confined to attacks across the two countries' common border, which extends northward from the eastern side of the gulf. As neither country gained the upper hand in land warfare, the field of combat shifted to the gulf in 1984. Each tried to knock out the other's ability to export oil, the financial lifeblood of both Iran and Iraq. In this latest phase of the conflict, known as the "tanker war," oil tankers belonging to other gulf nations and consumer nations have come under attack by Iraqi and Iranian gunners. When Iran

struck the Kuwaiti ship, the war escalated again. The attack prompted a U.S. retaliatory strike against an Iranian offshore oil platform, as well as a ban on Iranian imports to this country — mostly oil.

Of course, there are other forces behind the U.S. mission in the Persian Gulf. One is this country's ongoing contest with the Soviet Union for maximum influence in the Middle East, and particularly in Israel's ongoing struggle with its Arab neighbors. This consideration was clearly at work in the U.S. decision last March to assist Kuwait, which came only after the Soviet Union announced it was prepared to do so. Although the Soviet Union is a net oil exporter and has no direct stake in the free passage of oil through the Strait of Hormuz, it has recently improved relations with some traditionally pro-Western Arab oil producers, such as Kuwait. But Moscow is hedging its bets on the war's outcome: While continuing to arm the socialist regime of Saddam Hussein in Iraq, the Soviets have made overtures to Iran and last summer voted with the United States for a U.N. Security Council resolution calling for a cease-fire. The warming of Soviet relations with the region's powers, in addition to Moscow's offer to protect Kuwait's merchant fleet, pushed the Reagan administration to undertake the reflagging operation. *(See box, p. 98.)*

Another factor in U.S. policy in the gulf is the concern that an Iranian victory in the war would allow the regime of Ayatollah Ruhallah Khomeini to make good on his vow to spread the revolution of Islamic fundamentalism throughout the region. The U.S.-led flotilla that is protecting the sea lanes also is strengthening Iraq's hand in the war, and the

Iraqis have stepped up attacks on Iranian oil facilities.

But underlying the U.S.-Soviet contest in the Middle East and concerns about the spread of Islamic revolution is the Persian Gulf's strategic importance as energy supplier to the world. The region contains more than half of the world's proven oil reserves. Although other oil sources in less troubled areas — including the United States, the North Sea, Mexico and Venezuela — have filled much of the West's energy needs in recent years, these deposits are being depleted. Barring unforeseen developments in alternative energy sources, the oil producers of the region, including the combatants in the war and the Arab states on the western side of the gulf, will soon be in a position to control the oil market even more than the Organization of Petroleum Exporting Countries (OPEC) did in the 1970s.

War's impact on the West

When the United States accepted Kuwait's request to protect its tankers, America's European allies, who are also heavy oil consumers, initially condemned the operation as a military overreaction, motivated more by America's rivalry with the Soviet Union than a clear assessment of the risks involved in introducing military force in the Persian Gulf. But the European nations overcame their hesitancy to join the U.S. naval operations when their own ships came increasingly under fire toward the end of last summer.

By mid-October, Britain, France and Italy had joined the 41-warship American flotilla, while ships from Belgium and the Netherlands were on their way to the gulf. Japan and West Germany declined, citing constitutional limitations deriving from World War II on the extent of their foreign military actions. The presence of the six-nation fleet in the gulf underscores the Western stake in an escalating war that increasingly has centered on the destruction of oil supply lines.

Early in the war, Iraq was forced to curtail oil shipments from its main oil-loading facility on the Faw peninsula, a blow that cut Iraqi oil exports from more than 2.5 million barrels a day in 1980 to 1 million the next year. Iraq responded, however, by building a network of overland pipelines beyond striking range of Iranian artillery. By this year, the pipelines had enabled Iraq to build its oil exports back up to 1.8 million barrels a day.

Until recently, Iran had escaped serious damage to its oil traffic. Despite the widening of the war to the gulf in 1984, and disruptions caused by Iraqi air strikes last year, Iranian exports held steady at about their 1982 level of 2.2 million barrels a day. But since the recent arrival of

Public Opinion

Opinion polls have charted a growing approval of President Reagan's actions in the Persian Gulf and support for a U.S. military presence. About 75 percent of the public believes that the U.S. should maintain a military presence in the Gulf and a growing majority endorses the president's policy of escorting reflagged Kuwaiti oil tankers. The greatest shift in public opinion shows a majority of Americans now believe continued U.S. military presence in the Persian Gulf is important even if it carries the risk of war.

When asked about a U.S. military presence and the risk of war, respondents answered:

	June 29	Aug. 12	Oct. 19
U.S. should maintain military presence AND important enough to risk war	34%	34%	54%
U.S. should maintain military presence BUT NOT important enough to risk war	44	40	24
U.S. should NOT maintain military presence	20	25	17

Source: The Washington Post/ABC News

Western warships in the gulf, Iraq has stepped up attacks against Iran's main oil terminal on Kharg Island and other oil facilities, resulting in a falloff of Iranian oil exports by as much as 500,000 barrels a day.

In the past year, air strikes on ships in the gulf have become more numerous, especially Iranian attacks on ships doing business with Kuwait and Iraq's other Arab allies on the western side of the gulf. According to the Washington-based Center for Defense Information, more than 380 ships from 32 countries have been attacked by Iran or Iraq in the Persian Gulf and the Gulf of Oman since the war broke out in 1980. While most of the targets were Iranian, many others were foreign ships flying the flags of Panama or Liberia, where commercial registry is relatively cheap. Two of the tankers hit by gunfire were American vessels, and 17 belonged to the five European countries that have sent contingents to the area in recent weeks.

What would a cutoff mean?

Beyond the peril to individual ships, the oil-importing nations see a larger potential danger. What if the war does shut down the flow of oil through the Strait of Hormuz? Western nations and Japan have reduced their dependence on the Persian Gulf in recent years by learning to conserve oil and finding other suppliers. But memories of the disastrous economic shocks in the late 1970s remain vivid.

The major factor working in favor of consumers is the glutted condition of the oil market, which resulted from OPEC's price increases of the 1970s. High oil prices made it worthwhile to extract oil in areas outside the Middle East, such as the North Sea. As the consuming nations turned to these sources, demand for OPEC oil fell by 40 percent between 1979 and 1982 alone — a blow from which the cartel has yet to recover. Meanwhile, efforts to hold down production within the cartel failed, as producers were eager to maintain the flow of petrodollars into their economies. The result was an oil glut that caused prices to plunge.

Many experts predict that current overproduction will absorb the tanker war's destabilizing effects — even a shutdown in the gulf. "...[W]hile the common wisdom predicts oil-price increases as Persian Gulf hostilities continue, nothing will keep prices high if there is a glut of oil on the world market," say Hossein Askari, a professor of international finance at George Washington University, and Charles H. Wilbanks, a student at the Johns Hopkins University's School of Advanced International Studies. "Such a glut is likely to grow as OPEC and Saudi Arabia expand their production beyond their quota limits. This means there is ample reason to look for a significant and sustained drop in the price of oil in the months ahead." [1]

Another factor working in the oil consumers' favor is the fact that the Strait of Hormuz is less of a "choke point" than it was a decade ago. "Sources are available outside the gulf, and what comes from there does not all come by ship through the Strait of Hormuz," says Philip Garon, spokesman for the Paris-based International Energy Agency, an organization set up by 21 consuming nations after 1973 to coordinate efforts to avert future energy crises.

Of the 9.5 million barrels exported daily from the region in the second quarter of this year, Garon says, 2 million were pumped out through pipelines. Herrington says: "One of the things I found out on this trip is there are three or four major countries over there that are working hard on pipelines. By 1990 or 1992, about 7 to 8 million barrels of oil will be traveling out of the gulf by pipelines, not by tanker, and that is a big change in the geopolitical implications of what that oil means to us." [2]

Even before the outbreak of the war, a network of pipelines linked oil terminals in Saudi Arabia and Iraq with ports outside the gulf. Syria, Iraq's traditional adversary in the struggle for regional dominance, cut off the flow of Iraqi oil in two important pipelines that pass through Syrian territory on their way to Lebanese ports on the Mediterranean. The cutoff also shut down Saudi Arabia's overland route to the Mediterranean. But newer pipelines bypass Syria, and still others are being planned. An addition to a pipeline linking Iraqi oil fields with the Turkish port of Ceyhan on the Mediterranean has increased that vital line's capacity by half, bringing it to 1.5 million barrels a day by the end of last summer.

By stepping up hostile actions against Iraq's supporters in the region, Iran has encouraged further pipeline development. Saudi Arabia, which had delayed construction of a new pipeline that would carry Iraqi oil to the Saudi port of Yanbu on the Red Sea, decided to complete the project following last summer's violent demonstrations by Iranian pilgrims in the Saudi city of Mecca, Islam's holiest site.

Iran remains far more dependent than the other Persian Gulf nations on freedom of navigation through the Strait of Hormuz. The only existing pipeline Iran could conceivably use to export oil is a disused gas conduit to the Soviet Union. If it were extended, it could carry Iranian crude oil to ports on the Black Sea. But despite recent high-level exchanges between Iran and the Soviet Union, such an arrangement appears unlikely in the near future.

Although gulf producers still furnish two-thirds of all crude oil sold by OPEC, their share of the world market has shrunk. High oil prices in the 1970s encouraged the importing countries to search for new fields and open some that had been left untapped before the oil-price shocks because of high drilling costs. Oil production outside OPEC now yields more than 5 million barrels a day, mostly from a doubling of Mexican production and the full-scale exploitation by Britain and Norway of the fields under the North Sea. Brazil and India, which imported OPEC oil in the 1970s, increased their output and are now self-sufficient.

By turning elsewhere, some of the world's biggest oil-consuming nations have succeeded in greatly reducing their dependence on supplies shipped through the Strait of Hormuz. Although it has assumed the most visible military role in the gulf, the United States today depends on tanker-shipped crude oil from the gulf for only 5 percent of its imported oil. Only two industrial nations — Japan and Italy — still depend on it for more than a third of their imports.

Conservation efforts have also made the worldless dependent on Middle Eastern oil. According to U.S. Energy Department estimates, countries outside the Soviet bloc and China cut their total consumption of oil from a peak of 52 million barrels a day in 1979 to about 46 million by 1985. The 24 leading industrial nations' share fell from 42 million to 34 million barrels a day over the same period. Although the recession of the early 1980s explains much of this change, the decline in oil consumption was accompanied by the increased use of other energy sources. Worldwide nuclear energy production increased over the same period by an average 14 percent a year, while consumers also turned increasingly to coal, natural gas and hydroelectric power as substitutes for oil.

A joint oil-sharing program is another strategy undertaken by major industrial nations to lessen their dependence on freedom of navigation through Mideast waters. The main vehicle for this effort is the International Energy Agency's oil-sharing facility. Under the agency's emergency plan, a disruption in any member country's oil imports of 7 percent or more would trigger a coordinated drawdown of oil stockpiles member governments have set aside for this purpose.

As of Oct. 1, says agency spokesman Garon, the 24 industrial nations represented in the Organization for Economic Cooperation and Development (OECD) [3] possessed 443 million metric tons of oil, or 3 billion barrels, in government stockpiles and inventories owned by oil companies. These stockpiles, nearly 20 times bigger than inventories on hand in 1979, when the most recent price shock occurred, would meet the member countries' energy

Reflagging for Protection

Since the first oil embargo of 1973, American presidents have asserted that the free passage of oil through the Strait of Hormuz is a matter of U.S. national interest. But the current escort mission involving 41 American combat vessels in and around the Persian Gulf is the first instance of direct U.S. military involvement to ensure freedom of navigation through the strait. It may also be the first time the United States has introduced military force in any part of the world through the complex process of "reflagging."

In the past, shipowners who sought to sail their vessels under foreign flags did so for commercial purposes. All ships sailing in international waters must be registered under a national flag. Many shipowners chose to register their vessels in nations where taxes were lower, as in Panama or Liberia. Requests by foreigners to reflag their vessels under U.S. registry have been less common.

The Kuwaiti reflagging operation was undertaken solely to gain U.S. military protection for Kuwait's oil export trade. Under U.S. law, any American-registered vessel has access to the protection of the U.S. Navy.

Kuwait initially requested U.S. naval protection for 11 oil tankers last December, after its ships were fired on by Iranian gunboats. The United States declined immediate help, saying protection could be granted only after Kuwait completed normal reflagging procedures. Under U.S. law, a shipowner seeking to reflag a vessel must first establish a corporation in the United States and satisfy Coast Guard safety standards.

However, in early March, the Soviet Union agreed to lease two Soviet-flagged tankers to Kuwait. Soon after, the United States reversed its position. Although Kuwait did set up a corporation in the United States, the Delaware-based Chesapeake Shipping Corp., the Defense Department waived for one year the safety and other regulations normally required of reflagged vessels.

"Essentially, they had to paint a new name on the stern, hoist a new flag and hire an American captain," explains Sam Gardiner of the Center for Defense Information in Washington, D.C.

PERSIAN GULF OIL
Sea Routes and Pipelines

Black Sea

SOVIET UNION

SOVIET UNION

TURKEY

Caspian Sea

Ceyhan

Baniyas

Tripoli

SYRIA

Mediterranean Sea

Sidon

LEBANON

Tehran

Baghdad

IRAN

| Oil Pipeline | - - - |
| Gas Line | .... |

Closed to Mediterranean Sea

IRAQ

ISRAEL

JORDAN

Basra

Faw Peninsula

Closed to Mediterranean Sea

Kharg Island

0   250

MILES

KUWAIT

EGYPT

Strait of Hormuz

Manama

Persian Gulf

BAHRAIN

Yanbu

QATAR

Riyadh

UNITED ARAB EMIRATES

Red Sea

OMAN

SAUDI ARABIA

RELYING ON HORMUZ

	*Daily Imports, 1986 (Thousands of Barrels)	Percent of Oil Imports
JAPAN	2,226	52
ITALY	705	35
FRANCE	471	24
NETHERLANDS	438	24
SPAIN	210	20
WEST GERMANY	215	9
UNITED STATES	781	5
BRITAIN	102	3
CANADA	55	2

* Oil shipped through Strait of Hormuz
Source: House Armed Services Committee

NAVAL PRESENCE

	Combat Ships	Support Ships
UNITED STATES	41	15
FRANCE	10	4
BRITAIN	7	2
ITALY	6	2
BELGIUM	2	1
NETHERLANDS	2	—
SOVIET UNION	9	13

As of Oct. 23, 1987
Source: Center for Defense Information

NORTH YEMEN

SOUTH YEMEN

SUDAN

ETHIOPIA

Arabian Sea

AT ISSUE

Should the United States be policing the Persian Gulf on its own?

YES says Michael Sterner, former ambassador to the United Arab Emirates and deputy assistant secretary of state, now a consultant on international affairs. "The [reflagging] debate has focused on one interest — maintenance of the oil shipping lanes in the Persian Gulf — but has neglected a second that is equally important.

This is to insure the territorial integrity and political independence of the gulf's Arab states, which produce 80 percent of the oil that leaves the gulf and whose oil reserves are even more important for the future. We cannot afford to have these countries quarrel under the influence of a power whose purposes are hostile to the United States, whether that power is the Soviet Union or Iran. . . .

[T]he greatest danger to Western interests is the possibility of an Iranian victory over Iraq, which would extend Iran's influence throughout the Gulf and encourage Islamic extremist movements elsewhere in the Middle East. . . .

Some critics, pointing out correctly that gulf oil is at least as important to our allies as it is to us, have called for creation of a United Nations peacekeeping naval force to protect freedom of navigation in the gulf.

The presence of allied warships is a valuable symbol of Western political solidarity, but we must also be realistic.

Ultimately, only America has the naval and air power to provide an effective military deterrent, and we cannot allow the credibility of that deterrent to be enfeebled by the constraints of collective action. We have seen the difficulty even our own naval command had in devising rules of engagement for its ships. Can anyone believe that it would be feasible to arrive at a consensus among half a dozen naval powers about rules of engagement in the gulf's complex environment? . . .

Two successive presidents have declared that the gulf is vital to our interests and that we are prepared to use military force if necessary to protect those interests.

A superpower cannot keep saying these things and then not do anything when put to the test. Either the statements should not have been made or we must now be willing to back them up. . . .

The [Reagan] administration has not been very adroit about [selling this policy.] It is hung up between public professions of 'neutrality' and the obvious fact that our actions have 'tilted' toward Iraq. Its proclivity toward anti-Soviet rhetoric makes it describe the threat in the gulf as Soviet expansionism, even though this does not explain why we should be favoring one side in the Iran-Iraq conflict.

This public-relations dilemma is unfortunate . . . but it should not obscure what needs to be done in the gulf. The thrust of our policy is to maintain pressure on Iran in order to dissuade it from continuing to pursue the war. The task now is to carry out that policy in a way that demonstrates firmness while keeping diplomatic doors open for any sign of change in Iran's policy."

From an op-ed article in The New York Times, *June 24, 1987.*

NO say Cyrus R. Vance, secretary of state in the Carter administration, and Elliot L. Richardson, secretary of defense in the second Nixon administration. Both are now officers of the United Nations Association of the USA. "Neither the presence of Western and Soviet navies nor the initiation of United Nations diplomacy has stopped the [Iran-Iraq] war on land or at sea. Each day, more ships are attacked, more cities are bombed and more civilians die. An equilibrium of sorts has evolved, but it is neither stable nor permanent. . . . [T]he Western countries have demonstrated their commitment to keeping the sea lanes open and to aiding their friends in the region.

Now it is time for the next stage — for a bolder United Nations initiative before an unanticipated incident undoes these promising first steps toward concerted international action.

Our proposal for the provision of United Nations observers and lightly armed patrol boats, to be drawn from countries other than the United States and Soviet Union, does not contemplate the assembling of a United Nations armada of warships.

The parallel presence of naval contingents from major powers, however, could underline the message that attacks on unarmed commercial vessels, especially those flying the United Nations flag alongside their own, would be unacceptable.

A Security Council authorization of even a modest United Nations naval presence in the gulf would permit important Western countries now sitting on the sidelines to assist the joint undertaking. . . .

Such a mission would not require the United States to abandon its commitment to Kuwait or to beat a hasty retreat from the gulf. . . .

Furthermore, should the exchanges of fire between United States and Iranian forces continue to escalate, it is in our interest to have the international community firmly on our side, as we did in Korea.

That would be far easier to achieve if the Security Council authorized efforts to keep the sea lanes open before an incident rather than for the United States to seek international support after the fact.

By going it alone, the United States has only one sanction to impose: military escalation. By working through the United Nations, the alternatives range from diplomatic censure, economic sanctions, oil or arms embargoes to joint military action. . . .

Iranian leaders, moreover, should find it more palatable to defer to a United Nations presence than to an American one as part of a comprehensive peace settlement package. . . ."

From an op-ed article in The New York Times, *Oct. 20, 1987. The association is a non-profit organization that carries out research and educational programs on the United Nations and other multilateral institutions.*

needs for 164 days, nearly six months, greatly diminishing the immediate effect of a cutoff of Persian Gulf oil. "The Western countries are better prepared this time," he says.

Though better prepared than before, are the industrial nations prepared to withstand a cutoff? A congressional report issued in July concluded that "... closing the Strait of Hormuz could cause a net supply shortfall of about 4 million barrels per day, or roughly 9 percent of the free world's supply, even after resort to all the surplus capacity outside the Persian Gulf." Barring government intervention in the market, it predicted, "...the price of oil could double or triple to roughly $40 to $60 per barrel." [4]

Although the United States, the world's biggest consumer, depends on Persian Gulf oil for a small fraction of its imports, this country is affected by its trading partners' dependency on the region. Japan, the second-largest consumer, imports nearly all its oil — half of it from the Persian Gulf. Last year, Japan bought more than a third of the region's exports. Italy depends on the gulf for about a third of its oil, and France and the Netherlands import about a fourth of theirs from the gulf. *(See table, p. 99.)*

Moreover, despite the flurry of strikes against noncombatant tankers this year, Garon says the flow of Persian Gulf oil through the Strait of Hormuz is on the rise in the third quarter of this year. While data are not yet available for that period, 7.5 million barrels a day were shipped out of the gulf by tanker during the second quarter, 5.8 million destined for the 24 OECD countries.

A smaller, stronger cartel

If the risks of a Persian Gulf cutoff today are difficult to gauge, tomorrow's situation is clearer. It will favor the re-emergence of a smaller, more cohesive cartel centered on the Persian Gulf, with enhanced control over the world oil market. As most of OPEC's African, Asian and South American members exhaust their oil reserves, power within the cartel will be concentrated among Persian Gulf producers.

Last year's oil-price collapse and the glut of the oil market may have blurred Western perceptions of OPEC's potential strength as the world's dominant oil broker. Cheap oil has dulled Americans' memory of the long gas lines they endured in the 1970s, and consumption in the United States has steadily risen since 1983. At the same time, weak oil prices have discouraged production in this country, where oil is less accessible and thus more expensive to extract than in many other parts of the world.

As domestic production continues to decline, American dependence on oil imports is expected to rise from a third of the country's energy needs today to more than half in the next decade. At the same time, the position of gulf producers will improve. "You cannot downplay the importance of the gulf region," says Garon. "We are bound to be

OPEC Production and Reserves

	1986 Production (million barrels/day)	Reserves (million barrels)
Saudi Arabia	9.2	169,200
Kuwait	2.3	94,500
Iran	3.4	48,800
Iraq	1.9	47,100
United Arab Emirates	2.0	33,100
Venezuela	2.5	25,000
Libya	1.8	21,300
Nigeria	2.0	16,000
Algeria	1.2	8,800
Indonesia	1.5	8,300
Qatar	0.6	3,200
Ecuador	0.3	1,700
Gabon	0.2	600

Source: Energy Department

increasingly dependent on that region, especially as U.S. output and production in the North Sea decline."

While new deposits have been discovered in Norway and parts of northern Canada and Alaska, none promises to match the contribution made by Alaska's North Slope and the North Sea, which since 1975 have yielded 5 million barrels a day of non-OPEC crude oil. According to oil company statistics, domestic U.S. oil production may last for only nine more years, while Britain's offshore deposits in the North Sea may run out by the year 2010. [5] These estimates lead many oil analysts to predict that non-OPEC production will peak before the end of the 1980s. "Even if output does not then fall precipitously, there will be few if any non-OPEC countries, or for that matter, non-Persian Gulf OPEC countries that will have any export capacity by the mid-1990s," predicts George C. Georgiou, a professor of economics at Towson State University in Maryland. [6]

In the long run, the tightening of the oil market will reduce OPEC membership. Of the cartel's 13 members, Algeria, Ecuador, Gabon, Indonesia and Nigeria are already producing at near-capacity levels and their own needs will leave little for export. Of the members outside the Persian Gulf, only Venezuela and Libya have large enough oil reserves to assure their position as major exporters beyond the 1990s.

In contrast, the major Persian Gulf producers contain more than half the world's proven oil reserves. Kuwait, Iraq and Saudi Arabia are expected to continue pumping crude for 250, 104 and 99 more years, leading many experts to predict that the war-torn Persian Gulf will assume the dominant role in the world oil market as early as the mid-1990s.

By that time, the core OPEC producers may have strengthened their hand by diversifying their economies, especially through "downstreaming" within the oil industry by refining crude into gasoline and other petroleum derivatives and selling them at the retail level. Because

Past Coverage

■ **Oil Prices: Collapse and Consequences** examines the impact of Saudi Arabia's decision in December 1985 to abandon its traditional role as "swing producer" — that of cutting its oil production as necessary to try to maintain prices set by the Organization of Petroleum Exporting Countries (OPEC). As world oil production grew, prices fell, bringing relief for consumers but causing a recession in oil-producing areas, including parts of the United States. "Worse yet," notes author Richard C. Schroeder, "falling oil prices tend to discourage the development of new energy sources." E.R.R., 1986 Vol. I, pp. 245-64.

■ **Quest for Energy Independence** reviews American energy policy in the wake of the oil-price shocks of the mid to late 1970s. Although the United States has made "significant gains" in its effort to reduce energy consumption, writes Roger Thompson, "the nation is still vulnerable to another embargo or other disruption in its oil supply, and that vulnerability is likely to continue for the foreseeable future." E.R.R., 1983 Vol. II, pp. 965-84.

they own the reserves and can extract oil at relatively low cost, the gulf states also could produce petrochemicals and other products derived from oil at lower cost than many competitors.

Of all OPEC's core members, Kuwait has moved the furthest along the path of oil diversification. Since buying out Gulf Oil Corp.'s operations in Western Europe in 1981, state-owned Kuwait Petroleum Co. has spread its retail network to include some 5,000 "Q8" gas stations on the continent and plans to extend its operations to North America. [7] The sheikdom has also developed an extensive overseas oil exploration industry as well as a transportation industry that includes the tankers the U.S. forces are currently escorting through the gulf.

Downstreaming efforts in other gulf states have been less successful. Even Saudi Arabia, the region's leader in oil production and exports, has thus far failed to expand its economic base significantly. Although it has 10 refineries and produces more than half the gulf's liquefied natural gas, Saudi Arabia lags behind Kuwait in developing an extensive retail network for its oil and refined products.

For now, most OPEC members are still paying for the cartel's excessive price increases of the past. During the cartel's heyday, which lasted from 1973-85, more than $1 trillion flowed into the gulf region. But since the early 1980s, the oil glut has depressed the value of the region's oil exports: Saudi Arabia alone saw its economy shrink to just $70 billion in 1986, less than half the 1981 figure.

Saudi Arabia's plight worsened with changes in the country's production policy. In December 1985, the Saudis,

exasperated by their partners' refusal to honor production quotas, abandoned their role as "swing producer" — adjusting production to try to maintain steady oil prices within the cartel. The oil glut increased and prices fell.

Because the gulf states invested much of their earlier earnings in Western and Japanese banks and securities, they have been able to draw on these savings to soften the impact of falling oil revenues at home. Most have cut back on construction projects they undertook in the 1970s, while maintaining the free health care, education and other social services they have used to counter Iranian revolutionary ideas.

But the cushion provided by past oil revenues will not last forever. The other gulf nations' ability to follow Kuwait's lead into downstream operations will determine how strong a hold OPEC will have over the oil market in the next decade. As the past few years have shown, control over the extraction and sale of crude oil does not afford complete control over prices and demand.

There is one big obstacle to a comeback for the cartel: the war. As long as two of its members are locked in combat, Persian Gulf producers will be unable to plot an effective market strategy. The war has created some rifts that make pricing and production agreements among the contentious group of nations harder to reach than ever.

Iran is pushing OPEC to abandon its official price lid of $18 a barrel in the hope of boosting revenues for the war effort. Some other OPEC members, including Libya and Algeria, are supporting Iran's effort. Other members of the cartel, led by Saudi Arabia, Kuwait, the United Arab Emirates and Qatar, are trying to thwart the move in the interest of restoring market stability, as well as denying Iran an advantage over Iraq.

If prices are allowed to rise too far, these gulf states say, the consuming nations will be encouraged to develop alternative energy sources and loosen their long-term dependence on the oil producers with the biggest reserves. Saudi Arabia will press the other cartel members to honor their quotas. It will not be an easy case to make, however, because most of the cartel's members, including Kuwait and Iraq, are said to be producing above quota, and production limits are nearly impossible to detect or enforce.

NOTES

[1] The views of Askari and Wilbanks appeared in *The New York Times* Oct. 18, 1987.

[2] Herrington was interviewed Oct. 22, 1987, on the *MacNeil/Lehrer News Hour*.

[3] OECD members are the United States, Canada, Japan, France, Britain, Italy, West Germany, Austria, Belgium, Denmark, Finland, Greece, Iceland, Ireland, Luxembourg, the Netherlands, Norway, Portugal, Spain, Sweden, Switzerland, Turkey, Australia and New Zealand.

[4] The report, issued by the House Armed Services Defense Policy Panel and Investigations Subcommittee, is entitled "National Security Policy Implications of United States Operations in the Persian Gulf," July 1987.

[5] Published in the "BP Statistical Review of World Energy,"

[6] George C. Georgiou, "Oil Market Instability and a New OPEC," *World Policy Journal*, spring 1987, p. 304.

[7] See *The Wall Street Journal*, June 25, 1987, p. 1.

Graphics: cover, p. 95, UPI/Bettmann Newsphotos; p. 99, Roy Gallop.

RECOMMENDED READING

BOOKS

Hameed, Mazher A., *Arabia Imperiled: The Security Imperatives of the Arab Gulf States*, Middle East Assessments Group, 1986.

A Saudi analyst of international security issues looks at his country, the United Arab Emirates, Oman, Qatar, Bahrain and Kuwait — the six Arab oil-exporting lands on the western side of the Persian Gulf that collaborate in military and economic matters through the Gulf Cooperation Council. Hameed concludes that their oil has bolstered their position as "a conservative counterweight in the Arab world" to such radical Islamic regimes as Iran and Libya.

Stobaugh, Robert and Daniel Yergin, ed., *Energy Future*, Random House, 1979.

The challenge of developing alternative energy sources posed in this classic study by the Harvard Business School's energy project remains as relevant today as during the energy crisis of the late 1970s. The authors trace the increasing U.S. dependence on oil from the Middle East and analyze the feasibility of reducing that dependence.

ARTICLES

Georgiou, George C., "Oil Market Instability and a New OPEC," *World Policy Journal*, spring 1987.

A stronger oil cartel will emerge from the current disarray within the Organization of Petroleum Exporting Countries (OPEC), the author predicts. Because oil reserves in other parts of the world are fast running out at the same time the industrial nations increase their energy consumption, the Persian Gulf states will soon be in a position to dominate the market even more than they did in the 1970s.

Greider, William, "Up Shiites Creek," *Rolling Stone*, Oct. 22, 1987.

The author emphasizes the contradictions in U.S. policy toward the Iran-Iraq war and the difficulty of formulating alliances in a conflict that involves oil trade and superpower competition as well as a profound upheaval in social and political identities in the Middle East.

Morse, Edward L., "After the Fall: The Politics of Oil," *Foreign Affairs*, spring 1986.

Political differences within OPEC led to the oil price collapse of 1986 and could spell trouble for the cartel's future cohesion, the author predicts. Saudi Arabia, which has large oil reserves, wants to hold prices low enough so that consumer nations will lack the incentive to develop alternative energy sources. Other OPEC members are more interested in squeezing as much money as they can out of their reserves. Morse is managing director of the Petroleum Finance Company Ltd. in Washington, D.C.

REPORTS AND STUDIES

Energy Information Administration, "Monthly Energy Review," June 1987.

This U.S. Energy Department publication includes data on production, consumption, stocks, imports, exports and prices of the principal energy commodities in the United States for the first half of 1987. It also contains statistics on oil production by the major crude-oil exporters and imports by the largest industrial nations since 1973. Copies are available for $6.50 from the Superintendent of Documents, Government Printing Office, Washington, D.C. 20402-9325.

House Armed Services Committee Defense Policy Panel and Investigations Subcommittee, "National Security Policy Implications of United States Operations in the Persian Gulf," July 1987.

The committee's analysis of the U.S. reflagging of Kuwaiti tankers includes a concise description of oil routes through the Strait of Hormuz as well as the industrial nations' dependence on this source of oil. The report concludes that the Reagan administration's military presence in the gulf "is presumably based first on inhibiting Soviet expansion into the gulf and meddling in gulf-state politics, and perhaps only secondarily on improving relations with the Kuwaitis and other moderate gulf states." The report costs $3.25 and may be obtained from the Superintendent of Documents, Government Printing Office, Washington, D.C. 20402-9325.

International Energy Agency, "Annual Oil Market Report 1986," 1987.

This Paris-based organization, founded by 21 industrial nations of the Organization for Economic Cooperation and Development (OECD) in the wake of the 1973 OPEC oil embargo, collects worldwide energy data. This year's report finds: "Continued rising OECD consumption, combined with declining upstream activity [such as drilling and extraction] by its petroleum industries, would almost certainly presage an increased level of dependence on oil imports from high-reserve areas of the Middle East." Available from OECD Publications, 2 rue André-Pascal, 75775 PARIS CEDEX 16, France.

U.S. Energy Department, "Energy Security: A Report to the President of the United States," March 1987.

This report, prepared at President Reagan's request in the wake of declining domestic oil production and rising oil imports, examines the U.S. oil industry as well as alternative sources of energy, especially natural gas, electricity, coal and nuclear power. The report costs $16 and may be obtained from the Superintendent of Documents, Government Printing Office, Washington, D.C. 20402-9325.

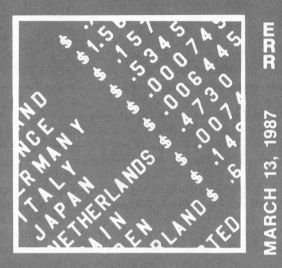

DOLLAR DIPLOMACY

World trade may be more stable with managed exchange rates, but U.S. benefits are uncertain. *106*

The Paris agreement has dual aims: stabilizing exchange rates and changing budget policies. *107*

Japan's 'comprehensive' plan to stimulate consumer spending isn't likely to materialize soon. *109*

West Germany's fears of inflation make it a reluctant partner in the Paris exchange-rate pact. *111*

France is hurting, but the weak American dollar has aided Britain's economy. *112*

America's deficit reduction pledge looms large as an obstacle to making the Paris agreement work. *114*

An exchange-rate pact
in Paris was a victory for

DOLLAR DIPLOMACY

but the goal of stable
world trade hinges
on economic pledges
that won't be easy to keep.

by Mary H. Cooper

For the moment, at least, the Paris agreement by six of the world's major industrial powers to stabilize exchange rates seems to be working. Since the Feb. 22 meeting in Paris, the dollar has held steady against the Japanese yen and the West German mark, the world's other two most frequently traded currencies, indicating that foreign exchange markets have taken the pact seriously.

The agreement to halt the dollar's plunge came just two years after it reached a peak, at a time when the soaring greenback allowed Americans to see the world on the cheap and develop a taste for luxury imports. But what was good for American consumers was not beneficial for U.S. industry. In early 1985, as the dollar was at its peak, sales of imported cars rose 15 percent in this country, where dollars went further in the purchase of foreign goods because of the American currency's appreciation. But meanwhile, U.S. products languished on foreign markets, where it took more yen, marks and other currencies to buy American.

In early 1985, when Treasury Secretary James A. Baker III undertook the task of reversing the dollar's upward course, and America's trading fortunes, he faced stiff opposition. Even among allies, one country's strong currency is another's ticket to greater prosperity and not something to be given up without a struggle. Seen from Japan and West Germany, the strong dollar was a godsend, allowing their export industries to capture a bigger market share from American producers.

But America's hand was stronger by September of that year, after Baker resorted to currency intervention — in essence putting large amounts of dollars into circulation by trading them for other currencies through the Federal Reserve System. With the dollar falling, America's trading partners were mindful that their exports were becoming increasingly expensive. At a meeting at New York's Plaza Hotel, America, Britain, France, Japan and West Germany agreed for the first time to try to stabilize exchange rates, and world trade, by jointly intervening in their various currencies. *(See pp. 110-111.)*

Although the goal of stability had not been realized, the incentive for cooperation was even stronger when the nations met again at Paris this February. During the previous 12 months, the dollar had plunged faster and farther than America's trading partners intended, and Baker's case for a new joint agreement was far more persuasive.

After months of bickering, including independent efforts by Japan and Germany to strengthen their currencies, and the collapse of the Plaza accord, the stage was set for another agreement. In it, the five trading partners and Canada, which endorsed the pact negotiated by the others, agreed to resume joint management of exchange rates. At Baker's urging, they also went a step further, agreeing that America, West Germany and Japan would make domestic policy changes that would bring more balance among world trade accounts.

The Paris agreement— which British finance minister Nigel Lawson dubbed "Plaza II" — was widely applauded as a difficult but necessary compromise. In theory, it is a significant step toward a jointly managed world economy.

But in reality, its success is far from assured, particularly because of the policy promises that make the agreement unique. Pledges by Germany and Japan to stimulate consumer spending face stiff resistance at home because they are seen as running counter to the economic interests of those export-driven economies.

In the United States, the terms of the agreement may also face stiff opposition. America's promise, in effect to make $63 billion in reductions of the U.S. federal budget deficit over the next two years, will depend on the ability of President Reagan and a Democratic-controlled Congress to agree on a tax and spending plan that meets that goal. Though the reductions are mandated by the 1985 Balanced Budget Act, wiping out that much budgetary red ink clearly will be no small task.

Meanwhile, the harm suffered by American industry when the dollar was strong continues to fuel calls for protective legislation. So far, the Reagan administration has been able to fend it off the main thrusts of protectionism, preferring instead to look for solutions in exchange rates and greater U.S. industrial "competitiveness." But if the exchange rate agreement does not bring relief, calls for protectionism almost certainly will intensify.

For American consumers, the weak dollar's impact has not yet been fully felt, as Japanese and European exporters of everything from bottled water to luxury automobiles have hesitated to pass along the higher price of their goods to the American buyer for fear of losing their foothold in a lucrative market. But the Paris agreement to hold exchange rates at about their present value could mean the era of bargain imports is coming to an end, forcing a change in American consumers' increasingly expensive taste for foreign imports. After all, the dollar's value had fallen about 50 percent against both the yen and the mark in the past two years.

Exchange rates and budget policy

The Paris agreement is the latest in a series of attempts to stabilize world currency values since 1973, when the system of fixed exchange rates set up under the 1944 Bretton Woods Agreement was abandoned. Since 1973, the world's currencies have been allowed to "float," rising and falling in value according to supply and demand. As the movement of currencies across national boundaries has increased with expanding global trade and investment, exchange rates have become more volatile, playing an ever more important role in world trade. For the United States, the impact has been especially great because the dollar is the principal currency of world trade.

The central component of the Paris accord is the agreement by the six trading partners that their currencies are now "within ranges broadly consistent with underlying economic fundamentals" and that they will act in concert to keep the dollar, mark and yen at about their present values. Although the parties were deliberately vague about how their agreement to "cooperate closely" will work, it presumably will entail intervention in currency markets by the U.S. Federal Reserve System and central banks in the other nations.

An important implication of the agreement is that the trading partners will stop trying to use exchange rate variations as a means of forcing one another to change their positions on trade. In the weeks leading up to the Paris meeting, for example, it was said that Treasury Secretary Baker had "talked the dollar down" in an attempt to pressure West Germany and Japan to increase their imports of American products. By publicly denying charges that the dollar was falling too far, too fast, Baker had signaled that the United States was not about to remove massive quantities of dollars from circulation. The currency markets concluded from his remarks that there was no impending shortage of U.S. currency, and the dollar's value continued to plummet, thus threatening the export-driven West German and Japanese economies.

The Paris agreement made no explicit mention of specific ranges of acceptable currency fluctuations — known as "reference zones" — which Baker has long argued should be adopted. But in effect, the parties appear to have adopted the reference zone principle or some-

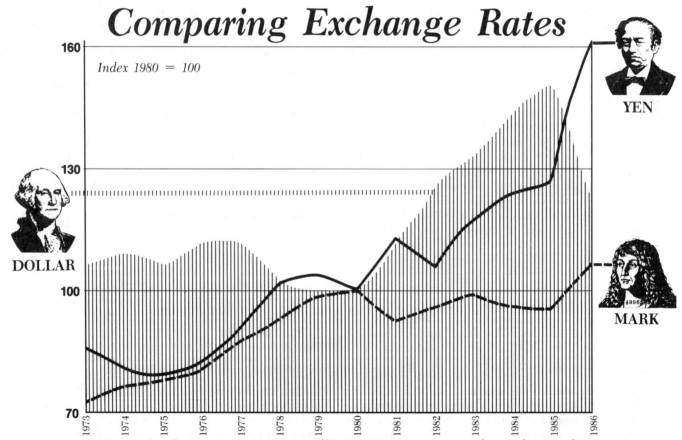

Comparing Exchange Rates

Index 1980 = 100

YEN

DOLLAR

MARK

Note: The graph shows fluctuations in American, Japanese and West German exchange rates, on an index with a base value of 100 in 1980. Data for the graph are trade-weighted "effective" exchange rates from the International Monetary Fund's Multilateral Exchange Rate Model.

HOW INTERVENTION WORKS

Central banks can raise or lower the value of a country's currency, its "exchange rate" with other currencies, by buying or selling large amounts of it, thus making its supply more scarce or more plentiful. In America, the decision to intervene in the foreign exchange market is made jointly by the chairman of the Federal Reserve Board and the Treasury secretary. The Federal Reserve Board then orders the Federal Reserve Bank of New York, its operating arm, to carry out the transaction. The bank's trading desk buys or sells dollars through 100 major commercial bank dealers in New York, including some U.S. branches of foreign banks. If the goal is to make the dollar appreciate in value, the New York bank buys up large amounts of dollars, using other currencies. Conversely, it can sell dollars in exchange for other currencies in an effort to flood the market and bring down the dollar's exchange rate.

thing very similar. Under a reference zone agreement, finance ministers and central bankers of participating countries would be required to consult on measures to be taken whenever a currency's value passes beyond the established upper or lower limits of the zone. Whatever the precise terms of the Paris agreement, both reference zones and similar "target zones," which would be more rigid, are likely to be subjects of discussion at the next annual economic summit meeting of heads of government in June.[1]

While the long-awaited agreement on exchange rate levels is the central component of the Paris accord, it alone cannot be expected to resolve the trade problems created by volatile exchange rates. Central banks intervene in currency markets by either buying or selling large amounts of a currency to raise or lower its value against that of other currencies. But in recent years, as the volume of private funds related to foreign trade and investment has swelled on foreign exchange markets, the impact of government intervention on exchange rates has diminished. If central bank intervention is inadequate to stabilize exchange rates, then coordination of domestic economic policy — the other component of the Paris agreement — becomes all the more significant.

In that part of the Paris accord, Japan and Germany both agreed to take steps which Baker had pushed for months but which both countries had resisted. While the United States posted a $170 billion trade deficit last year, Japan and West Germany enjoyed trade surpluses of $89 billion and $63 billion. By increasing their own consumer and business demand, the United States has argued, both trading partners could buy more American goods and services and bring the three countries' trade accounts into closer balance.

From the American point of view, West Germany made the more striking policy reversal of the two trading partners. After vehemently resisting Baker's pleas for months, West Germany pledged to stimulate domestic growth by increasing the amount of tax cuts already planned for 1988 and by proceeding with a new tax reform measure that would give West German consumers more money to spend.

Japan's commitment to stimulate its economy with a "comprehensive" program was less specific and, to date, has resulted in no legislative proposal. Although the Bank of Japan cut its discount rate — the interest charged banks for short-term loans — by 0.5 percent to a postwar low of 2.5 percent the day before the Paris meeting, this move was not expected to have a significant impact on Japanese consumer demand because interest rates were already low. "[West] Germany has made a clear policy change in the right direction," said David D. Hale, chief economist of Kemper Financial Services in Chicago. "Japan is the real slowpoke."

In both West Germany and Japan, however, the pledges given at Paris face stiff political opposition. Both those economies were largely destroyed during World War II, and in the decades since both have emerged as major industrial powers on the basis of exports. For this reason, they are reluctant to adopt policies that would undercut their competitiveness on export markets. Current Japanese and West German budget policies are aimed not at consumer spending but at consumer saving, which provides investment capital for export industries.

Although the two countries reluctantly acceded to U.S. demands on exchange rates and fiscal policy, Japan and Germany continue to blame the United States for the trade and currency imbalances. By running huge federal budget deficits, they say, the United States created its own trade dilemma. By introducing policies to encourage savings rather than spending, they say, Washington could curtail the American consumer's appetite for imports without seeking budget policy concessions from its trading partners. Given these arguments, it will not be easy for the West German and Japanese governments to carry out the tax reform measures, spending cuts and interest rate reductions they promised in Paris.

Japan's 'comprehensive' economic plan

In Japan, the high yen — which has appreciated from 260 to about 150 yen to the dollar since early 1985 — has become a subject of widespread concern. American critics point to Japan's growing trade surplus with the United States, up from $19 billion in 1984 to $58.6 last year and the largest of any U.S. trading partner. But the falling dollar has hurt Japan worse than the other parties to the Paris agreement because it is the most dependent on exports to the American market, which account for nearly half of all Japan's foreign sales. Rising prices for Japanese exports, it is feared, could lead the economy into recession. Although Japan's economy continued to grow last year, industrial production fell slightly for the first time since 1975 and unemployment rose to 6 percent, the highest level since the end of World War II. According to the Democratic Socialist Party, 705 Japanese companies have gone bankrupt in the two years since the yen began to appreciate against the dollar.

Amid concerns for the well-being of Japan's economy, Finance Minister Kiichi Miyazawa's Paris commitment to introduce "comprehensive" stimulative measures to the Japanese economy faces high political obstacles. The Japanese parliament, officially the Diet, has not even begun to discuss a tax reform and budget proposal, submitted shortly before the Paris meeting, that would have some stimulative effects. According to Masakazu Hayashi, counselor for financial affairs at the Japanese Embassy in Washington, the Nakasone government will not propose any additional stimulative measures until parliament votes on the budget and tax measure.

That proposal contains tax rate cuts. According to Hale, of Kemper Financial Services, it is an important step toward fiscal policy coordination by the two trading partners. If enacted, the proposal, together with the U.S. federal tax reform law that took effect in January, will bring about "fewer divergences in the microeconomic components of the two countries' fiscal systems than at any time since the Second World War." [2]

But the proposal's approval is far from certain. The

HOW U.S. PRESSURE ON THE DOLLAR...

Despite their position that the burden of correcting the low dollar rests on the United States, the Europeans and Japanese had little room to negotiate for better terms in Paris. As the dollar has fallen in the past year, their export industries have suffered, and fears of further damage to their trade positions prompted them to accept some of the U.S. demands.

An important factor in the dollar's fall has been a policy shift by the Reagan administration. In the president's first term, the United States adhered to a hands-off, free-market policy on exchange rates, proclaiming an end to the Carter administration's practice of intervening in currency markets to correct dollar fluctuations. The strong dollar, Reagan said early in his first term, was a sign that his policy of cutting taxes and government spending at home had restored international confidence in the American economy.

When the dollar soared against the mark and the yen in the early 1980s, pushed up in large part by high U.S. interest rates, the administration continued its policy of non-intervention until the rising flood of imports pushed the U.S. trade balance into deficit and forced a change of position. In January 1985, shortly before Treasury Secretary Donald T. Regan switched jobs with White House Chief of Staff James A. Baker III, Regan announced that the United States would intervene in the foreign exchange market to push down the dollar. In the wake of this policy reversal, the dollar began its decline after peaking in February 1985, when it traded for 263 yen and 3.44 marks.

Alarmed by the rising trade deficit, Baker sought greater coordination from America's trading partners to bring down the dollar's value. A September 1985 accord in New York, which was a vaguely worded agreement to coordinate exchange rate intervention between Baker and his counterparts from Britain, France, Japan and West Germany, convinced the foreign exchange markets that the trading partners would intervene heavily, pushing the dollar even faster on its downward path. However, the

Plaza accord — named for the New York hotel where it was reached —fell apart in early 1986, as Japan and West Germany began to intervene, without success, to stem their own currencies' rapid appreciation.

Treasury Secretary James A. Baker III

Some U.S. officials, including Federal Reserve Board Chairman Paul A. Volcker, began to warn of the dangers presented by a "free fall" of the dollar. If the dollar declines too fast, he has said, foreign investors may panic and withdraw their money from U.S. investments, especially government securities, leaving the Treasury with insufficient funds to finance the federal budget deficit. Under such a worst-case scenario, the Fed would be forced either to create more money, fueling inflation, or raise interest rates in an effort to attract investors. Either course could prove devastating to the American economy.

Although the dollar's fall continued throughout 1986, it had no noticeable impact on the growing U.S. trade deficit. (Changes in currency values tend to have a delayed opposition parties to Prime Minister Yasuhiro Nakasone's Liberal Democratic Party oppose it on the ground that a new sales tax, which is part of the proposal, would have a disproportionate impact on poorer citizens. Because the government is currently preoccupied with "making a great effort to persuade the opposition" to accept the sales tax, Hayashi said, "so far it has had no time to study new proposals for stimulating our economy."

Because the debate over the sales tax proposal could doom Nakasone's ambitions for re-election when his term expires in October, he may modify or retract the proposal, dimming prospects that Japan will enact any meaningful stimulative economic measures this year. Other measures advocated by critics of Japan's savings-oriented policy, such as easing restrictions on consumer loans and making financing for housing more accessible, seem unlikely to be considered in the foreseeable future.

Meanwhile, resentment grows in Japan over what is widely viewed as American highhandedness in Baker's "benign neglect" of the falling dollar. "If we continue like this, we will be slave laborers to the world forever," said one Japanese banker. "What Nakasone did was make one unilateral concession after another to President Reagan, always yielding to the U.S. demand that Japan be the one to initiate changes," another critic charged. "This is simply an extension of the attitude that has characterized Japanese relations with the U.S. since the close of the Pacific war." [3]

...SET THE STAGE FOR PARIS ACCORD

effect on trade patterns, in part because several years may pass between an initial order for a product, its manufacture and its delivery to the export market. Also, exporters often prefer to reduce their profits rather than risk losing

> *"We'd like to see other industrialized countries that have big surpluses taking more exports from the United States," Baker said in January.*

market share.) As the trade deficit continued to grow, the Reagan administration found it increasingly hard to resist calls for protectionist legislation. Acknowledging the limited effectiveness of exchange rate intervention alone in correcting the trade deficit, Baker pressed Japan and West Germany to stimulate consumption. He was rebuffed by both countries, which expressed fear that such stimulative measures as tax cuts and lower interest rates would fuel inflation.

By the end of 1986, however, both West Germany and Japan were beginning to suffer the consequences of their currencies' appreciation against the dollar. Unemployment rose and economic growth slowed in both countries as their exporting industries were forced by the loss of

profits to lay off workers and cut production. Efforts by the government of Japanese Prime Minister Yasuhiro Nakasone to depress the yen's value by exchange rate intervention proved fruitless, and the yen appreciated to a record of just under 150 to the dollar. Finance Minister Kiichi Miyazawa met with Baker in Washington in October and gave Japan's commitment to lower interest rates and introduce additional measures to stimulate the Japanese economy. It was also reported that the two sides agreed privately to adopt a "reference zone" — an idea most of the United States' other chief trading partners have so far rebuffed — and to take steps to hold the dollar's value within that zone of 150 to 163 yen.

The dollar's plunge accelerated this January, as it fell by 7.4 percent against the mark and 4.4 percent against the yen amid reports that Baker — disappointed by Japan's failure to stimulate its economy — was refraining from stemming the currency's fall to press Japan and West Germany to take further action. The same month, the seven nations belonging to the European Monetary System — Belgium, France, Italy, Ireland, Luxembourg, the Netherlands and West Germany — whose currencies are roughly pegged to the West German mark, were forced to realign their currencies under pressure from the mark's rise against the dollar. After the yen dipped below 150 against the dollar on Jan. 16, Miyazawa again traveled to Washington, but this time obtained no apparent commitment from Baker to stem the dollar's fall.

The Treasury secretary explained his tough stand on the dollar: "The United States has taken 60 percent of the increase in exports from lesser developed countries around the world. We'd like to see some of those exports going somewhere else as well and we'd like to see other industrialized countries that have big surpluses taking more exports from the United States." [4] By mid-February the dollar had fallen still further against the yen and the mark, setting the stage for the Paris agreement combining exchange rate intervention with domestic policy changes.

Inflation fear limits
West Germany's cooperation

West Germany, which is less dependent on the U.S. market for its exports than Japan, long resisted Baker's calls for a more stimulative domestic policy, refusing, for example, to join the United States and Japan in a currency stabilization agreement they made last October. West German officials cite fear of inflation as their main reason for refusing to go along with U.S. proposals, often recalling the last time West Germany bowed to American pleas to encourage consumption at home. After West Germany accepted President Carter's request that it serve as a "locomotive" to rescue the falling dollar in 1977-78, that country experienced inflation that was high by West German standards, though not as high as in the United States or the rest of Europe. One reason the fear of inflation is especially sharp in West Germany is the memory of post-World War I runaway inflation, which was the highest ever recorded anywhere.

Though reluctant to run the risk of an inflationary spiral, West Germany offered greater concessions in Paris in terms of domestic budget policy than Japan. On Feb. 25, just three days after the new pact, Gerhard Stoltenberg, the West German finance minister, went beyond his Paris commitment to increase the size of tax cuts scheduled for next year. He announced a $24 billion tax reform package to take effect between 1988 and 1990. The agreement resolved a dispute that had split the center-right governing coalition led by Chancellor Helmut Kohl since it was returned to power in elections held Jan. 25.

However, the tax cuts, which would cost about 19 billion marks ($10.3 billion), would be paid for in large part by reductions in West Germany's relatively high public expenditures. "This will be hard to attain," a West German government official explained. "Each subsidy has its own political history that comes back to haunt you when you try to cut it." Faced with slowing economic growth caused in large part by the mark's increasing value against the dollar, he said, there are growing demands for subsidies. West German farmers, for example, are calling for higher subsidies to compensate for their cuts in agricultural production. And shipbuilders are asking for more government support to see them through the worldwide slump in that industry.

Adding to the political obstacles facing tax reform in West Germany are this year's elections, in four states, all of which depend to some degree on subsidies. In an effort to win the voters' support in these states, the German official said, "the government has announced the tax-cut goodies first and will not propose the subsidy cuts necessary to pay for them until after the elections," the last of which will be held in September.

The Kohl government, whose slim election victory is blamed on a recent weakening of the economy, is a reluctant party to the Paris agreement and remains ambivalent on its prospects for success. "The dollar is much too low now," the official said, "but we are realistic enough not to expect major rises in the near future." The German government is blunt in its negative assessment of the U.S. contribution to policy coordination, especially its failure to come to grips with the federal budget deficit. "The missing part of the agreement is a commitment by the Reagan administration to raise taxes," the German official said. Criticizing the administration's insistence that low taxes are vital to U.S. economic growth, the official added, "Europeans in their simple-mindedness see things differently, that taxes must be raised to cut the budget deficit."

Until recently, the Kohl government rebuffed American calls to stimulate the West German economy, saying it was already growing fast enough. The falling dollar, however, pushed West Germany into the agreement with its trading partners. As the dollar has plummeted from its 1985 peak of 3.46 marks to about 1.80 today, West German exporters have faced the same dilemma as the Japanese: either lose markets to competitors with weaker currencies or absorb the cost of the high mark by trimming profits and cutting production. West German Unemployment, already high by U.S. standards, shot up from 8.9 percent in December to 10 percent in January. Despite a record trade surplus last year, growth in exports, which account for 30 percent of the West German economy, was a disappointing 0.06 percent, and many observers predict the beginning of a recession by this summer.

How France, Britain
and Canada are faring

West Germany's faltering performance is of special concern to Britain and France, the other European parties to the Paris agreement, because West Germany is the region's leading economic power, fueling growth among its neighbors. Further linking France's economic health to that of West Germany, the franc is loosely pegged to the mark through the European Monetary System (EMS). As the mark has appreciated against the dollar, so has the French currency, reducing the competitiveness of French exports. The falling dollar's effects began to be felt toward the end of last year. French unemployment rose above 10 percent at the end of 1986, as industrial production fell in the last quarter of the year. Italy's lira also is pegged to the mark through the EMS. But in contrast to France, Italy has continued to grow at a healthy pace, leading many analysts to predict that it may overtake Britain this year in total output.

The British pound sterling, which has been superseded by the mark as Western Europe's dominant currency, has been kept independent of the EMS by Prime Minister Margaret Thatcher's Conservative government in the belief that the pound would maintain a better value outside the system. The pound has in fact weakened as the other European currencies have risen, giving British industry a needed shot in the arm. As a result, British exports to West Germany, other European countries and Japan have

Press Watch

Views From Abroad

COORDINATING THE FLOAT

"Washington's insistence on the need for economic policy coordination signifies its recognition of two points: that the United States should no longer adopt policies unilaterally without concern for other countries' wishes as it has tended to do in the past, and that even if it implements such policies, it will not be able to achieve its objectives without the support of the other major industrial countries," writes Japanese economist **NAKATANI IWAO.** "In short, the United States has tacitly acknowledged the end of the postwar Pax Americana. The September [1985 Plaza] agreement on joint intervention was a turning point for the United States. Realizing that America's external imbalances had swollen to intolerable levels, the U.S. administration acknowledged the need to coordinate its policies with those of other countries in order to realign currencies. . . . After 13 years of floating exchange rates, we now know that the power of the float to correct external imbalances is not as great as it was made out to be. Floating rates alone have been unable to correct the mounting surpluses of Japan and West Germany and the persistent deficits of other industrial countries, most notably, the United States. . . . 'Coordination' has a nice ring to it, but in practice it will sometimes mean sacrificing domestic interests for the international good. In the age of concerted leadership, there will inevitably be conflicts between the prerogatives of national sovereignty and the demands of international coordination." From "Policy Coordination: An Idea Whose Time Has Come," an article in the Japanese monthly, *Keizai Semina*, July 1986, pp. 14-18.

FOR TARGET ZONES

U.S. Treasury Secretary James A. Baker III's "assumption has been that, prodded hard enough, [Japan and West Germany] will run the inflationary risk of boosting their economies by increasing public spending or cutting taxes and interest rates to keep their factories running," writes **THE ECONOMIST.** "The by-product for America is that Japanese and West German shoppers would then buy more made-in-America goods. If Japan and West Germany prove uncooperative, he himself is implying that the dollar might then fall so fast and so far that it sends America and the world spinning towards recession. . . . It is time to stop pushing currencies to and fro. Instead, let America, Japan and West Germany push their economic policies into line with the present, roughly correct pattern of exchange rates . . . How then to impose the needed policy convergence? Two ideas keep cropping up. One is to turn the economic indicators that the IMF [International Monetary Fund] collects on the big economies into promised targets: governments would aim for agreed inflation rates, current-account balances, growth rates and so on. This is too complex and much too ambitious. Tussles over procedure would become a substitute for action. Because of Congress, America could not be bound in this way. . . . Exchange-rate target zones are a better bet. Governments would promise to hold currencies within agreed bands, using exchange-market intervention followed by changes in interest rates if necessary. That commitment would then force other changes in policy, but it would be up to governments to choose them."

From "Awful Truth About Exchange Rates," in the British magazine *The Economist*, Jan. 24, 1987, pp. 16-17.

OLD EUROPE'S PLIGHT

"In the industrialized world, contracting government debt is no longer the silent process, without repercussions, that it once was," writes West German editor **RENATE MERKLEIN** in the Oct. 20 *Der Spiegel.* "It generally leads to diminished savings and, as a result, makes capital scarcer and more expensive. This means that credit-hungry treasuries hurt not just their own citizens but other countries as well; capital does not respect national borders. The greatest offender in this regard is the U.S. The sums that its federal, state and local governments have gobbled up at home and abroad since 1982 have run as high as $140 billion a year — an amount equal to the gross national product of Belgium. Now the European countries are borrowing heavily, and Japan is doing its part. . . . But contrary to the widespread notion that only the U.S. federal deficit is creating problems, the fiscal situation in Europe is worse than in the U.S. and more dangerous than in the Far East. In Japan and in the U.S., government spending is equal to only about a third of the GNP [gross national product]. In the EEC [European Economic Community] countries, state spending has increased from a third of the GNP, on the average, in 1970 to more than half today. . . . Young America and the youngest industrial nation of them all, Japan, are not as involved in this vicious circle as is old Europe. . . . Both countries will have to pay for further high deficits, as will the world. But in both countries, the tax burden on the typical citizen is far lower than in Europe — so low that raising taxes, obviously a highly unpopular alternative to government spending cuts, does not appear to be completely senseless. . . ." From the *World Press Review*, December 1986, pp. 31-33.

Korea and Taiwan: Fortunate Exceptions

While most of the major strong-currency countries have been feeling the pinch as the dollar has depreciated over the past year, for Taiwan and South Korea the plunge has been beneficial. Because their currencies have fallen along with the dollar, the exports of these newly industrialized trading nations have become increasingly competitive against those of Japan and some West European nations.

Exporters on the island of Taiwan have gained a strong foothold in Japan and Western Europe as a result of the falling dollar, to which Taiwan's dollar is loosely pegged. Taiwan's trade surplus with the United States, to which Taiwan ships half its exports, reached a record $13.6 billion in 1986. The trade imbalance has brought Taiwan under heavy fire by U.S. critics of its stiff tariffs, which block U.S. and other imports. Although Taiwan is now counted among the nine major industrial powers and enjoyed the third-largest trade surplus with the United States after Japan and Canada last year, Taiwan still receives trade preferences the United States grants developing countries to help their export industries. Under pressure from Washington, the Taiwanese government has intervened in the local foreign exchange market, causing an 11 percent appreciation of the Taiwan dollar against the U.S. dollar last year.

Although South Korea's currency, the won, is not officially pegged to the dollar, it has fallen in tandem with the U.S. currency as a result of successive devaluations aimed at enhancing the country's export industries. Unlike Taiwan, however, South Korea has resisted U.S. pressure to raise the won's value. Exports to Japan and Western Europe allowed South Korea to register its first trade surplus in years in 1986, bringing in capital it needs to reduce its $45 billion national debt.

The good fortune of Taiwan and South Korea did not escape the notice of the parties to the Paris exchange rate agreement. In their closing statement they added their voice to the pressure on the newly industrialized nation to assume some of the burdens of industrial development and expanding trade. The statement urged the newly industrialized countries to "allow their currencies to reflect more fully underlying economic fundamentals."

increased, contributing to Britain's falling unemployment and rising productivity and profits. The dollar has fallen by 12 percent against the pound over the past year, less than it has relative to other currencies.

Canada, which is America's biggest trading partner and the sixth party to the Paris agreement, has seen its currency firm only slightly against the dollar. Thus its trade position has been relatively unchanged. Though Canada endorsed the pact, it was not in on the negotiations.

In a note of discord in Paris, Italy refused to endorse the agreement, saying its and Canada's exclusion from the negotiations violated an understanding reached last May that any discussion of exchange rate management would include all of the so-called Group of Seven nations, which have been coordinating economic policy since 1975.

U.S. deficit-reduction pledge looms large

In the United States, the weak dollar has yet to benefit U.S. export industries significantly. "There are straws in the wind," said Lawrence A. Fox, vice president in charge of international economic affairs for the National Association of Manufacturers. Signs of improvement attributable to the falling dollar are beginning to appear among chemicals and some other basic commodities as well as in European orders for U.S. producer goods, he said. "But last year exports grew by just 2 percent, while imports grew by 7 percent, so we are not yet back to 1981 trade levels."

Although the United States is less dependent than its major trading partners on exports, they are increasingly important for the country's economic health. In addition, industries that are not heavily export-dependent are being displaced from the domestic market by more efficient foreign competitors. Calls for government protection are thus likely to mount, despite the Reagan administration's warning that protectionist legislation would set off a trade war between the United States and its trading partners.

To many European observers, the coming budget negotiations between the President and Congress loom as a major obstacle to the Paris agreement. "It is impossible to tie Congress by an agreement with five or six ministers of finance," the West German official observed. In contrast, he added, European governments have much more leverage over their parliaments. In Britain and West Germany, for example, the prime minister or chancellor is named by the majority in parliament, which thus has a moral obligation to support the government. "European leaders confer with parliament before meetings like the one in Paris and thus they go to them with their parliaments' firm support; the United States has no such guarantee," the official concluded.

Indeed, Treasury Secretary Baker faces an uphill battle with Congress over his pledge that America will meet the budget targets that were mandated by the 1985 Balanced Budget Act. Many observers say both tax increases and spending cuts are needed to meet the $108 billion

deficit target for fiscal 1988. In Congress, House Speaker Jim Wright, D-Texas, has come out in support of a tax hike. But the administration continues to reject the idea. In the absence of a tax increase, the Congressional Budget Office estimates that government spending will have to be cut by $63 billion if the target is to be met, a goal few congressional observers say is feasible.

As they confronted the task of drafting the fiscal 1988 budget resolution in late February, the House and Senate Budget Committee chairmen, Rep. William H. Gray III, D-Pa., and Sen. Lawton Chiles, D-Fla., said they expected to obtain no more than a $36 billion-$40 billion cut. Further diminishing chances the deficit target will be met is the prospect of the 1988 presidential election. With an eye on that race, members of both parties in Congress likely will be reluctant to support spending cuts or tax increases.

Nevertheless, Federal Reserve Board chairman Paul A. Volcker continues to caution that deficit reduction cannot be put off much longer. Although he concedes that the $108 billion target may be unrealistic, he has warned that any reduction in the trade deficit brought on by the dollar's fall will not benefit the economy unless the budget deficit is reduced at the same time and by roughly the same amount. Because a shrinking trade deficit would be accompanied by a reduction in the volume of foreign capital flowing into the United States, the Fed chairman warns, the government's borrowing must also shrink to avoid competing too strongly with private business for a smaller supply of lendable funds. "The clear implication would be congested capital markets, higher interest rates, strong inflationary dangers, and threats to growth," Volcker told the Senate Budget Committee on Feb. 25.

Meanwhile, administration hopes of deflecting calls for protectionist legislation appear increasingly dim. Last year was the fifth in a row in which Americans bought more goods and services from other countries than they sold overseas. Recent statistics indicate that another record trade deficit may be set in 1987. The administration, which last year vetoed a bill passed by Congress that would have curbed textile imports and some other commodities, this year has introduced its own trade bill in an attempt to fend off Democratic-sponsored proposals calling for import restrictions.[5] In another move aimed at derailing protectionism, the administration has launched a campaign aimed at improving U.S. industrial competitiveness.

NOTES

[1] For an analysis of target zones, see John Williamson, "The Exchange Rate System," Institute for International Economics, September 1983.

[2] David D. Hale, "Tax Reform in the U.S. and Japan: The Movement Towards International Tax Convergence," paper presented before the U.S.-Japan Consultative Group on International Monetary Affairs, San Diego, Calif., February 1987.

[3] From the Japanese newspaper *Nihon Keizai Shimbun*, Jan. 17, 1987, cited in *World Press Review*, March 1987, p. 45.

[4] Baker was interviewed Jan. 26, 1987, on the "MacNeil/Lehrer NewsHour."

[5] The Reagan administration's trade proposal was introduced Feb. 19 in both the House (HR 1155) and Senate (S 539). Cosponsors are Senate Minority Leader Robert Dole, R-Kan., and House Minority Leader Robert H. Michel, R-Ill.

Graphics: cover, Charles Moseley; p. 107, S. Dmitri Lipczenko.

BOOKS

Kaufman, Henry, *Interest Rates, the Markets, and the New Financial World*, Times Books, 1986. Wall Street's noted prognosticator writes of the effects of financial market deregulation on international capital flows.

Strange, Susan, *Casino Capitalism*, Basil Blackwell, 1986. An examination of the international financial system, including the foreign exchange market and attempts at exchange rate management, concludes it is a largely unstable system heavily influenced by speculation.

ARTICLES

Brownstein, Vivian, "Fortune Forecast: Where the Dollar Is Headed — With Luck," *Fortune*, Feb. 16, 1987. An analysis of the dollar's fall just before the Paris exchange-rate agreement was reached.

Dryden, Steven J., "The Risks of a Free-Fall," *Business Week*, Feb. 2, 1987. An analysis of the pressures that ultimately forced America's allies to the negotiating table in Paris.

Durant, Andrew, and Ira Kaminow, "The Dollar and the Search for Stability: What Are the Implications for Japan?" *The JAMA Forum* (published by the Japan Automobile Manufacturers Association Inc.), Jan. 10, 1987. The authors challenge the Reagan administration's call for policy changes in Japan and West Germany, saying the United States "has suffered no loss of sovereignty over the way it conducts domestic economic policy."

Fallows, James, "The Rice Plot," *The Atlantic*, January 1987. Japan's housing shortage and lack of consumer spending incentives are traced to steep agricultural subsidies.

Hale, David D., "The United States in Opposition, or, Can Mr. Baker Prevent Germany and Japan From Pushing the World Back into Recession," *Japan Economic Journal*, January 1987. The author, an economist at Kemper Financial Services, supports Treasury Secretary James A. Baker III's efforts to drive down the dollar as more of a "low risk economic game plan during 1987" than that of his Japanese and German counterparts.

REPORTS/STUDIES

Ito, Takatoshi, "The Intra-Daily Exchange Rate Dynamics and Monetary Policies After the G5 Agreement," National Bureau of Economic Research, October 1986. A University of Minnesota professor presents evidence that central banks are unable to manage exchange rates by coordinated intervention alone.

INDEX